MEDIATION AND NEGOTIATION:
REPRESENTING YOUR CLIENTS

Michael P. Silver

with the assistance of
Peter G. Barton

Butterworths

Toronto and Vancouver

Mediation and Negotiation: Representing Your Clients
© Butterworths Canada Ltd. 2001
April 2001

The Butterworth Group of Companies

Canada:
75 Clegg Road, MARKHAM, Ontario L6G 1A1
and
1721-808 Nelson St., Box 12148, VANCOUVER, B.C. V6Z 2H2
Australia:
Butterworths Pty Ltd., SYDNEY
Ireland:
Butterworth (Ireland) Ltd., DUBLIN
Malaysia:
Malayan Law Journal Sdn Bhd, KUALA LUMPUR
New Zealand:
Butterworths of New Zealand Ltd., WELLINGTON
Singapore:
Butterworths Asia, SINGAPORE
South Africa:
Butterworth Publishers (Pty.) Ltd., DURBAN
United Kingdom:
Butterworth & Co. (Publishers) Ltd., LONDON
United States:
LEXIS Publishing, CHARLOTTESVILLE, Virginia

National Library of Canada Cataloguing in Publication Data

Silver, Michael P. 1960-
    Mediation and negotiation: representing your clients

Includes bibliographical references and index.
ISBN 0-433-43789-8

1. Mediation – Canada. 2. Negotiation – Canada. 3. Dispute resolution (Law) – Canada.
I. Title.

KE8615.S54 2001   347.71'09   C2001-930203-7
KF9084.S54 2001

Printed and bound in Canada.

DEDICATION

For my daughter, Alexandra, and my son, Jeremy, and in memory of Carol Annibale, who will be sorely missed.

PREFACE

A critic cannot be fair in the ordinary sense of the word. It is only about things that do not interest one that one can give a really unbiased opinion, which is no doubt the reason why an unbiased opinion is always absolutely valueless.[1]

Why write this book? The objective reason is as follows: alternative dispute resolution (ADR) and specifically mediation are fast becoming integrated into traditional litigation practice and into the resolving of disputes in society generally. Apart from mandatory government programs and Law Society rules requiring solicitor-client discussion of ADR, it is a process about which lawyers, especially litigators, now have to know something.

It would be as ridiculous to say to a client or to another lawyer, "I don't like to mediate" or "I don't believe in ADR" as it would to advertise that you do not believe in cross-examination, do not like to do discoveries, or do not feel comfortable with legal research!

The skills involved in a good representation of a client have come to include negotiation and mediation skills, which are as much a part of the litigator's toolbox as anything a litigator may normally be called upon to do. Learning and practising these skills is, therefore, important to the well-trained litigator.

But an appreciation of negotiation and mediation skills is also useful to the layperson, who will have to be directly involved in the process if he or she is embroiled in a dispute. Whether he or she works to resolve a dispute on his or her own or with the aid of a lawyer, the nuts and bolts and ins and outs of it all are highly relevant and important to achieving a good outcome.

This book is, therefore, meant to serve as a teaching tool to both lawyer and layperson alike. It is hoped that you will gain a greater understanding of and respect for mediation and the role it can play in resolving civil disputes.

Because mediation is the most widely used and talked about means of alternative dispute resolution, because it is so flexible and effective in dealing with the greatest variety of disputes, and because within its boundaries it can encompass so many different techniques, the terms "alternative" and "ADR" used throughout this book shall refer specifically to mediation. These terms may, therefore, also be used interchangeably.

Furthermore, the discussions in this book will primarily focus on the civil dispute (*i.e.*, one in which there is a legal cause of action, though not necessarily one in which litigation has commenced). Apart from being the type of dispute with which most of us will be embroiled,[2] it is one area of disputation in which

---

[1] Oscar Wilde, *The Critic As Artist*, Part II.

[2] The chances are that most people will be involved as a party in a litigious dispute during the course of their lives. It may be a family law dispute (*e.g.*, marriage breakdown), commercial dispute (*e.g.*, breach of contract, failure to honour a debt, a shareholder or partnership dispute), a personal injury case (*e.g.*, motor vehicle collision), perhaps a wrongful dismissal from employment (layoff or firing), estates case (contestations under a will) or even professional negligence (*i.e.*, actions against professionals such as doctors, lawyers, contractors, engineers, *etc.*).

mediation is now being made mandatory through government-sponsored and enacted rules requiring parties to a lawsuit to have a mediation at an early stage in the litigation. In a very real sense, the world of civil litigation is now leading the way in ADR by institutionalizing mediation and demonstrating its effectiveness at resolving the most varied and complex of society's disputes — those in which the conduct is actionable and which form the subject of litigation before the courts.

The subjective reason for writing this book, however, was no less relevant to me. Indeed, it culminates something of a personal journey. Once upon a time, I was a litigator at a downtown Toronto firm. My practice was a mixed bag of commercial, personal injury, medical malpractice, environmental and administrative litigation. The people at our firm worked hard and were very proud of their work. Being a litigator was in essence my entire life. It kept me very busy and was all-consuming. In law school, not a word about ADR had ever been uttered. Settlement was not a part of our legal education, and, though settlements did occur in practice, achieving them was not a part of our firm culture and certainly not something we as associates received any training to accomplish.

Notwithstanding, as I took more mediation/negotiation courses, I came to agree with the statement attributed to Mahatma Gandhi, himself a lawyer, that "the best thing a lawyer can do for his clients is to get them to settle".[3]

As the years went on, I became increasingly disenchanted with what I was doing with my career. And since litigating was not just my career, but my life, I was growing disenchanted with my whole life's direction. I began to notice that though we billed a lot of money (more than even I on an associate's salary could afford), we often did not get good results for the client, even worse *sometimes we did not ever get results of any kind at all*. The cases just kept dragging on for years. They would get mired in interlocutory motions or never-ending discoveries, or they would sometimes essentially be shelved and put in abeyance (due to a client not paying promptly, the "dog's breakfast" nature of the file, or inaction on the part of the plaintiff).

However, as with many things in life, a general dissatisfaction was insufficient to provoke a response; it took a number of seminal events to get me to adjust my thinking. Some of these involved some bizarre and unfair adjudication. Others illustrated the inefficiencies of the litigation process. I will mention just three examples, though there were quite a few more. Anyone who has litigated is likely to have examples of their own; thus it is hoped that the litigator reader can relate to these career changing episodes.

One of these cases proved to be a quintessential lesson on discoveries. We had been retained to do the trial, but the discoveries (two weeks' worth) had been done by another firm. The case involved a husband and wife together going to a solicitor, and the husband providing instructions for his will to leave everything to the wife. When he died, it turned out that he had left much of his estate to others; consequently, the wife sued the lawyer for breach of fiduciary duty allegedly owed to her. The lawyer, however, claimed he owed her no duty be-

---

[3]   G. Ohsawa, *Gandhi: The Eternal Youth*, trans. K.G. Burns (Oroville, Calif.: George Ohsawa Macrobiotic Foundation, 1986) at 111.

cause he was only the husband's solicitor, not hers. A day before the trial, I was asked to find anything of relevance in the voluminous discovery transcripts (over one foot high). I had no idea what to look for and thought I might as well begin at the beginning. At page 2 (of thousands) and about one minute into the first examination, the lawyer was asked, "Are you Ms.____'s friend?" Most likely annoyed by her lawsuit and feeling a certain amount of personal betrayal, he replied, *"No, no, I was not her friend; I was more like her lawyer!"* The rest of the transcript was superfluous — the key answer was right there on page 2! If he was her lawyer, then he owed her the fiduciary duty. The rest of the discoveries were just window dressing. The case was tried for a few days after which settlement discussions finally took place. After hundreds of thousands of dollars in fees, the dispute was settled with an apology from the lawyer, one dollar and the return of a desk.[4]

In a dispute over an agreement of purchase and sale for industrial condominium units, the opposing lawyer seemingly became obsessed against our client and our firm. The case was at best a dispute over $25,000, but that amount was spent on fees many times over, since we were in motions court almost weekly. The opposing lawyer lost most of the motions, and as a result, a number of cost and other orders against his client and himself personally were registered. However, none of these was paid. With each new motion, more orders would accumulate. Outrageous things happened. The lawyer proceeded to read my own notes — while they were upside down — during a discovery, resulting in my cancelling the discovery. He infuriated a judge by implying that the judge had had an off-the-record substantive discussion with me in his absence. Finally, a judge on one of the motions, upon hearing the litany of proceedings, orders and alleged unbecoming conduct, took it upon himself to refer this lawyer to the Law Society. When I finally met the other parties for the first time at a cross-examination (they were, by this time, represented by different counsel), I initiated a settlement discussion that successfully concluded later that day.

Finally, in a major and novel case involving constitutional and administrative law arguments, which took months at trial, the judge who rendered the decision had ignored most of our arguments and even some of our witnesses. The decision bore little resemblance to the record and to the law submitted, was internally inconsistent and was brief in its treatment of the important issues. A respected law professor who later reviewed the decision thought that if the trial had been a law school course, and the reasons for judgment were given as an answer on an examination, the judge would have failed.

Events such as these convinced me that a *strict reliance* on adjudication was flawed. Each of these clients paid hundreds of thousands of dollars in legal fees. None of them had bad cases — in fact, their cases were strong. And contrary to what the reader may be thinking right now, our legal services were competent. There were real needs behind the bringing of these cases, and, of course, these needs and interests were never addressed. How could they be? The workings of

---

[4]   These items were provided in part because they mattered to the wife, but also because the assets (various businesses and shareholdings) not left to the wife had plummeted in value since the husband's death.

the system did not facilitate that. Or, at least, they did not do so until far too late in the process.

And so it was with a certain sense of personal mission that I left legal practice and took a job as one of the two full-time mediators (we were called Dispute Resolution Officers) with the Toronto ADR Centre, which was the first pilot project (between the Ministry of the Attorney General and the Ontario Court of Justice) to test and evaluate the efficacy of mandatory mediation of civil disputes. Below is a quote from one of the promotional communiqués:

> The ADR Centre is the court system's response to the public's desire "to have conflicts resolved, but not necessarily tried." It will provide institutional support to lawyers who hitherto have been left on their own to negotiate settlements. The ADR Centre is a free of charge, court provided facilitation of the crucial settlement efforts of the profession.
>
> The new ADR Centre is a tremendous opportunity for litigants and counsel, being the vehicle by which the Ontario Court will help the parties to achieve a tailor-made solution which is more likely to satisfy the parties' essential interests. The ADR process occurs at a stage in the proceeding before much time and money have been expended. The Centre will facilitate what statistics show is likely to happen anyway, namely a settlement of the action, but at a time, for a cost and in a manner which is likely to be more efficient and satisfying.
>
> ADR is not just another hurdle to be overcome in the litigation process. It is the court sponsored mechanism by which the already present hurdles in the litigation process can be avoided through early settlement.
>
> The ADR Centre is in effect a "New Justice Product", allowing lawyers to offer their clients an important and accessible service from an adjunct of the Ontario Court. In this era of cutbacks, it is a remarkable step towards a multi-door courthouse in which counsel and litigants can choose the door appropriate for their case and in which a trial (and the litigation leading up to trial) is but one of the available options for dispute resolution.
>
> In short, it is hoped that the ADR Centre will prove itself an invaluable part of a well managed court system."[5]

The Toronto ADR Centre proved that mediation could work and could do so on a mandatory basis.[6] In fact, the mandatory nature of the process was a distinct

---

[5]   This communiqué was written by the author as part of the material given to counsel and to the parties upon a case's random selection for a mediation within the program.

[6]   During the evaluation period (the first 10 months of 1995), about half the cases that were referred to the Centre at random settled, with a further 17 per cent settling on their own before the ADR session. The mean time to achieve a settlement occurring at the Centre was 124–129 days. The mean time for case disposition for non-mediated cases in the General Division, including case managed cases, is at least twice as long and sometimes much longer.

   Satisfaction levels were very high. Over 95 per cent of lawyers and clients said that they would use the Centre again, and over 96 per cent of lawyers found the mediations to be fair. More than 70 per cent of lawyers and 75 per cent of parties believed that their case would have settled at a higher cost if it had not been referred to the Centre; in fact 14 per cent of lawyers estimated these savings to the client to be over $100,000. Even with cases that did not settle, 71.5

advantage. Parties did not feel that they had anything to lose by suggesting a settlement discussion. Through mediating nearly a thousand cases of all descriptions at the Centre, I realized that ADR made real sense and did some wonderful things to help people deal with their pressing problems.

Sometimes it is as important to undo what has been done as it was to have initially done it. Because of ADR's popularity and current mandating in some jurisdictions (specifically mediation), some parts of the old adversarial system may currently be in the process of realignment. I make no apologies for this: we may very well be dismantling that which was carefully constructed over the last few centuries. But as a new millennium has begun, perhaps the time is ripe for such a sea change. The maxim, "if it ain't broke, don't fix it" does not apply. The traditional litigious adversary system is broken in some important respects, and it does need to be fixed. ADR is the needed repair.

It finally became clear to me that bringing people together and helping them to resolve problems was a noble task to which to devote one's career. There is so much conflict, so much strife in society. If we all make a little bit of a contribution towards making things better for each other, then maybe we will survive this tumultuous period in our history.

As people, we are different, think differently, emote differently and have different goals and interests. We also live in a world where there are fixed or limited resources. That is fundamentally why there is conflict amongst the human race. However, the following statement by John F. Kennedy is probably the best articulation of what we do have in common — and why we need to find ways to get along:

> For the final analysis, our most basic common link is that we all inhabit this small planet. We all breathe the same air. We all cherish our children's future. And we are all mortal.[7]

While ADR is not a panacea for all of society's ills, it is a useful tool to help resolve even the most difficult of disputes more efficiently and with greater regard to the needs of the disputants. That is why it is worth knowing something about.

Michael P. Silver
April 2001

---

per cent of lawyers agreed that the mediation had, nonetheless, provided an important settlement opportunity.

There was no significant dissatisfaction among lawyers or litigants with mandatory referral to ADR in the pilot project, nor with the timing of the referral after the close of pleadings and before discoveries. The evaluation also showed that settlement was successful over a wide range of case types, with varying complexities and dollar values. Over half of lawyers and parties cited the skill of the mediator as the key reason settlement was reached.

The evaluators, therefore, recommended mandatory referral of cases at the close of pleadings, without any institutional screening (J. Macfarlane, "Court-Based Mediation for Civil Cases: An Evaluation of the Ontario Court (General Division) ADR Centre", Faculty of Law, University of Windsor, November 1995; and the Executive Summary of the Evaluation of the ADR Centre, prepared by Christine Hart).

[7] J. F. Kennedy, commencement address (American University, Washington, D.C., 10 June 1963).

ACKNOWLEDGMENTS

I wish to thank a number of people without whom this book would never have materialized. First, my wife, Sandy Mahr, who ran the house while giving me the much needed intensive time to write the book. She is my rock and my redeemer!

Without Peter Barton, this book would never have been completed. Peter and I go back almost 20 years, and he is as young in spirit and refreshingly unconventional now as back then. Like manna from heaven, he appeared on the scene just at the right time, when I was deadlocked on the project. He offered salvation by agreeing to revisit the text and getting it ready for publication. My heartfelt thanks go out to him.

I would also like to thank Gary Caplan, Paul Iacono, Jim Davidson and Leslie Dizgun, each of whom has contributed to this book, and with whom I have for years enjoyed bantering about the concepts contained within.

Many thanks are also extended to Peggy Buchan and Rose Knecht of Butterworths for their tireless editing and commitment to making the text the best it could be.

I would also like to thank Ophir Bar-Moshe, whose initial support at Butterworths was very helpful.

I would like to thank Peter MacDonald, Jack Daiter and the students of the Ryerson Dispute Resolution course whom we have taught together through the years for their insight and the ideas brought out in class discussion. Many of these ideas and insights are represented herein.

A word of thanks goes to my ADR Centre colleagues, in particular Norman Ross, with whom many experiences were shared.

There are a number of judges, masters and professors without whose active encouragement I would never have entered mediation. Their encouragement changed my life, and I am grateful for their guidance: Ontario Chief Justice Roy McMurtry, for being an especially involved and caring mentor for most of my professional life; Justices Gerald Day, Warren Winkler, Kathy Feldman, Jim MacPherson, Jim Farley, Stephen Borins; Masters David Sandler and Bassel Clarke; and Professor Sir David Williams (my Cambridge thesis advisor and a former Vice-Chancellor of the University) have all provided inspiration and help over the years.

Finally, I would like to thank all the people with whom I have ever mediated, without whom I would never have developed the deep appreciation I have for the value of mediation, and without whom I would never have had the opportunity to listen, watch and learn.

TABLE OF CONTENTS

Part I

NEGOTIATION

Chapter 1

INTRODUCTION

Our deepest fear is not that we are inadequate. Our deepest fear is that we are
powerful beyond measure. It is our light, not our darkness, that most frightens us.
We ask ourselves, who am I to be brilliant, gorgeous, talented and fabulous? Actually, who are you not to be? You are a child of God. Your playing small doesn't
serve the world. There is nothing enlightened about shrinking so that other people
won't feel insecure around you. We are born to make manifest the glory of God
that is within us. It's not just in some of us; it's in everyone. And as we let our
own light shine, we unconsciously give other people permission to do the same.
As we are liberated from our own fear, our presence automatically liberates others.[1]

Probably more than any other quote, the one above captures the essence of
empowerment. In a very meaningful way, this book is about empowerment.
What then, does another ADR book such as this one have to do with
empowerment? The answer is — everything!

TRADITIONAL ADJUDICATION

The "alternative" in Alternative Dispute Resolution (ADR) is supposed to represent the alternative to traditional adjudicative litigation. Traditional litigation in
most common law jurisdictions has become extremely cumbersome, lengthy,
costly, and to a great extent, self-perpetuating. This is not a knock on the common law legal system, which has become dominant in most of the British colonized world. Indeed, that system has many virtues as compared with some of the
alternatives.[2] However, expensive, complex litigation ruled by endless procedural rules and wrangling, teams of lawyers and clogged courts requiring years
to get to trial are not a necessary corollary to being involved in a dispute. There
are other ways to solve problems.

---

[1]   M. Williamson, *A Return to Love: Reflections on the Principles of a Course in Miracles* (New
     York: Harper Collins, 1996) from Chapter 7, Section 3. This quote is often attributed to Nelson
     Mandela in his 1994 Inaugural Address.
[2]   Many would argue that the common law system of jurisprudence is a positive byproduct of Brit-
     ish imperialism — such systems of law were established all over the British Empire, on which,
     in the early part of the 20th century, "the sun never set". Common law systems are based on
     prior precedents (*stare decisis*), which provide certainty in the law. However, because each case
     is considered *de novo*, there is scope for innovation and flexibility, either in the manner in which
     prior precedents are interpreted or by distinguishing the case at bar from earlier decisions.

At the core of these "other ways" is the concept of personal empowerment[3] — the idea of breaking free from the shackles of a litigation system that has come to embody, in many though not all cases, not the betterment of those involved within it, but more of a kind of self-sustaining tedium to which the courts, lawyers and the parties themselves have become hostage.

What is meant by an alternative to traditional adjudication? We are not talking about the extreme alternatives, such as medieval style trial by battle or by ordeal, or vigilantism. We are talking here about other ways and alternatives which are compatible with a modern civil society that is organized by the rule of law — in which individuals have both liberties and positive rights,[4] as well as legal and social obligations.

In the context of a "civil society", both rights and interests bear upon the ultimate resolution of a dispute. By this we mean rights emanating from legal, historical, precedential or policy sources, and interests deriving from the needs, desires, frame of reference and subset of potential actions/inactions from which a party is at liberty to choose. Rights and interests are the key ingredients in the mix, giving rise to the specific resolution of a dispute from the myriad of possible resolutions that could conceivably exist.

The criticism of traditional court adjudication is that it is too rights based. Accordingly, as potential resolution focuses myopically on rights, time and money are wasted, and procedural potholes arise, making ultimate resolution highly cumbersome.[5] This development begged the question of how relevant to the disputants the sometimes arcane debates over various "rights" were. For example, the first report of Ontario's Civil Justice Review found that the average piece of litigation comprised 2.5 interlocutory motions in court.[6] How many litigants really cared about these appearances and, indeed, how many even knew in any detail what transpired at them?

An unbalanced rights-based approach to resolving disputes entails a number of significant problems. While settlements of cases are nothing new (approximately 97.5 per cent of all cases settle before trial), the problem has been that cases do not settle early in the process, resulting in clogged courts (especially motions courts) and much wasted expenditure of time and money. The costs are borne not only by the litigation system and the government providing the infra-

---

[3] Throughout the book, reference will be made to personal, or individual, concepts. These, of course, also apply to corporate interests, as corporations are considered to be legal persons and have standing before the courts.

[4] A liberty is that which a person is free to do because there is no law or restriction against doing it. Were a restriction to be enacted, however, the liberty would disappear. A right is a positive ability to do a thing, the source of which is usually legal and from which individuals are specifically enabled to do something.

[5] A quick example of this can be found by comparing the time required for a mediation of a substantive and somewhat complex case with the time taken to adjudicate it — in court or even arbitration. Anyone involved in these processes knows that it takes far longer (at least twice as long, and sometimes much more) to bring out the relevant facts and evidence in a rights-based mode, with the *pro forma* examination, cross-examination and re-examination. Questions take much longer to be answered, and a lot of ultimately superfluous information is delved into. A mediation is much more effective at getting at what is at the bottom of the issues in dispute.

[6] Ontario Civil Justice Review, *Civil Justice Review: First Report* (Toronto: Ontario Civil Justice Review, 1995).

structure, but by the litigants themselves, and by lawyers who often have to compromise on billings after their fees have climbed beyond initial expectations. It has been estimated that the total legal bills to the parties in an average Superior Court of Justice lawsuit (including those that settle before trial) are in the $40,000–50,000 range.[7]

The reasons for these problems include the nature of the adversarial system which encourages parties to assert their case at its highest extreme; the tendency to take positions or make threats from which it is later difficult to extricate oneself; the delays in the system;[8] the business costs facing law firms; and what has been described as an "increasing failure of Canadian society to resolve conflict without official intervention."[9] Until now, the sole mechanism available for the resolution of disputes has been the adjudicatory process, which has become inaccessible for many who literally cannot afford to have a dispute!

Further, within the adjudicatory process, there are only winners and losers. "Intermediate solutions, compromise and tailored outcomes to accommodate the parties' best interests are simply not available to judges."[10] Given the limited extent to which cost awards indemnify a successful party, even winners can feel like losers.

ALTERNATIVES

Accordingly, what is being referred to as "alternative" is an alternative to traditional adjudication with its emphasis on pure rights analyses. Mediation is a catalyst to negotiation. While negotiation can be a daunting process, a good mediator can help parties reach an agreement.

Negotiation can take many forms depending on the role taken by the neutral third party (neutral). The following diagram of the Dispute Resolution Continuum outlines the differences:

---

[7] *Ministry of the Attorney General Investment Strategy: Alternative Dispute Resolution*, June 29, 1993.

[8] There was once a backlog of over 10,000 civil cases in the Toronto Region (General Division) — *Ministry of the Attorney General Investment Strategy: Alternative Dispute Resolution*, June 29, 1994.

[9] G.W. Adams and N.L. Bussin, "Alternative Dispute Resolution and Canadian Courts: A Time For Change" (Cornell Lectures, Ithaca, N.Y.), 11 July 1994.

[10] *Ibid.*

DISPUTE RESOLUTION CONTINUUM

Unassisted Negotiation — Facilitation — Conciliation — Mediation (Facilitative / Evaluative) — Early Neutral Evaluation — Non-binding Arbitration — Binding Arbitration — Adjudication

On the left of the continuum we find completely unassisted negotiation — there is no neutral third party involved at all. As we move towards the right, the intervention of a neutral third party increases, as does the evaluative component of the intervention. With facilitation and conciliation, the neutral acts more as a convenor, ensuring that everybody gets heard and that the discussion is kept on track. There is virtually no evaluative component to the intervention. In the middle, we find mediation. The left goal post is more facilitative, and the right is more evaluative. This is, in fact, the beauty of mediation, for it encompasses both the facilitative and the evaluative. Accordingly, mediation encompasses a very flexible response and level of third-party intervention, enabling it to best meet the demands of a given dispute. The commitment and assertiveness of the third-party neutral can vary, on a case-by-case basis, so as to best accommodate a specific dispute. This makes mediation adaptable and most effective, no matter what kind of dispute or whoever the parties may be.

As we move to the right, we encounter the evaluative modes of dispute resolution. The least adjudicatory of these is early neutral evaluation, in which a respected authority (such as a judge, arbitrator or expert) provides a neutral evaluation/opinion of a particular point that is a stumbling block — the determination of which will help pave the way for a more broad resolution. Next, we find arbitration, of which non-binding is more facilitative (because it is only advisory) and, therefore, on the left, and of which binding is completely evaluative and, therefore, on the right. On the far right of the continuum we find adjudication, in which the third-party neutral is in complete control, and to whom the parties have handed complete responsibility for imposing a resolution to the dispute.

ADR and mediation are fundamentally processes which utilize negotiation. It is, therefore, essential to have an understanding of the main principles of negotiation in order to understand mediation. An analogy would be the requirement of an understanding of math in order to comprehend physics. There is an inextricable link. Therefore, negotiation is dealt with both in Part I, "Negotiation", and Part II, "Mediation".

The book will examine the best approach to getting what you want from a mediated negotiation. Accordingly, it should appeal to counsel (who will increasingly be representing clients or planning mediation with clients) and to laypeople. The focus will be on how to negotiate (setting out the basics of negotiation and how it relates to the mediation process), what to expect in a mediation and how the mediation process unfolds. The book will also examine the negotiation stage from the perspective of the party to the legal dispute. Although you may have legal training, it is important for you to know how your client views the dispute and how your view of it may differ, and why. You should know how he or she has tried to resolve it and why this has failed, thus leading to your involvement. Knowing how far the process of his or her dispute has gone will make you a more effective problem-solver.

This book contains many suggestions on how to negotiate and maximize the outcome of a mediation. Counsel may find that within their role as advocate, they really have to "do the thinking" for their clients by making and conveying offers or representations at a mediation. This can apply if the client is an individual or a sophisticated corporation. After solicitor-client discussions, counsel may have to carry the load on the client's behalf, by thinking out and acting upon the many suggestions and considerations contained herein.

Dispersed throughout the discussion will be real life examples and problems. This will help to illustrate the problems and solutions discussed and should provide for a better read. The contents are very much a product of the author's and contributors' own experience and deductions from common sense.

Because our mediation experience is primarily in mediating civil disputes, and because the variety of disputes encountered in the litigation context is so interesting and extensive, the examples cited will relate primarily to actionable disputes. Examples of litigation highlight the omnipresent alternative to a settlement, which, of course, comes with many incumbent risks and costs. Litigious disputes are a good backdrop for the discussion of interests and for the canvassing of alternatives inherent in any discussion of interest-based dispute resolution.

Chapter 2

NEGOTIATION BASICS

OBJECTIVES OF DISPUTE RESOLUTION

It is obvious that people seek to resolve the disputes in which they are involved to their liking. Accordingly, the most general objective to a negotiation is to actualize wants and needs. Apart from achieving what you want, negotiation entails a number of realizable objectives. Any successful settlement encompasses the realization of at least some of the following objectives — for that is why the dispute is settled.

Fairness

Essential to any process of negotiation is the perception of fairness. It applies not only to the outcome but also to the dispute resolution process used to arrive at that outcome. In other words, the parties to the dispute have expectations that the result will be fair to them *and* that the process will treat them fairly. In particular, they want to feel that they have had some control over the process.

Fundamental to fair process is the absence of any conflict of interest on the part of a third-party neutral. We have all seen this in the adjudicative model — "justice must be seen to be done", and any perception of a conflict is usually sufficient for the adjudicator to remove himself or herself from the matter. In mediation, any potential conflict that might arouse feelings of partiality or lack of neutrality by the mediator on the part of the disputants requires the mediator to disclose the potential conflict. The parties must then decide whether or not to proceed.[1]

Objective criteria can often form the basis of what is fair in a negotiation. For example, legal principles and precedents are often utilized to suggest what might be fair (and are imposed by an adjudicator in a litigious dispute if there is no settlement). Past dealings between the parties themselves and past practices within the sector, community, industry or relevant group are also of value. Such practices, especially if previously arrived at consensually, are good indices of the tolerances of the parties and of the disputants' fundamental values. It will later be seen how these affect negotiations on legal disputes.

---

[1] See the CBAO Mediators' Code of Conduct (Appendix V).

Efficiency

Efficiency is a goal in itself, in terms of time, money, the expending of energy and other ways. Part of the reason for the introduction of mandatory mediation in litigation is the inefficiency of the litigation process in resolving disputes. Cases can take years to get to trial and can bankrupt parties before the matter ever gets adjudicated. Even though most cases never see a trial (over 97 per cent of claims launched never get tried), they tend to settle late in the litigation after much time and money have been spent. Additionally, and of concern to Ontario's courts prior to the implementation of mandatory mediation, many cases were settled for the wrong reasons, such as for the bankruptcy, or even for the death or illness of a party. Many cases simply ran out of steam and were abandoned ignominiously. None of these outcomes was impressive from a quality of justice perspective. As in business, in which efficiency is a veritable goal and upon which the existence of a business may depend, it is important for any good mode of dispute resolution to achieve an outcome in an efficient manner.

Costs of Litigation

An example of the inefficiencies of litigation is in the area of costs. The basic principles of costs are the discretion of the court and the indemnity principle. What the latter means is that if you lose, you are at fault — you should have realized that you had a bad case; now you must indemnify the winning side. Costs in the usual scale awarded in trials indemnify the winner up to 33-50 per cent. What this means is that the losing party pays up to 33-50 per cent of the actual legal costs of the winner (called recoverable costs).

For example, assume a two-day Superior Court trial, preceded by pleadings, one or two motions, discoveries, pre-trials, *etc.* Also, assume the average cost to each party to be about $30,000. If the judgment was $40,000, the winner gets that amount, less the winning party's non-recoverable costs, *i.e.*, the amount billed by his or her lawyer not covered by the costs recoverable from the other side. This difference is called a non-recoverable cost.

For instance, if the winner's legal costs were $30,000, he or she would be indemnified to roughly one-third to half that amount, or $12,000. Non-recoverable costs would then be $18,000. The net recovery of the winner would be $40,000 less $18,000 (non-recoverable costs), equalling only $22,000. The loser pays the judgment of $40,000, plus interest, plus the $12,000 assessed by the court, plus his or her own legal bill for roughly another $30,000, equalling approximately $82,000, which is twice what the trial judge thought the case was worth. Obviously, there is a downside of going to trial — for both sides.

Privacy

A further possible objective is privacy. Many parties shun the publicity that the openness of the litigation system entails. Cases can achieve attention from the print and broadcast media, and judicial decisions can find their way into reported decisions (which can then also be the subject of media attention). Reported decisions and the goings-on in court are also discussed within the community. The only sure way to keep a dispute and/or its resolution confidential is to achieve it privately, with as little fuss and as much discretion as possible. In addition to outcomes negotiated directly by the parties about which the world at large knows very little, mediated settlements can remain completely confidential. The mediator is sworn to secrecy, and the parties generally sign a confidentiality agreement before proceeding; indeed, the parties may make confidentiality a term of the settlement.[2]

Preserving, or Even Enhancing Relationships

This can also be an objective. According to a 1993 statement by the then Prime Minister Yizchak Rabin, it is not always true that we "negotiate with our enemies and not with our friends". However, even when we do, it may be a goal, or at least a contemplated by-product, that the relationship will improve somewhat. We have all experienced an improved friendship/relationship with someone with whom we have had a conflict that was subsequently resolved amicably. Sometimes the relationship is, in fact, stronger for having gone through the process of resolving the conflict. The phenomenon at work may involve a certain sense of relief from having resolved a conflict or may truly represent an increase in the quality of the relationship due to improved understanding. In either case, where a relationship is likely to continue, or where people will be forced to deal with one another again, maintaining the relationship can be very important (obvious examples include management and union, separated spouses with children, or buyers and sellers within the same distinct business community). Relationships are what drive human societies. Enhancing, creating or simply preserving relationships is a goal in itself.[3]

Satisfying Interests

Achieving an outcome which satisfies at least some of the needs and interests which were at play in involving the party in the dispute is a crucial objective. These interests are what prompt the party to get involved in the dispute in the first place. Settlement proposals which do not do this either fail to win agreement or obtain very bad agreements. Later, we will examine the concept of the

---

[2] Mediation confidentiality agreements usually have a provision similar to the following (see Appendix IV):

CONFIDENTIALITY

The parties agree that all communications and documents shared, which are not otherwise discoverable, shall be without prejudice and shall be kept confidential as against the outside world, and shall not be used in discovery, cross examination, in an affidavit, at trial, in this or any other proceeding, or in any other way.

The mediator's notes and recollections cannot be subpoenaed in this or any other proceeding.

[3] A case that illustrates the importance of relationships and the value of a negotiated agreement was one in which a financially troubled son owed his retired father a lot of money. Members of the family had not spoken for six years. An agreement was finally reached that had everyone embracing. The happiness was palpable; the relationships had been restored. The son was given time to pay a discounted debt, and the father had certainty that the debt would be paid and he could continue his retirement in more comfort.

best alternative to a negotiated agreement (BATNA)[4] — the idea being that if your alternative to an agreement is as good or better than any agreement on the table, then it is better not to agree. The assessment and evaluation of core interests is essential in determining the worth of any agreement.

WHAT IS AT STAKE IN A LEGAL DISPUTE?

The case problems described later in this chapter illustrate how needs, goals and interests are brought to the fore in dealing with and potentially resolving disputes. First, it is important to understand how the strength or weakness of one's legal case affects the negotiation.

Laws affect all of us in many ways. Some affect us more directly than others. We buy items from stores; we lease cars, or apartments; we get involved in accidents; we make wills; we try to arrange our financial affairs to survive and even to flourish; we pay taxes; and we seek benefits such as health insurance, employment insurance, *etc.*

All of these activities bring us into contact with other people. If something goes wrong, we sometimes look to others for relief.[5]

If the law, whether judge-made or legislative, provides us with a cause of action, we may sue in court. If the law provides some other remedy, such as an appeal to a government tribunal, we may pursue that route. Our "legal" case may be stronger if we can back up our claims with court action, but even in disputes with a government department about benefits, the law may be on our side. This will help in our dispute with that department.

There may be many reasons why we don't prolong our disputes about legal matters with others.

1. We can't really convince anyone that our side of the story is to be believed.
2. The law does not favour us.
3. We have some alternative which is more acceptable. If, for example, we get fired from our job and get a better job the next day, it might not be in our interests to push a dispute with our former employer if there is little for us to gain, since our financial loss is zero.
4. We don't like conflict.
5. We feel powerless — what is the point?
6. We may want to continue a relationship with the other person and don't want to risk it.
7. We don't like risks generally.
8. We are very tolerant and forgiving.

---

[4]   The term BATNA was originated by the Harvard Negotiation Project in its seminal book: R. Fisher, W. Ury and B. Patton, *Getting to Yes: Negotiating Agreement Without Giving In*, 2nd ed. (New York: Penguin Books, 1991).

[5]   As with most of the topics in this book, there is a large volume of literature on the process of how a conflict becomes a dispute, and how the dispute evolves. See, in particular, W. Felstiner, R. Abel and A. Saray, "The Emergence and Transformation of Disputes: Naming, Blaming Claiming...", (1980-1) 15 Law & Soc'y Rev. 631, and J. Macfarlane, ed., *Dispute Resolution* (Toronto: Emond-Montgomery, 1999), c. 1.

Each legal dispute in which we find ourselves will have two sides and each side will have a perspective about what happened, who is correct, what the individual wants, what the other should do, and where and how it should be resolved. It is unlikely that both sides will view the dispute in the same way. Each will consider or be influenced by a range of factors from the specific to the more general. These can be characterized as *rights*, *interests*, and *values*.

The following two examples illustrate how the perspective of a party can be broken down into rights, interests and values. It is useful to identify each of these when exploring creative resolutions to a dispute. Unless underlying interests and values are recognized and addressed, the parties are unlikely to settle.

For example, let us suppose in May 2001, Maria decides that in September she will leave her home in Sault Ste. Marie and go to London to start a three-year community college course. She is 19, and she will be away from home for the first time. She is planning to finance her education through student loans and does not drive a car. She must decide by August 15 whether to go to school, for that is when the first year's tuition is payable. Maria's course will take three years to complete. She comes to London looking for a place to live. She talks to Janine, who has an older house near the campus. In the basement of the house is a small one-bedroom apartment which was used for two years by Janine's son, who is now married and living elsewhere. Unknown to Janine, the stove is broken. Janine works as a human resources specialist for a local hospital but has been on sick leave for two months while her broken leg heals. Her sick leave will run out in June, and she may not be able to get back to work until October.

In May, Maria and Janine talk and agree on a rent of $500, parking, if Maria gets a car, and a start date of September 1. They do not discuss utilities. Maria thinks they are included, and Janine has not considered it. On August 3, Janine has learned that the stove is broken, calls Maria and tells her that they can split the cost of a replacement. She also tells her that utilities will be an extra $50 per month and that she will need a security deposit of one month's rent in advance, plus rent for September. Maria is upset and wonders what to do. She refuses to pay the extra amounts. They now have a dispute.

From Maria's point of view, she thinks the following:

1. She has a lease on terms discussed in May. Utilities would be included and a stove provided. She saw one there in May.
2. Security deposits may be illegal.
3. Rent is good.
4. It will be hard to find another place in August.
5. She will lose a week of work if she has to go to London in August.
6. She may decide not to go to school this year. She has to decide by the 15th.
7. She does not have much money to waste.
8. She thinks Janine is being unfair and even greedy about the stove.
9. If she likes the place, she would like to stay three years.
10. She would like to know what her plans are, have them settled.

Janine's perspective is as follows:

1. Maria would be a good tenant, who might stay three years.
2. She has financial pressures, needs the extra security deposit money now.
3. She assumes Maria would pay utilities, now that she thinks of it.
4. She does not want an unhappy tenant in her basement making noise, causing damage.
5. She would like some financial certainty in her life.
6. She might not find another tenant until October.

The issues here can be broken into groups:

A.   1.   Is there a lease yet?
    2.   Is a security deposit lawful? Is last month's rent?
    3.   Is there any law about utilities?
B.   4.   Both have financial pressure and time pressures.
    5.   Each has reasons for wanting the deal to go ahead and to last for three years.
C.   6.   Maria thinks Janine is being unfair and greedy. She wants to be treated fairly.
    7.   Both want some security in their lives, some certainty.
    8.   Janine wants her home to be under her control and to be peaceful.

Group A includes the narrow issues, in this case characterized as legal ones. If there is no law about utilities, it is still an issue. We will refer to these issues as "rights" issues.

Group B includes *why* they are taking certain positions on "A" issues. We will call these the "interests" of the parties.

Group C includes deeper, longer-term factors. These are called *values* or *goals*. Deeper values and needs lie behind our interests. They include identity, security, happiness, peace of mind, physical well-being, social approval and a sense of belonging.

The number of rights issues is not fixed at the start of the dispute. The number may increase or decrease, as we will see. Our example does not include such possible issues as paying rent over the school term rather than over a full year, pets, subletting, decorating, *etc.* Maria and Janine have a choice in August: agree about what was agreed to in May, and its significance, or work out something in August which will satisfy their interests (B list) and values or goals (C list). Which approach will be best for both of them?

Let us take a particular type of dispute as a further example of rights, interests and values. In a medical malpractice dispute, the first instinct may be to delineate only the monetary interests on both sides. However there can be more to it, as demonstrated below.

A plaintiff claiming malpractice against a doctor and hospital may have interests that extend beyond the need for compensation. Depending on the psychology of the plaintiff, these interests may include:

- revenge
- altruism — *i.e.*, not to let this happen to someone else or to change medical policies for the better
- desire for more information about what happened
- an apology — *i.e.*, a reckoning by those who committed the harm
- in some cases, a crusade against the medical establishment

Likewise, the interests of the doctor and the hospital may extend beyond minimizing financial exposure and may include:

- preserving professional reputation/esteem with colleagues
- avoiding being victimized
- having one's methodology vindicated
- having an opportunity to explain what happened

As will be discussed in more detail in Chapter 5, "Probing Underlying Interests", it is critical to assess the unmet interests which are driving the dispute, and not to focus solely on the rights issues.

Chapter 3

NEGOTIATOR STYLES

In the previous chapter, the example involving Maria and Janine illustrated how interests, needs and goals could potentially drive how and if a resolution of a dispute is achieved. Additionally, the negotiating styles that Maria and Janine would utilize would also have a bearing on whether an agreement is reached and would impact on the shape and scope of the settlement as well as how it was achieved.

Whether you are negotiating your way through a legal dispute by yourself or acting for someone else as a legal professional or expert negotiator, you will have your own style. This will have an important influence on the strategy you use and on the tactics used to implement the strategy. Your personality and style will usually translate into your strategy — if you are aggressive, you may prefer a competitive strategy. It is useful, however, to be able to adopt more than one strategy and to use tactics that might seem "out of character" with your personality, where required. Following are the various styles of negotiating:

STYLES	CHARACTERISTICS	APPROPRIATE USE	PROBLEMS
• Competing	• Assertive • Uncooperative	• Get your own way	• Hurts relationships • Agreement may be undermined
• Accommodating	• Cooperative	• Build relations	• Exploited
• Avoiding	• Unassertive • Uncooperative	• Prevent conflict • Decide without enough info	• Agreements less likely
• Compromising	• Modestly assertive and cooperative	• Reach agreement quickly	• Problems recur
• Collaborating	• Assertive • Cooperative	• Fully explore issues/relationships	• Takes more time/energy • Others refuse to engage

WHICH NEGOTIATOR TYPE ARE YOU?

Let us look at the behavioural or attitudinal aspects of the different negotiator styles. Below is an exercise that illustrates essentially three types of negotiator.

Examine the three options which follow, as well as the specific attitudes and strategies listed under each, and ask yourself, "would this be likely to get me what I want from a negotiation?" Simply answer this question with a yes or a no with respect to each example of an attitude or strategy.

Keep track of the answers under each option. When you have finished, tally up the answers for each option and see how many positive responses you have for each.

What is it you are trying to do in a negotiation?
(Assume that you are trying to get your way. You are trying to get what you want. What would be the best way to do it?)

Option A	Option B	Option C
i) get angry and accusatory	i) completely trust the other side — "they may know more than you"	i) adopt the attitude that it is both sides versus the problem at hand
ii) adopt a me/us versus them attitude	ii) view the other side as friends	ii) create an atmosphere of collaboration and joint problem-solving
iii) create an atmosphere of mistrust, competition	iii) make concessions to cultivate the relationship	iii) utilize fairness/objective criteria
iv) take a hardline, uncompromising approach	iv) make offers — if the other side does not like an offer you have made, make another one it will like	iv) be soft on the people, hard on the problem
v) "my way or the highway"	v) avoid a contest of wills	v) explore each party's multiple interests — substantive, procedural and emotional/psychological — attempt to combine these interests in a variety of ways

vi) victory at all costs — including your own ("scorched earth policy")	vi) insist on agreement — that is the goal — at any cost, including your own	vi) focus on interests and get around the rigidity of limiting yourself to set positions
vii) make decisions based on threats, coercion, pressure, manipulation	vii) disclose your bottom line, preferably early	vii) utilize principled offers — with some rationale/ substantive basis behind them
viii) "if they want something, it must be bad for me"	viii) try to please the other side	viii) treat all parties with respect, but do not be afraid to communicate real concerns/feelings

Most people, after doing this exercise, come to the conclusion that Option C, which we will designate as the "Type C" negotiator, has the best chance of succeeding in a negotiation by arriving at a satisfactory agreement. There should be more positive responses to the question "Would this get me what I want" with Type C. The other types — Type A and Type B — can be characterized as the "hardball, positional bargainer"[1] and the "ineffective negotiator" respectively. Neither of these approaches is very effective in the long run.

COMPARING NEGOTIATOR TYPES

What happens when a Type A negotiator meets another Type A negotiator? There will probably not be an agreement, and if there is one, it may only be achieved through coercion or other unattractive means, which, of course, may affect the durability of the agreement as well as the satisfaction rating from the parties.

What happens when Type B negotiators confront one another? There again may be no agreement at all because the parties may not be directed enough to achieve one. Any agreement that is reached may miss essential issues remaining to be resolved; this can also affect the durability of the agreement. The parties may have to come back to the table in short order.

When we have Type C negotiators up against one another, we have an interest-based, principled negotiation[2] in which alternatives are canvassed, risks are

---

[1] The positional bargainer takes a position and insists on that initial position, without considering underlying interests.

[2] Interest-based principled negotiation seeks to realize the interests of a party to a dispute, as opposed to simply maximizing a position taken. Proposals which are made are not arbitrary, but are based on a cogent rationale which has at its root the underlying interests motivating the party.

assessed and the outstanding issues are addressed head on. There is a good chance for reaching a durable, satisfying agreement.

What happens when a Type A encounters a Type B? Generally, Type Bs will be demolished, as the more hardline, positional stance of Type As will tend to dominate Type Bs, who may give in vainly, hoping for some kind of improved relationship. Type Bs are vulnerable, and Type As tend to pounce on any vulnerabilities.

When a Type A encounters a Type C, however, the Type C principled negotiator can handle it. Type Cs will not capitulate and will not respond to pressure tactics; nevertheless, they will address the issues in dispute and attempt to work out a compromise that satisfies the parties' interests. Perhaps no agreement with the Type A negotiator will emerge, but there is a higher chance of an agreement and a much greater likelihood of a deal which is satisfactory to both Type C and Type A.

When a Type B meets up with a Type C, there will often be an agreement, perhaps skewed in favour of the Type C, but not such that the deal is unfair to the point that it may not be durable or enforceable.

USING ELEMENTS FROM ALL TYPES

Of course, these are all generalizations. In reality, people may exhibit a bit of each negotiator type, depending on moods and on the circumstances. But that fact also serves to make the analogy a useful one — because when negotiating, you need to have an idea about how your behaviour is influencing events and how productively you are handling the negotiation.

As mentioned, there may be elements to each negotiator type that are usefully employed in a negotiation. For example, it may be appropriate to make concessions to cultivate a relationship (a Type B trait) if the relationship interest is of prime importance. Negotiating with your mother or spouse comes to mind! Equally, becoming angry and accusatory may have its place in an adversarial context when it is necessary to delineate lines over which you do not want the other side to cross, and the crossing of which makes the alternatives to an agreement better than any potential agreement. Every context is unique. However, the general rule is that a principled Type C negotiator will be far better able to handle other types of negotiators and will be far better at achieving his or her core interests through negotiated agreements.

A study of negotiation style was conducted by the author G.R. Williams to see if it was possible to identify characteristics that would make one more effective than another.[3] He used aggressive versus cooperative, and, although both could be effective, a good settlement was more likely with a cooperative style;

---

[3]   G. R. Williams, "Style and Effectiveness in Negotiation" in L. Hall, ed., *Negotiation: Strategies for Mutual Gain: the Basic Seminar of the Harvard Program on Negotiation* (Newbury Park, Calif.: Sage, 1993) and G.R. Williams, *Legal Negotiation and Settlement* (St. Paul, Minn.: West Pub. Co., 1983).

however, some caution was required if the other side was using an aggressive style.

What he found to be ineffective in a cooperative style were traits such as "gentle, obliging, patient, forgiving, and trustful". In negotiation, it is possible to be too trusting and too "nice", like the type B negotiator above.

He also found that it was possible to be ineffective when being too aggressive. The traits of an ineffective but aggressive negotiator included "argumentative, quarrelsome, demanding, egotistical, headstrong, intolerant, hostile". These people were too bull-headed to recognize the need to make some concessions, if a settlement was possible.

If you find your style to be less effective than desired, consider using another style to help you. It will not mean that you are a worthless person. Indeed, you may be a wonderful person. It just means that your style of personality does not help you in negotiations.

Finally, every good cooperative negotiator is also a good aggressive negotiator.[4] There are several reasons for this. One is that it shows the other side that you will not let yourself be pushed into unmet concessions. If you keep being too cooperative, the other side will keep pushing. Another is that if you do not show your teeth once in a while, the entire range of issues will be decided against you, and there will be nothing left for you. A third reason is that sometimes the best tactic is to maintain your cooperation for only as long as the other side is doing the same. Meet aggressive behaviour with firmness. Finally, there will be some key issues upon which you will have decided how far to go. A walk-away alternative firmly held will keep you from going beyond your limits.

There are many good reasons to try to maintain a cooperative style and to turn the negotiation from positional to principled wherever possible. One of the best of these is found in the psychological principle of "liking". It is suggested that people prefer to say yes to those they know and like.[5] Thus, a positive relationship with the other side may be more effective in helping to obtain agreement to your proposals. If you are an aggressive negotiator, you risk having the other side begin to dislike you, and you limit your effectiveness.

The conclusion to be drawn from this discussion of negotiator styles is that it is important to be aware of your own style, as well as that of the opposing party. Where circumstances dictate, consider adopting a different style to optimize your chances of success. While a cooperative approach usually works best, there are times when it is necessary to take an aggressive stance.

---

[4]   R. E. Hawkins, "Negotiation" in P. Emond, ed., *Commercial Dispute Resolution* (Aurora, Ont.: Canada Law Book, 1989) at 62.

[5]   R. Birke and C.R. Fox, "Psychological Principles in Negotiating Civil Settlements" (1999) 4 Harv. Negotiation Law Rev. 1 at n. 201-05.

Chapter 4

POSITIONAL VERSUS INTEREST-BASED (PRINCIPLED) BARGAINING

As touched on in the previous chapter, there are two contrasting models of how to negotiate: positional[1] (also called value claiming, distributive, adversarial, or zero sum) and principled[2] (also called interest based, problem solving, integrative, value creating, and win-win). It should be emphasized that these are models with their own methods of negotiating. No negotiator uses one model to the exclusion of the other. A better settlement would probably be possible where *principled* negotiating is the overall choice of both parties, although each party may use tactics derived from *positional* negotiating to its advantage during the process.

THE POSITIONAL MODEL

Much of a lawyer's experience and much of the literature on negotiating focuses on bargaining in a transaction. One party has something that the other wants, and they work it out. They see the number of issues as fairly limited, much like cutting up a pie. If one party gets a bigger piece, the other will get a smaller one. The parties jockey for position. This concept of negotiating has been carried

---

[1]   See, generally, H. Raiffa, *The Art and Science of Negotiation* (Cambridge, Mass.: Harvard U. Press, 1982); G. Lowenthal, "A General Theory of Negotiation Process, Strategy and Behaviour" (1982) 1 U. Kansas L. Rev. 69; L. Boulle and K.J. Kelly, *Mediation: Principles, Process, Practice*, Canadian ed. (Toronto: Butterworths, 1998) at 53; C. Menkel-Meadow, "Toward Another View of Legal Negotiation: The Structure of Problem Solving" (1983-84) 31 U.C.L.A. L. Rev. 754 at 783; C.B. Craver, *Effective Legal Negotiation and Settlement* 3rd. ed. (Charlottesville, VA: Michie, 1993); D. Pruitt, *Negotiation Behaviour* (New York: Academic Press, 1981); D. Gifford, "A Context-Based Theory of Strategy Selection in Legal Negotiation" (1985) 46 Ohio State L.J. 41; G. Wetlaufer, "The Limits of Integrative Bargaining" (1996) 85 Geo. L.J. 369; J.J. White "The Pros and Cons of Getting to Yes" (1984) 34 J. Legal Ed. 115; M. Deutsch, *The Resolution of Conflict* (New Haven: Yale University Press, 1973).
      An excellent foundation paper discussing the issue of dispute resolution and law is S. Sibley and A. Sarat, "Dispute Processing in Law and Legal Scholarship" (1988-89) 66 Denver U.L. Rev. 437.
[2]   See C. Menkel-Meadow, "Toward Another View of Legal Negotiation: The Structure of Problem Solving" (1983-84) 31 U.C.L.A. L. Rev. 754 at 783, and R. Fisher, W. Ury and B. Patton, *Getting to Yes: Negotiating Agreement Without Giving In*, 2nd ed. (New York: Penquin, 1991). This volume, first published in 1983, expounds the concept of principled negotiation stressed in *Mediation and Negotiation: Representing Your Clients*.

over from transactional bargaining to dispute resolution. However, it does not travel well. Think about some of its underpinnings:

1. The size of the pie (the number of issues and their size) is limited.
2. Your gains minus my losses equals zero (zero-sum).[3]
3. The idea is not just to win but to "win big".
4. The focus is on what happened in the past, limiting the scope of resolutions and restricting creativity.
5. The tactics used, which will discourage maintenance of long-term relationships, include:

- do not make the first offer
- make the first one high
- do not make the first concession
- give less than you get each time you concede
- do not disclose any information to the other side unless it is to your advantage
- use bluff, misleading statements and threats
- be the one to draft the terms of settlement
- keep one item back to throw in at the end once you have settled (the "nibble")

The positional model is based largely upon transactional bargaining and deals with a one-off situation in which no future relationship between the parties is likely.

As you can see, this style will favour the aggressive style of negotiator and will often result in a settlement in the middle, between the two opening offers. More often, the dispute is not resolved and, therefore, moves on toward the court house.

THE PRINCIPLED (INTEREST-BASED) MODEL

The other polar model, *principled* negotiation, rejects the zero-sum concept and assumes that a dispute is always about more than narrow rights issues. It recognizes that money may be a "proxy" for more basic needs and values, and that narrow remedies might not address these. Principled negotiation involves doing the following:

1. Negotiate about what really drives the parties — their interests — why they are pursuing their "rights".

---

[3] This is based upon economics and on "game theory". The text that started it all is J. von Neumann and O. Morgenstern, *The Theory of Games and Economic Behaviour* (Princeton: Princeton University Press, 1944). Another useful source is M. Bacharach, *Economics and the Theory of Games* (London: Macmillan, 1976).

2. Enlarge the number of options — develop creative remedies that address the real concerns of both sides. Let them identify these to each other.
3. Disclose some information to the other side — try to persuade, using motivational argument.

The advantages of the principled approach are as follows:

1. It is possible to achieve a gain without a corresponding loss to the other side. When all of the value has been extracted from the dispute, a Pareto-optimal solution will have been achieved (win-win).[4]
2. Ongoing relationships can be maintained, in whole or in part, because some trust is required when disclosing information.

In essence, there is little harm in trying principled negotiation, even in acrimonious or intractable disputes, with some caution. If settlement efforts fail, you can always fall back to positional bargaining and future adjudication. However, as a note of caution, many negotiators still assume that the pie size is fixed and that a gain for the other side means a loss to them. This means that you will spend much of your time trying to convince the other party to engage in principled negotiation, using methods that will be described in Chapter 7.[5]

THE "NEGOTIATOR'S DILEMMA"

As indicated earlier, most negotiations involve a mix of models and may involve a mix of negotiator styles. However, there is a tension between the two models which may affect all negotiations. The dilemma faced by each negotiator is that her or she knows that if both parties use principled negotiation, an agreement will be likely, and it will be a good one for both sides. But the negotiator may also think that if he or she uses positional bargaining while the other side uses principled bargaining alone, he or she will do even better for his or her side. This occurs because the negotiator is able to take advantage of the openness of and the information disclosed by the other side. This difficulty, which is called the "Negotiator's Dilemma", is illustrated below.[6]

---

[4] Beyond this stage, a benefit to one comes at a cost to the other. See R. Birke and C.R. Fox "Psychological Principles in Negotiating Civil Settlements" 4 Harv. Negotiation Law Rev. 1, and A.M. Polinsky, *An Introduction to Law and Economics*, 2nd ed. (Boston: Little, Brown, 1989). The name Pareto is that of an Italian economist.

[5] See R. Birke and C.R. Fox "Psychological Principles in Negotiating Civil Settlements" 4 Harv. Negotiation Law Rev. 1, and M. Bazerman and M. Neale, "Heuristics in Negotiation: Limitations to Effective Dispute Resolution" in M.H. Bazerman and R.J. Lewicki, eds., *Negotiating in Organizations* (Beverly Hills: Sage Publications, 1983).

[6] See D. Lax and J. Sebenius, *The Manager as Negotiator: Bargaining for Cooperation and Competitive Gain* (New York: Free Press; London: Collier Macmillan, 1986) "Managing the Negotiator's Dilemma" in *Negotiation Analysis* (1986).

Others have done studies on a similar game called the "Prisoner's Dilemma" (R. Axelrod, *The Evolution of Cooperation* (New York: Basic Books, 1984).

Model Used by Party A		Model Used by Party B	
		Principled	Positional
	Principled	Good / Good	Great / Terrible
	Positional	Terrible / Great	Mediocre / Mediocre

Result for Party A is in lower left of each box.
Result for Party B is in upper right of each box.

The matrix set out above serves as a warning to negotiators whose style is cooperative to be a bit cautious sometimes. As we will see, positional bargaining can and does play an important role in negotiating and mediating an interest-based solution.[7]

USING THE PRINCIPLED MODEL EFFECTIVELY

Not only strike while the iron is hot, but make it hot by striking.[8]

In any negotiation, regardless of the approach used, the ultimate goal is to get what you want. If this goal is absent, the negotiation will not take place because the issue is not worth pursuing. If this goal is unclear, the objectives will be muddied, which can lead to all sorts of bad results.[9] But how do you conduct yourself at the negotiation when you want to use the principled approach? How can you ensure that you will achieve what you want out of a negotiation?

"Cautious cooperation" will maximize the chances of success at a negotiation, no matter who the other side is. This is highly useful because it is likely that you will encounter all sorts of negotiators with all sorts of different behaviour patterns — some functional and some dysfunctional. The better adapted your own general attitudinal approach to negotiations, the more likely you will succeed no matter what behaviours the other side demonstrates.

When offers are being made, the "principled approach" maximizes the chances of success because it appeals to the merits of the arguments advanced

---

[7]   This will be discussed in detail in Chapter 7, with respect to the use of the "mutual gains" approach.

[8]   Oliver Cromwell in F.L. Knowles, ed., *The Value of Courage* (Boston: H.M. Caldwell Co., 1905) at 13.

[9]   In the 1970s, the Trudeau government approached the members of the European Union in an effort to forge new trade links and areas of partnership. The stated aim was to create a "contractual link". When, after some diplomatic lobbying, Canada's quest was finally given some air time by Germany and France, Trudeau was asked exactly what he meant and what he sought to negotiate on Canada's behalf. The response, however, was the same — "a contractual link". This, of course, was too vague, and little came of the idea. While increased exports may have been the underlying interest, the goal of the negotiations had not been properly worked out. Canada had not ascertained precisely what it wanted, and it arguably lost a real opportunity to better specific trade ties with Europe.

by the parties to a negotiation. This grounds the negotiation in the reality of the issues involved in the dispute, which has a salutary and, indeed, satisfying impact on the conduct of the negotiations.[10] It also plays to the need to deflate intense emotions and to come to rational decisions — both of which are essential in order to achieve agreement in an adversarial dispute.

Principled offers involve some rationale or basis for their making. For example, when you present the offer, you explain how it is based or calculated, and why it is important to you, as opposed to making a straight demand without explanation. In this way, offers are not arbitrary and, therefore, do not carry with them all the risk of alienation inherent in an arbitrary offer. There is always an explanation, a calculation or a theory behind a principled offer. These offers tend to work better at resolving disputes (especially after the first exchanges of offers have been made) because they indicate that thought and compromise have gone into their crafting — and that fact alone may lessen the acrimony and help to evolve a negotiating climate that is rational and conducive to settlement. Making principled offers also gives each side the opportunity to demonstrate that it has listened to the other side and to incorporate something of the other side's argument or position in the offer. This enables a carrot or an olive branch to be demonstrably extended and moves the parties closer together. It also makes it easier for a party to emphasize what is important about its own arguments or views of what constitutes a fair resolution, in that the thrust of the party's own position may be reflected in the principled offers made. Because the offer is broken down and is available for all to see how it was arrived at, it has an educative function that is lacking in offers that just toss numbers or concepts back and forth.[11]

For example, where the insurer of a long-term disability policy denies liability for paying the policy benefit (due to medical or technical reasons to do with the policy or with the representations made when applying for it), a settlement is made based on the payment of a lump sum, comprising arrears and a present value for the future payments due under the policy. If we assume there is an arguable case for the presence of a long-term disability under the relevant policy, a number of options for a settlement exist, including:

---

[10]   The November 1995 evaluation conducted on the Toronto ADR Centre (See J. Macfarlane, "Court-Based Mediation for Civil Cases: An Evaluation of the Ontario Court (General Division) ADR Centre", Faculty of Law, University of Windsor, November 1995) revealed that the parties and counsel at a mediation found the process much more satisfying and productive if the merits of the parties' cases were thoroughly canvassed. This is really no surprise, as people are devoted to the arguments that drive the dispute, or even create the dispute, and it is not realistic, even in an interest-based or facilitative process, to abandon those arguments. They are relevant in determining a party's interests and alternatives to an agreement by constituting the basis of an honest risk assessment.

[11]   There is a computer service now available which relays to parties in litigation three settlement numbers respectively. The service collects a fee if one of the three numbers comes close to matching one of the other party's three numbers. The problem with this approach, apart from how to compare offers in a case where the numbers have to be broken down or where elements other than numbers are essential to the integrity of the offer, is that there is no opportunity to make the offers principled. The missing ingredient is the examination of interests and of that which is really important to the parties.

1. a payment of a portion or all of the arrears (to take the claimant up to the time where the disability may have ended)
2. payment of arrears and a number of years into the future (perhaps based on the claimant's or physician's opinion of when improvement might occur)
3. taking the arrears and present value of the future and discounting the total by a percentage akin to the risks on the medical or other issues
4. taking payment up to a date referred to in the medical opinions about when the claimant may be able to return to work
5. attributing a "buy out price" for the surrender of the policy
6. adding an exclusion to the existing policy for the disability in question

All of the above options could constitute the rationale for an offer. Rather than simply trade numbers back and forth, these theories could reflect some objective reality of the case or could be structured so as to recognize a particular argument or interest advanced by a party. In any event, making an offer using one or more of the above rationales, in isolation or in combination, will render it a principled offer. Nevertheless, however principled an offer may be, there is no guarantee of acceptance. Often, quite a few principled offers have to be traded back and forth until the gap is narrowed and a settlement is forthcoming. It can, paradoxically, also be the case that after a while, principled offers are of less importance, and the remaining gap (after there has been some significant movement) is bridged by simply splitting the difference or by some other equally effective "unprincipled" idea.

While the principled approach works best most of the time, positional negotiation can also play a role, despite its shortcomings. This chapter has illustrated the power of interest-based (or principled) negotiation to achieve agreement where the more traditional positional model fails. The next chapter discusses how to identify the underlying interests of the parties to enable you to negotiate using the principled approach.

Chapter 5

PROBING UNDERLYING INTERESTS

Interest-based resolutions focus on the underlying interests of the parties — their wants, needs and expectations. A party's interests are usually a compendium for what is motivating the party in the dispute, and what the party really needs to achieve from the dispute. A party's interests are not always readily apparent, yet it is crucial that interests be identified before interest-based resolutions can be sought. This chapter explores the process of identifying interests.

People do not enter into disputes without reason. In a rational setting, people have an objective, a goal, or a cause — although they may not have clearly articulated it or may have juxtaposed it with other less obvious interests. There is something they desire to be achieved by being involved in the dispute.

INTERESTS NOT WORTH PURSUING

People usually let the matter go when they have little or no interest to be served through disputation and they have a readily available and satisfactory alternative. For example, a person may have hated his or her last car — it may have broken down frequently and rusted out prematurely — but does not make an issue of it and sue the manufacturer. He or she simply purchases a different make of car and never returns to the maker of the model that gave so much trouble (think how many other countless times something has bothered you — a shoddy item of merchandise, a rude person behind a counter, a nonsensical explanation, *etc.*) Rational individuals do not "pick a fight" or become embroiled in a dispute every time something untoward happens. They let the matter pass because there is nothing to gain by entering into a dispute. In a complex and busy world, this is as much a matter of self-preservation as anything else.[1]

NEGOTIATION NOT ALWAYS APPROPRIATE

There is another kind of abstinence from disputation which has nothing to do with the need to ignore the trivial. A party may refuse to negotiate because no interests are served by negotiating. For example, a wildlife photographer on a safari tour bus had a dispute with a particularly obnoxious fellow passenger. The

---

[1]   Indeed, we may have a generalized interest in not entering into a dispute every time we encounter conflict, otherwise we would become obsessed and dominated by every little thing that bothered us, and we would become completely dysfunctional in short order.

photographer needed the tinted window open in order to take pictures, and the other tourist wanted the window closed, to maximize the effect of the air conditioning and to minimize dust.

The photographer assessed the situation: opportunities for taking pictures of wildlife were unpredictable and fleeting, requiring leaving the window open at all times; the tourist had a repugnant personality and was disliked by most people on the bus; the tourist did not pose a physical threat to the photographer; and the photographer was not at risk of being ostracized by others on the bus as a result of refusing to compromise.

In this example, any compromise involving keeping the window closed would have spoiled picture-taking opportunities, which were deemed far more valuable than the benefits of accommodating the tourist. There were no negotiations because no interests would have been served in negotiating. There was no desirable relationship to preserve, no avoidance of harm or trouble to achieve and no gain to be had at any level by negotiating a compromise. There was barely any downside, but a lot of upside to *not* negotiating.

As a further example, in World War II, the Allies insisted on unconditional surrender and refused to negotiate, despite several high-level efforts by the Nazis to explore a separate peace. There were no Allied interests to be served by sharing a world with a Nazi-dominated and heavily armed Germany. Such a peace could not have endured for long.

On a more mundane level, if a party is wrongfully dismissed from employment but obtains an identical paying job the following day, though there has still been a wrongful dismissal, it is unlikely to be pursued because the damages would be nominal at best, the employee having fully mitigated by acquiring the new job. No negotiations are needed because there is no interest served by negotiating. Conversely, if a 10-year employee with an open and shut wrongful dismissal case is faced with an employer who steadfastly refuses to provide any more termination pay than that required by the *Ontario Employment Standards Act*, there may also be no interests advanced by negotiating. The employee would have better success in court, beyond any level attainable by way of negotiation, provided he or she has not fully mitigated.

LEGAL MERITS

The legal merits in an interest-based negotiation are not irrelevant. Indeed, they make up one of the important interests to be considered.[2] An interesting result from the evaluation conducted by the Toronto ADR Centre was that parties and counsel were more satisfied with the mediation process when the merits had had a full hearing than when they were dealt with peripherally. People are in a dispute for a reason, and one of those reasons is likely that they think they are right. It is,

---

2 See generally R. Mnookin and K. Kornhauser, "Bargaining in the Shadow of the Law: The Case of Divorce" (1979) 88 Yale L.J. 950, and G. Goodpaster, "Lawsuits as Negotiations" (1992) 8 Negot. J. 221.

therefore, folly to assume that the merits of the different viewpoints in a dispute can be shelved when it comes time to deal with the resolution of the dispute.

Interest-based bargaining is all about assessing alternatives. If a given settlement meets or exceeds likely litigation outcomes, then the matter should resolve. If any potential deal falls short of likely litigation outcomes, then the case should not settle. The alternative to a given settlement is continued litigation; therefore, it becomes imperative to assess possible litigation outcomes (both legal and financial). This cannot be done without evaluating the merits/arguments presented — including the facts, the law and the evidence, as well as any issues of credibility.

Principled offers should, therefore, reflect an assessment of the merits as well as of any other relevant interests. It is also important to emphasize your own arguments. However, this should not be done myopically or without an openness to be persuaded by the other side or to realize greater exposure than initially anticipated. Listening to what the other side is saying is as important as cogently making your own submission.

NON-LEGAL INTERESTS

As stated earlier, it is possible for other interests to overshadow the legal merits involved in a dispute. Parties to a contract where one party has a clear case for breach of contract may settle on terms not related to the relative merits because of the commercial advantages for doing so. An employee may settle for less than he or she is entitled to because he or she knows he or she is going to get another job the following week and, therefore, stands to attain double recovery. A long-term disability carrier that settles for a large lump sum when the evidence of a disability is scant may do so because it wants the relatively young and injury/sickness prone policyholder to surrender the policy — thereby letting the insurer off the hook with future claims. Accordingly, the merits are really akin to one of the interests at play in the mediation — an interest with a direct bearing on the alternatives faced by a party and on the party's aversion to risk. What this means is that subject to doing something against the law, the legal merits need not be the driving force in the negotiation. In the landlord-tenant example illustrated in Chapter 2 (with Maria and Janine), if there was no lease, and if Janine insisted on that strict legal position, she would find herself without a tenant in September — a pyrrhic victory!

WHAT ARE "INTERESTS"?

Interests are what drive our behaviour. We behave in certain ways to satisfy our interests, usually according to some sort of subjective or objective hierarchy. Wants and needs are a part of this, with wants being a manifestation of our deeper needs. For example, a homeowner may *want* marble bathrooms in the house he or she purchased, but *needs* a house that has plumbing. The need is the proverbial trunk upon which the various branches of wants spring forth.

Accordingly, wants can be sacrificed in a compromise leading to an agreement, as long as our core needs are met.

A party to acrimonious litigation may want to "get even" with the other side, that is, to obtain revenge. The core need here may be for self-actualization, and to build up self-esteem. In other words, realization of a personal goal which is driving the more superficial "want". Accordingly, receipt of adequate compensation through a settlement may suffice to enhance the needed self-esteem, thus dispelling the "want" for revenge.

Interestingly, as crucial as interests are to what is behind a dispute, the ascertainment of a person's interests is often something of an afterthought. People often jump blindly into disputes, knowing at some level that they have to be there, but not stopping to quite figure out why. This is because they often react instinctively or with a gut feeling. People know that they do not want to be taken advantage of or treated lightly, but their assessment of their interests may not be any deeper than that.

If a person slips and falls and is injured, he or she brings an action for damages because of anger or fear, or because a lawyer advises it. He or she may have a vague concept of the need for compensation but the real interests have not been addressed.

ASCERTAINING INTERESTS

The assessment of your own interests is much more an intellectual exercise than an intuitive one. The process of reasoning out alternatives and canvassing what is sometimes a multiplicity of driving forces, and prioritizing them, requires intellectual thought and rigour. It is a rational rather than an emotional process. In fact, it is helpful to try to completely divorce emotion from the process, because emotion may serve to cloud the reasoning required to make informed choices about which interests are important and which to pursue.[3] Without an emotional detachment, it can be easy to fall into the trap of misjudging one's interests and erroneously solving a temporary problem with a permanent solution.

Ascertaining interests is not always easy and is often hard work. It can usually benefit from the assistance of a third-party neutral who will in some detail review the party's expectations, desires, goals and the like. Why is a third-party neutral helpful? Like cutting one's hair, it is hard to do it to oneself. An objective, fair and dynamic process of questions posed and questions answered is difficult to engage in alone. When dealing with one's own interests, there is a tendency to assume that one has it all in one's head — that one has already done it and knows why one is disputing. However, this is seldom the case, because few people have the self-discipline or objectivity to thoroughly review their situation and the context in which they are disputing, and to determine what they can get out of it and what goals they need to achieve. People seem to find it helpful to bounce their thinking off someone not attached to the dispute (lawyers are not the ideal persons to assist the client with this because they are filling the

---

[3]   See Chapter 6, "Planning for the Negotiation".

role of an advocate) and to have someone throw back at them challenges to the assumptions underlying their thinking. Hence, the benefit of using a neutral.

The neutral also helps the party to reformulate its thinking so that it is able to develop a hierarchy of needs, based on a rigorous comparison of what it perceives to be the driving force behind its involvement in the dispute.

For example, a contractor may have been sued for damages when he walked off the job for non-payment, which non-payment arose when certain things were not done according to the contract specifications. The plaintiff's real interest, however, may have been completing the project, getting it done less expensively or having certain specifications changed. Or it may have been something less obvious. In a construction case involving the above scenario, the real interest of the owner was to see the subtrade, which had dug the foundation, get paid. It had inflamed the owner's sense of decency that the subtrade had done that work and had not gotten paid. The case settled for not a dime to the owner plaintiff, but on an agreement that the general contractor was to pay the subtrade the invoice it had rendered.[4]

Ironically, a key element to an honest canvassing of interests is a hard look at the risks associated with the dispute. This is ironic because inherent in the interest-based process is an overlay of rights-based analysis. An interest canvassing cannot be properly done without a risk assessment. If the risks in pursuing the dispute outweigh the interests served by being involved in the dispute, then something has to give.

For example, NATO bombed Serbia in a purported effort to halt Serbia's ethnic cleansing of Kosovar Albanians. If the Soviet Union still existed, and had threatened war with NATO if NATO attacked Serbia, it could be argued that NATO would probably never have gotten involved with Kosovo. NATO's interests would have been defined differently. The risk of conflict with the Soviets, and the incumbent risk of nuclear war, would have far outweighed the humanitarian interests of NATO in helping Kosovar Albanians.

In expensive and drawn-out litigation, the risks of losing and of exposure to large cost awards, as well as the delay in time, ought to be fully taken into account. Accordingly, one's interest in a lawsuit that will be difficult or impossible to win may be to get out gracefully with as little cost as possible — in other words, damage control. Conversely, if the case is a winner, one's interests may be more focused on obtaining compensation so as to better one's quality of life, or on seeing a legal obligation performed.

The cynic would say that there is always an interest on the part of the plaintiff in getting as much compensation as possible, and on the part of the defendant in minimizing the payout. This equates to a "greed interest". This, of course, is true — but only to a certain extent. A person who has suffered a catastrophic injury is not motivated by greed, but by fear and by his or her future needs. A long-term disability claimant (in a case where the disability is not manufactured or exaggerated) is motivated less by sheer greed than by fear of being unable to work remuneratively, and may possibly also be motivated by

---

[4] Amazingly, the owner and the contractor which was the subtrade that had dug the foundation were completely at arms length from each other and had never met!

vengeance against the insurer whom he or she believes should have maintained the benefits. A party to a cancelled contract may want less to get even than to simply be put back into the position he or she would have been in had the contract been honoured. There is a subtle difference here from a greed interest, and it can be seen that the real interests permit a number of settlement possibilities that unadulterated greed cannot.

Interests are subjective and personal, and therefore not always what you might reasonably assume them to be. For example, in a disability case mediated by the author, the insurer eventually offered to put the plaintiff back on full benefits, and to pay the arrears with interest and costs. This was all that the plaintiff could ever hope to achieve in the litigation — he had "won". However, this was not where his interests lay. He had a child about to enter college and had no cash for the tuition and expenses. The entrance opportunity would not last forever, and the plaintiff was desirous of a closer relationship with the child, with whom he had been distant for some time. Accordingly, the plaintiff wanted a lump sum settlement, even if it meant absorbing a substantial discount in the amount which might ultimately be paid if he were to be put back on benefits.

Another example is an estate case, also mediated by the author. A family had been embroiled in very bitter litigation for years and was in danger of completely dwindling the value of the mother's estate. About the only thing which the middle-aged children and their families could agree on was that the family was dysfunctional, and that they wanted to do something to rectify that. Accordingly, the children eventually agreed to completely bypass their own generation and worked out a formula for leaving everything to the grandchildren.

In the above two examples, something other than personal greed was at work. Where greed really is the only interest, far less can be done creatively to fashion a settlement.

Questions to Uncover Interests

While we may need outside help in assessing our own interests, it can often be easier to decipher the interests of the other side. This can be done with some simple questions and requests for clarification, such as:

1. "Why would you say that?"
2. "Help me to understand what you are saying."
3. "What do you really need here?"
4. "What concerns do you have?"
5. What would be wrong with.....?"
6. "As I understand it, you are saying that you have an interest in...."
7. "What is really the best way to achieve that for you?"
8. "What do you really want this litigation/dispute to do for you?"
9. "What I am hearing you say is..."
10. "What is your objective in calling for that?"

In summary, in order to maximize your outcome from a negotiation, you must probe the interests of both sides and attempt to craft a solution which meets some of these interests. For a discussion of the three different types of interests with which a party may be confronted, see Chapter 6, "Planning for the Negotiation".

Chapter 6

PLANNING FOR THE NEGOTIATION

Experienced negotiators will tell you that the key to success in a negotiation is planning,[1] planning, planning. While flexibility is essential, it is crucial to enter the process with a strong idea of what the best outcome for you is likely to be. Concepts that are explored in this chapter include understanding your best and worst alternatives to a negotiated agreement, the utility of identifying as many interests as possible and how to categorize and prioritize them, avoiding making assumptions about the opposing party, and using "independent" standards to legitimize your position.

CANVASSING BATNAS AND WATNAS

> Let the fear of danger be a spur to prevent it; he that fears not, gives advantage to the danger.[2]

The single most important lesson for negotiating well is to know your "walk-away" alternatives to an agreement and to constantly compare any settlement proposal on the table with those alternatives. Seldom is there only one alternative to an agreement. For example, the alternative to a settlement in a litigious context is litigation, but this likely entails a number of scenarios, some favourable, some not so favourable, depending on the adjudicated result. There is often an element of uncertainty in determining precisely what the alternatives are going to be, and this, therefore, requires the parties to do some educated speculation. Assessing alternatives can become an exercise in probabilities and priorities.

As basic as this concept seems, it is incredible to see intelligent parties, even institutional litigants, ignore their alternatives and look at proposed settlements in isolation — a very dangerous practice. The bottom line is — if you are ignorant about what will likely happen if there is no agreement and do not rate the desirability of that option — how will you know whether a settlement proposal is advantageous and meets your interests?[3]

---

[1] W. Ury, *Getting Past No, Negotiating with Difficult People* (New York: Bantam, 1991).
[2] Francis Quarles (1592-1644).
[3] For example, during the 1962 Cuban Missile Crisis, President Kennedy rejected the option of a surprise bombing of Cuba prior to Cuba's missiles becoming operational. This was because no general could assure him that every missile would be destroyed and that the Soviets would do nothing in response. A Soviet response, and an American counter-response, could have escalated into nuclear war. The alternatives to an agreement over the missiles were terrible to contemplate, and, fortunately, Kennedy did not ignore them.

Best Alternative to a Negotiated Agreement (BATNA)

There are two broad alternatives to consider. The first, the BATNA (best alternative to a negotiated agreement), is the litmus test by which to evaluate any proposed settlement. For example, a wrongfully dismissed employee with 20 years' service, a high income and no cause alleged by the employer knows with some degree of certainty (albeit not 100 per cent certainty) what a court might award. If offered one week/year of service, the employee's BATNA exceeds the offer (because the court would very likely award an entitlement to far more notice and, therefore, more payment in lieu of notice). The employee is better off not agreeing — the best alternative to the agreement is better than the agreement itself. If, however, the employee is offered three-and-a-half weeks per year of service, the BATNA (which might approximate one month per year of service) is not much better, and when non-recoverable legal costs and a helpful reference are factored in, the BATNA may be no better than the alternative. In this case, it may be wise to take the offer. If the employer were to offer one month per year of service, pay the amount so as to minimize taxes, provide a reference letter and active assistance in looking for another job as well as introduce the employee to a prospect of immediate employment (in which case the employee could obtain a windfall of the lump sum paid as damages because no income from the newly obtained job could be deducted if the lump sum was agreed to and paid), then the BATNA is clearly worse than the proposal, and the employee would be foolish not to agree.

Assessing BATNAs necessarily involves conducting a risk assessment and challenging the assumptions inherent in a party's position. Which alternative is likely to happen is sometimes difficult to predict, but the prediction is essential, or at least it is essential in order to develop a short list of possibilities which have a reasonable (*i.e.*, not remote) chance of occurring. It is the most likely short list of alternatives to which a settlement proposal must be compared.

The exception to this is where a BATNA is so favourable, despite fewer chances of it occurring, that the prospect of its occurrence, given the immense gain obtainable, is worth favouring over a prospective settlement which offers less. Accordingly, the parties least anxious to settle and who have some alternatives tend to bargain hardest.

Worst Alternative to a Negotiated Agreement (WATNA)

The other concept is the WATNA (worst alternative to a negotiated agreement). If the WATNA is very unfavourable, even though it may be remote, it may be worthwhile to accept a lesser settlement which precludes that unfavourable result from occurring. This will be a function of the parties' aversion to risk and the nature of that risk. As illustrated at the end of World War II, much of the Japanese military wanted to continue fighting, but the dropping of two atomic bombs, and the prospect of a rain of ruin on Japan's cities, was so terrible an

---

Instead, Kennedy pursued a naval blockade of Cuba that bought time, and enabled a negotiated outcome — the removal of U.S. missiles in Turkey and a pledge never to invade Cuba in exchange for the removal of the Soviet missiles in Cuba.

alternative that the Japanese accepted the terms of an unconditional surrender.[4] In terms of mediation, a litigant facing financial ruin from a lost court battle may decide, even if the prospect of a complete loss seems unlikely, to accept a compromise so as to avoid the WATNA. If the WATNA is more likely than not, then the decision on what to accept in an agreement is easier still.

Is it knowledge of the WATNA or BATNA that is of greater utility to a party faced with a decision on whether to accept, reject or amend a given settlement proposal? Interestingly, despite all the focus in the literature on BATNAs, it seems that the WATNA is far more operational. This is becaue people are instinctively more concerned with what might go wrong. Fear seems a better motivator than pleasure. This is not readily apparent because a party in a mediation usually tries to impress the mediator — as well as the other side and anyone else who will listen —that the party has a good case and is willing to take it to trial. The party purports to minimize the risks and downplay the consequences. However, when it comes time to make the tough decision on whether to accept a given proposal which the parties have struggled to negotiate for some time, it is the fear of failure which motivates the party to make the last clear compromise and accept an agreement that meets some of the party's interests and at least avoids the WATNA from occurring.

For example, an employer who dismissed an employee without cause faced an action for wrongful dismissal, the main issue being compensation to be paid for stock options which would have vested during the period of reasonable notice. The employer, however, had language in the stock option agreements which precluded its exercise after cessation of employment, even if the cessation was unlawful. However, rather than subject such favourable language to scrutiny by the courts (where it could very well be struck out), the employer paid a settlement and, in so doing, was able to continue to purport to rely on the exclusionary language with all its dealers across Canada in the future.

Another illustration of this would be helpful here: In a long-term disability case, the claimant alleges that he or she is disabled within the terms of the policy; the insurer alleges that the claimant can work and is not entitled to benefits. There may be other reasons for the various arguments, as well. The BATNA facing the claimant is to be paid any arrears with pre-judgment interest and to be put back on the monthly benefit. There will inevitably be non-recoverable legal costs. Under the policy, the insurer is free to attempt rehabilitation and may continue to rechallenge the disability. For the claimant, this means a life of independent medical exams, surveillance and a cramped lifestyle. The WATNA for the claimant is to lose, with all the cost consequences that may entail, and with no benefit or lump sum payable at all. For a party who truly believes in his or her inability to work, such a result would be a disaster.

---

[4] In fact, the Americans only had two operational bombs (with a third not ready until some months later). It was decided that they should be dropped in rapid succession (in the event that Japan did not surrender after the first one) so as to convey the impression that the United States had an unlimited number of bombs and could rain one down every couple of days until Japan was completely destroyed. It was a gamble that paid off, as the Japanese were seemingly convinced of this and apparently surrendered to avoid it. The WATNA was so terrible for Japan, and appeared so likely, that even unconditional surrender seemed better.

The insurer's BATNA is to win, but this entails non-recoverable costs; in many cases, the claimant is left with the policy still in force which means that the insurer may be faced with another similar disability claim in the future. Of greater significance to the insurer is the WATNA if the claimant is victorious, especially if the claimant is young, as this would mean that the insurer will face many years of potential payout once the claimant's benefits are ordered reinstated.

When such cases are settled (and they often are once all the medical documentation is assembled), it is not so much what the parties hope *to gain* that are the factors for comparison. It is what the parties hope *to avoid* — for the claimant hopes to avoid a loss (it costs money and provides zero future security) and the insurer hopes to avert a loss (it entails years of payout).

The point at which disputes settle, sometimes called the point or area of mutual gain, is supposed to be where each party is sufficiently satisfied with the agreement to enter into it. However, many agreements involve the parties being quite unhappy with the agreement. There is a certain amount of truth to the old adage, "if both parties are unhappy, it must be a good agreement". But why, then, are people agreeing to what makes then unhappy?

The reason is simple: because their alternatives to an agreement are so poor, the agreement still represents their best option. A disability claimant who would make a bad witness — with damaging surveillance and weak medical reports may settle for a low lump sum (as a proportion of the total present value of the entitlement) because the litigation alternatives are poor.

On the graph below are different hypothetical points of mutual gain (the settlement line) at which both parties recognize that settlement is in their best interests and are likely to enter into an agreement. Agreement where both parties have poor BATNAs or significant WATNAs are on the left side of the graph. Agreements that surpass BATNA or avoid WATNA altogether are on the right.

SETTLEMENT LINE

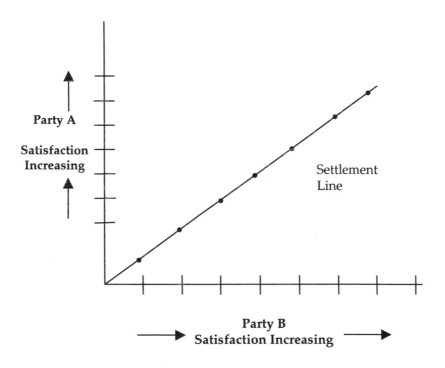

Improving Your BATNA/WATNA and Worsening That of Your Opponent

It is perfectly legitimate for a party to take lawful steps to better his or her BATNA, to lessen his or her WATNA, and to even worsen the other side's WATNA as well as to hurt the other side's BATNA! All this can be done by taking steps to improve arguments (by obtaining an expert report, achieving an interlocutory victory in a motion before the court or creating alternatives in the event the negotiations do not bear fruit). For example, an employee about to negotiate a raise may want to line up another potential job as a fallback. A homeowner's claim for damages from the contractor who has walked off the job may want to obtain some estimates of the cost of completion before negotiating with the new contractor.

As an historical illustration, after the Six Day War, the Israelis retained the captured "occupied territories" of Sinai, the West Bank and the Golan Heights, in part to use as bargaining chips in future peace negotiations. All three territories have, are, or may figure prominently in peace discussions with Egypt, the Palestinians and Syria respectively. The seizure of the territories consequently worsened Israel's neighbours' WATNA — no agreement meant continued loss of territory — and, to some extent, improved Israel's BATNA — no agreement meant continued retention of the territory and room for expansion and security buffers.[5]

As you can see, the more options that are on the table and the more alternatives there are to settling by negotiation, the more likely it is that negotiation will succeed. Thinking about your best alternatives is not the same as thinking about the bottom line. For that, the focus is on the dispute as it has been framed. If litigation has started, it will be framed narrowly, looking back at what happened. The bottom line, sometimes called the reservation point, will be a necessary although not restricting figure if other creative solutions that respond to interests are permitted. It is also difficult to make a realistic assessment of the chances of success in litigation until you know more about the case for the other side. It may be that BATNAs will be hard to assess until well into the negotiation process, and that it will be hard to take steps to improve it.

UNIVERSAL FACTORS AND AVOIDING ERRONEOUS ASSUMPTIONS

Almost all negotiations have the following factors at work:[6]

---

[5]   R. Fisher, W. Ury and B. Patton, *Getting to Yes: Negotiating Agreement Without Giving In* (New York: Penguin, 1991), discusses these concepts thoroughly. Reservation points and BATNA may be the same if the dispute is viewed solely in monetary terms. See I. Ayers and B. Nalebuff, "Common Knowledge as a Barrier to Negotiation" (1997) 44 U.C.L.A. L. Rev. 1631 at 1642.

[6]   Various people have tried to analyze litigation from the perspective of looking at these factors and trying to see if it is possible to set up categories which are more likely to settle early. Because there are so many variables, a generalization has proved to be elusive. See C. Menkel-

1. Time pressures
2. Costs issues
3. Strength of the legal arguments
4. Number of issues
5. Similarities and differences in culture and gender
6. Value of the dispute to you
7. Voluntariness — are you there by choice?
8. Public visibility
9. Accountability — Are the negotiators accountable to others?
10. Routineness — Is the problem unique or routine?
11. Power — How can one side use it in the negotiation?
12. Personality and style of the negotiator
13. Options other than settling
14. Motivation to settle or to continue fighting

When negotiating, consider these items not just from your perspective, but from that of the other side(s) to the dispute. Specifically, if you are negotiating for yourself, you should beware of assuming that the other side sees these items in the same way you do. Your perception will be influenced by all of your previous experiences, particularly those relating to other conflicts and how they were resolved. There have been many studies and much written on the influence of culture and gender on how people see disputes, how they interpret the actions and words of others and how they expect the disputes to be resolved. Many conclude that broad stereotypes are likely to be inaccurate; yet, they are used all the time. Assumptions are commonly made that people from a particular place act or think differently, or that men share a common view of the world that differs from that of women. Rather than adopt these stereotypes which alter all perceptions and expectations, it would be prudent to recognize that everyone has his or her own individual "culture" and no two people see events in the same way. In other words, it can be foolhardy to automatically assume that the other side views the dispute in a particular way solely because of culture or gender. When trying to assess what the other side in a negotiation will do, avoid making broad assumptions, and, instead, wait for real information. Failure to recognize that the other side has its own unique viewpoint, which it holds as firmly as you hold your own, will make resolving the dispute far more difficult.[7]

When planning your strategy for the negotiation, try not to second guess what the other side will do. Instead, focus on your own objectives, as your assumptions regarding the other party's strategy may be in error because of misperception or lack of information. Reactive bargaining (responding only) will make you less flexible.

---

[7]
Meadow, "Toward Another View of Legal Negotiation: The Structure of Problem Solving" (1984) 31 UCLA Law Rev. 754.

These issues are canvassed in J. Macfarlane, ed., Dispute Resolution (Toronto: Emond-Montgomery, 1999) at 25-35, 76-87, and by the same author, "Why Do People Settle" (2000) 46 McGill L.J., and C.B. Craver, "The Impact of Ethnic and Gender-based Factors" in *Effective Legal Negotiation and Settlement*, 3rd ed. (Charlottesville, VA: Michie, 1993) at 281.

Also, consider whether your own expectations of how you would like the dispute to be resolved are realistic or distorted by your individual perspective.

THE THREE TYPES OF INTERESTS

If you identify your own interests, and try to identify those of the other side, you will find that there are three types: shared interests; different interests; and opposing interests.

Shared Interests

Shared interests are the easiest to deal with because a given idea for settlement will coincide with the shared interests of both parties, reduce conflict and help resolve part or all of the dispute. Examples could include a desire to avoid publicity, or a need to minimize financial exposure or to maximize financial gain. Cases which settle by having both parties walk away from their respective claims usually involve a shared interest in minimizing risk and/or financial exposure. In one case, the parties involved could agree on only one thing (unrelated to the issues in the litigation): this was their support of a specific charity. They elected to settle by agreeing to donate a given amount to that charity. In another case involving a mortgagor and a mortgagee suing for the amount of the debt and faced with a likely deficiency after power of sale proceedings, the parties decided to form a partnership to develop and market the property because of a shared interest in making money — a shared interest which was more powerful than their interests involved in simply "winning" the litigation. Shared interests can be dovetailed in obvious or creative ways to arrive at solutions that are acceptable to all parties.

Different Interests

Different interests can be left to coexist within a settlement because their realization does not prevent the other side from achieving its goals and helps to achieve something for at least one of the parties. For example, in a long-term disability case, the claimant will have an interest in obtaining enough money to provide financial security in light of the disability, and the insurance company may have an interest in the surrender of the policy so as to avoid future claims for the disability (which might recur and be more serious or better substantiated). The interests are different, but a given lump sum settlement may achieve both without harming either. This can be illustrated by the international example of Saddam Hussein's interest in remaining in power after the 1991 Gulf War and the Coalition's interest in preventing Iraqi air incursions into Kuwait or into Kurdish territory in the north. This led to the agreement on "No Fly Zones" within Iraq's boundaries. Different interests were melded into one agreement which allowed both parties to pursue their separate objectives, at least for a while.

Opposing Interests

Opposing interests are difficult (if not sometimes impossible) to reconcile and often cannot exist compatibly within the same settlement. A property insurer faced with potential fraud on the part of the insured may have a strong interest in establishing a reputation and an internal policy of not paying a claim at all in light of a fraud. The insured, on the other hand, has an interest in maximizing the amount of the payout. Thus, the interests are diametrically opposed and may doom negotiations. Another example is a dispute between a developer and a ratepayer group dedicated to preserving the natural state of an area slated for development. The interests involved oppose one another. The only way to deal with opposing interests is to be creative and to find a solution that somehow allows both interests to be satisfied. As in the first example, the insurer might pay the claimant its non-recoverable legal costs likely to be incurred in defending the claim, but nothing towards the actual claim itself. In the second example, a portion of the land could be set aside for wilderness preservation.

The process of exploring creative solutions can be challenging and usually requires the intervention of a mediator who assertively reviews with the parties their alternatives to an agreement and helps to assess whether a given settlement proposal meets or exceeds those alternatives.

It is not necessary to satisfy absolutely *all* of your interests in a negotiation. This is, in fact, rarely achievable in a complex negotiation where the parties have assorted and varied interests. However, what might be obtainable is an agreement that satisfies *some* of your interests; the question will be which ones, and how important would these be as compared with the best alternatives to an agreement?

PRIORITIZING INTERESTS

When trying to establish priorities among your aims, you will find that some are more difficult to weigh than others. Monetary issues are easier than non-monetary ones. How, for example, do you put a value on goodwill of a business or on your need to have the opposing party acknowledge some wrong-doing? Here, you may have to create an artificial scale and subjectively order what you are seeking. This will be your list from which to develop your plans. You should also speculate on the other side's list.[8]

Because some issues are linked, it may be helpful to consider various packages of issues and objectives. For example, payment of money may involve issues of taxation and estate planning. Custody and access tend to be linked.

You will find that some issues, or packages of issues, will be less important than others. These lesser interests can be "trade-off" or "throw-away" issues. If the other side values them more than you do, and they are higher on their list,

---

[8]   On scoring systems, see R. Birke and C.R. Fox, "Psychological Principles in Negotiating Civil Settlements" 4 Harv. Negotiation Law Rev. 1 at 46, and H. Raiffa, *The Art and Science of Negotiation* (Cambridge, Mass.: Harvard University Press, 1982).

conceding on such an issue may spur the other side into making concessions as well, and provide momentum for further progress.

Ideally, when planning, you will be able to establish priorities in what you will seek as you resolve your legal dispute. This is not easy. How do you reconcile your wish to further your own interests with the need to consider those of the other side? You may share the interests that the dispute should come to an end and that costs should be kept to a minimum, and perhaps some others, but what determines why you choose to compromise on one interest to obtain another? It is often necessary to objectively value key interests in a way that both parties consider fair.

Independent Standards

The writings on principled negotiation suggest that to prioritize interests it is essential to carefully consider independent standards or objective criteria. The other side is more likely to accept a solution, and you are more likely to be comfortable with it if it can be said to be the right thing to do — in terms of fairness, legality, honour, business gain, *etc.* Utilizing independent standards to assess what is fair or appropriate is often productive.

Reasons for Using Independent Standards

- It lets parties save face when departing from previous "positions" in that it allows parties to defer to an objective explanation for the need for compromise.
- It allows parties to rationalize compromise.
- It educates parties and performs a persuasive function.
- It makes a resolution that will fit with the "law"and be more acceptable to both.

Examples of Independent Standards

1. *Law.* Let a neutral legal expert give an opinion on the legal, evidentiary and factual issues creating the impasse.
2. *Accounting Principles and Market Value.* Have an accountant, actuary, business valuator, appraiser or other professional make findings or come to conclusions, such as the market value of a business.
3. *Precedent.* Examine the history of similar disputes with the disputants or similar parties.
4. *Professional Standards.* Have a consultant, engineer, contractor, scientist or planner develop a plan to which the parties will agree to adhere.
5. *Scientific Finding.* Retain experts to give an opinion on the central issues of the dispute. Often, this can descend into a "war of the experts", and the value, at least from a mutual buy-in perspective, is minimal. This is often the case with conflicting medical opinions in a personal injury, medical malpractice or long-term disability case. It is optimal to agree on an expert and let that report be binding, but in practice, especially in a

litigious context, this is rare, especially with medical reports. Where this "common expert" concept works best is with opinions in which there is little room for any subjective evaluation, such as is sometimes the case with a business valuation or real estate appraisal.

6. *Reciprocity.* Allow the complainant to do to the other party what the other party is alleged to have done to the complainant. In other words, employ a reciprocity rule. For example, in one case, departing employees had established their own competing company and had taken with them the employer's customer list. The employer alleged that this was a breach of fiduciary duty and contrary to the non-competition clause of the employment agreement. However, in the interim, the employees' company had become a viable entity with an expanded customer base. It was agreed that the employer should be able to do to the employees' company what the employees had done to the employer — namely, to take the new entity's customer list (a result which no court would ever have awarded!).

7. *Shared Cultural or Religious Values.* Objective criteria need not come only from law or from experts. They may also come from shared cultural or religious values. By way of example, consider this: A company fired an employee for cause. It had a strong case involving serious misconduct. The employee disputed the facts, and litigation resulted. It turned out that the principals in the company, who belonged to the same religious group as the employee, strongly believed in having the employee "come clean". Recognizing the shared religious value, the parties negotiated a settlement in which the employee admitted what he did, but in return got a good financial settlement where his legal basis for doing so was weak. The religious norm had a strong influence in making the settlement acceptable to both sides.

As we can see, planning involves an assessment of many factors, as well as creation of an overall strategy. At the actual negotiation, which we will examine in the next chapter, things move quickly.

Chapter 7

THE NEGOTIATION PROCESS

> Negotiations are required when there is a genuine desire to solve a problem and an unpalatable alternative.[1]

The negotiation process requires participants to identify issues about which they differ, to educate each other about their needs and interests, to generate possible settlement options and to bargain over the terms of a final agreement.

So far, not much has been said about what to expect from the process, as contrasted with what to expect in result. As we will see, the tactics and arguments used revolve around power, rights and interests.[2] The parties may also have different views with respect to the norms usually involved in negotiations, including equality, fairness, equity and egalitarianism. Such differences can be impediments to the negotiation process.

FAIRNESS

Earlier, in Chapter 2, "Negotiation Basics", we encountered one of these norms: fairness. Most people involved in a legal dispute want to be treated fairly, with dignity and respect, during the process. They may even want to treat the other side in the same way, once they clear away the negative emotions. It is particularly important in a dispute between two people in an ongoing relationship with each other that they both share this norm. Being treated poorly at some stage of the process may unduly influence a decision about whether to accept an offer because people are more sensitive to how fairly they have been treated than to how they have faired in objective terms, on the merits.[3]

Other difficulties arise because the parties have different ideas about what is fair. People tend to overestimate their own ability to control outcomes which are, in fact, determined by factors beyond their control, and in which they define and use terms such as "fairness" to their own advantage. This principle is called "egocentric bias".

The parties may also have some ideas about equality, that is, they may think that they should be about equal in terms of individual concessions and the timing

---

[1] Albert Einstein, *Out of My Later Years* (New York: Wings Books, 1956).
[2] G.T. Lowenthal, "A General Theory of Negotiation Process, Strategy and Behavior" (1982) 31 U. Kan. L. Rev. 69.
[3] See R. Birke and C.R. Fox, "Psychological Principles in Negotiating Civil Settlements" (1999) 4 Harv. Negotiation Law Rev. 1.

of concessions, as well as in terms of total concessions. With some interests, however, it may be difficult to evaluate the weight of the concession. Non-monetary issues such as dignity, apology and recognition as a person are examples. Here, each side has a level of hope or aspiration with respect to it, and some idea of whether the other side matches it.

Speaking in general terms, an agreement is much more likely when both sides share the same norms of the process and have the same understanding about what they mean. Opposing norms on the other hand cause far more problems than opposing interests, which may be accommodated, as discussed earlier.

It may be useful to discuss these norms with the other side before the negotiation. If you both have different ideas about these basic norms of the process, you will waste a lot of time in misunderstandings. Some authors suggest preliminary meetings with the other side to clear up process issues and to set the ground rules for the negotiation. Preliminary process meetings may also allow you to get a read on the other side and may allay some of your fears.

CONDITIONS FAVOURABLE TO NEGOTIATION

Once you have mapped out your basic strategy, and plan to use a principled approach whenever possible, you will need to know how negotiations are conducted. One of the first issues to be considered is whether you should be there at all. What factors will make it more likely that your negotiation will be successful? Below is a list of conditions, some of which will be considered in more detail later.

1. *The right people with full authority to settle must participate.* For negotiations to be productive, the attendees must include those with full knowledge of the events or transactions in issue, and those with full authority to decide at the negotiation upon a wide variety of monetary and non-monetary settlement options. If a critical party is either absent or unwilling to commit to good faith bargaining, a settlement is less likely. A "mediation/negotiation ghost" — someone who is not physically present, but whose presence, nonetheless, exerts an influence — can doom a negotiation. This is because it gives the negotiator the opportunity to buy some time by saying "I'll have to check this", and to come back with more demands. If you have ever bought a car and had the salesperson do this, you will recognize the tactic.

2. *People must be ready to negotiate.* This means they must be psychologically prepared to talk, and also prepared for the negotiation. If adequate or necessary information is not available, or when a negotiation strategy has not been thought out, success is less likely, and people may be reluctant to even begin the process.

3. *For agreement to be reached on issues on which people disagree, there must be some means of influencing the other party/parties.* This

influence can be negative (for example, the power to inflict a litigation loss and, hence, undesirable pain and costs), or it can be neutral (such as asking thought-provoking questions, providing needed information or obtaining expert opinions). The influence exerted can also be positive — by providing rewards of some sort for the desired behaviour or outcome.

4. *The parties must be able to agree on some common interests, or at least agree to disagree on certain interests or issues.* Another way of putting this is that shared interests can be merged or dovetailed, and differing interests can either be ignored, compromised or met. The realization of one party's interest does not necessarily negate the other's interest. However, opposing interests are much more difficult to deal with because realizing one's interest may exclude the realization of the other party's interest.

5. *There must be a will to settle or at least an objective or subjective reason to settle.* This could be referred to as "Settlement DNA" (discussed later in this chapter) because it can lie dormant for a long time, evolve or be triggered with a catalyst of some sort. Settlement DNA is any objective or subjective interest in resolution. It can be a cash flow problem, unwanted or unsustainable risks, a desire to promote a relationship, a desire to save time or money, a need to save face, *etc.* The negative consequences of not settling must be more significant than those entailed in the sacrifices made to reach agreement. Put another way, the agreement on the table must be at least as good as or better than the party's best alternative to an agreement. If a party is better off not settling as opposed to accepting the terms of the best negotiated agreement able to be reached, the party should continue to litigate. Occasionally, a party is so invested in a conflict relationship that maintaining the conflict is of greater value than settling and ending it.

6. *People negotiate because the alternative means of resolution as to outcome are unpredictable.* This scenario is usually present in litigation where both or all sides have some merit to their perspectives on the dispute and there are a variety of ways in which a court could decide the case. A one-sided victory is either unpredictable or not very likely. Accordingly, it makes sense to negotiate and avoid the risk of losing or doing poorly in court. Negotiation is more certain than going to court because by reaching an agreement, the party will have at least achieved something for itself.

7. *Negotiations are important where there is some urgency or pressure to reach a decision.* Urgency may be imposed by either internal or external time constraints. External constraints include court dates, litigation deadlines or imminent administrative decisions. Internal constraints may be artificially set to enhance the motivation to settle. For negotiations to be successfully concluded, the parties must feel a joint sense of urgency

and be aware that they are vulnerable to adverse consequences or to loss of benefits if a decision is not reached.

8. *Psychological barriers to settlement, such as low self-esteem, or strong and intense negative emotions or feelings about another party must be dealt with or reduced to increase the chance of a settlement.* In addition to intellectual intelligence, what is relevant to a party's ability to assess interests and risks and to make decisions in often difficult circumstances is emotional intelligence. This includes attributes such as self-awareness (*i.e.*, an understanding of one's own values and goals) and the ability to manage emotions, control impulses, show empathy and skilfully connect with others.[4] Emotional intelligence is as important to a party's ability to harness settlement DNA and to make decisions about one's interests as are intellectual abilities. Where emotional intelligence is low or subdued, the chances of settlement are reduced.

9. *Issues must be negotiable, and each party must feel that there has been some recognition of its perspective on the dispute.* If negotiations appear to have only win/lose settlement possibilities so that none (or few) of a party's needs will be met as a result of participation, that party will become reluctant and will have little reason to reach an agreement. Participants need to feel that there are acceptable settlement options open to them as a result of participating in the process, and that the other side recognizes their needs. The concept of "recognition" involves the other side recognizing that a party has a perspective that is different from its own, and considering that perspective as well as its own.

10. *Participants must have the resources to negotiate.* These include the intellectual and emotional abilities to deal with the substance and dynamics of the negotiation, as well as representation, money, access to information and time. Power imbalances between the parties that are not "equalized", for example, the redressing of such imbalances through the intervention of a third-party neutral, can render a negotiation futile.

11. *The agreement must be durable and able to be implemented.* An agreement which is beyond the capabilities of a party to comply with, which is so complex that no one understands it, or which continues to require people who cannot maintain a relationship to work together, has little chance of being followed. Parties to a negotiation must be able to agree on a realistic and workable plan.

---

[4] See D. Goleman, "What Makes a Leader" (November-December 1998) Harvard Business Review 93 at 97, and D. Goleman, "The Emotional Intelligence of Leaders" (Fall 1998) 10 Leader to Leader 20, in which the author argues that emotional intelligence can be measured, and that some studies indicate that today's children are showing signs of being more impulsive, disobedient, angry, lonely and sad. If true, one could speculate that interest-based negotiation will be more difficult in the future.

12. *The negotiations must occur in a context where it is appropriate to negotiate.* There are rare examples of situations where it would be inappropriate or offensive to negotiate, or where there is absolutely nothing to be gained by negotiating, or to be lost by not doing so. Such a situation might occur where the other side simply cannot be trusted to implement the agreement, or where there is a suspicion that the agreement is being entered into only to buy time for a future transgression of some sort.[5] On a more general level, where it is known beforehand that a party at a negotiation will simply reiterate a previously rejected offer or require the other side to bargain against itself without making proposals of its own, or where there is a history of broken agreements, the climate may be inappropriate.

CONDITIONS UNFAVOURABLE TO NEGOTIATION

There are other factors that raise the question of whether you should negotiate at all. In some cases, negotiations should perhaps not be held. These include:

1. Power imbalances that are so excessive that one side fears the other.[6]

2. Nuisance cases in which one side is entirely "out to lunch". (Since there is no bargaining range, there is nowhere to start.)[7]

3. Pure value conflicts in which two strongly held principles collide. (Some resolution may be possible, but only if the principles are bypassed or their significance in the dispute[8] is minimized.)

4. Cases in which critical facts are in dispute. (Here again, until facts are clarified, or parties agree that they are not critical, there will be no bargaining range.)[9]

---

[5] In World War II, the Allies demanded unconditional surrender from the Axis powers. Negotiation was not appropriate under the extreme circumstances of this situation, as there was no value or durability to a relationship with Hitler.

[6] The example used here is often that of a family dispute in which one partner is dominated by the other. The use of power in a negotiation is an attempt to coerce an agreement and may not be related to the merits of the dispute at all, thus leading to a settlement that has little chance of succeeding in practice. Use of power as part of negotiating is done by both principled and positional negotiators. See, C.L. Karrass, *The Negotiating Game* (New York: World Pub. Co., 1970) at 56.

[7] One should distinguish between a case brought to establish a new area of law, where only a court can do so, from a case where there is no chance of success because even an extension of existing law will not cover the claims or defences. In both cases, negotiation is probably of little use.

[8] You should be wary when someone says "It is a matter of principle" because, although oft-stated, it is usually not the case. A case involving an affirmative action program and a resisting employer might be an example. The difficulty with principles is that they almost always come in conflicting pairs. My "right to privacy" may conflict with your "right to freedom of expression". Your "right to strike" will conflict with my "right to manage my business". Here, the conflicting "principles" are freedom of expression or association and free enterprise economics.

[9] Since most cases settle in spite of credibility and factual issues, perhaps the significance of this category is overstated.

5. Cases of great public interest, such as those involving an abuse of power by a public body. (Here, negotiation may be possible, but ratification of the settlement by an elected body may be necessary[10] to satisfy the public interest.)

6. Where one side needs to establish a principle or send a message to others.[11]

7. Where there is no "recognition" by the one side, or the other.[12]

In addition, factors #3, #5 and #6, above, raise the issue as to whether it is legitimate ever to negotiate cases in which legal issues are at stake. According to one author, a controversy on this issue has arisen, largely in academic circles.[13] Obviously, however, negotiation to settle most legal disputes outside court does occur.

Once it has been determined that negotiation is a worthwhile pursuit, it is useful to understand the different stages of the process.

NEGOTIATION STAGES

Like any process, a negotiation often follows a pattern. One author describes it as follows:[14]

---

[10] The recent Nisga'a treaty in B.C. is an example. The settlement of land claims should, arguably, have legislative support.

[11] See W. Coyne Jr., "Using Settlement Counsel for Early Dispute Resolution" (1999) 15 Negotiation Journal 10 at 12.

[12] Although factor #1, above, referring to power imbalances, may be one example of this, there are many others. "Recognition" means the willingness of one side to accept that there are points of view of the dispute other than its own, and to consider these seriously. See R.A. Baruch Bush and J.P. Folger, *The Promise of Mediation* (San Francisco: Jossey-Bass, 1994). Where legitimate recognition does exist, both sides will, perhaps, see their dispute in a new light (a "transformative" effect) . This is the thesis of Bush and Fogler, who have spent a lot of time examining how mediations can change people. Gary Caplan, however, in his essay in this book, casts doubt on the validity of that proposition (see Appendix II).

[13] See O. Fiss, "Against Settlement" (1984) 93 Yale L.J. 1073 and "Out of Eden" (1985) 94 Yale L.J. 1969. See also C. Menkel-Meadow, "For and Against Settlement" (1985) 33 UCLA L. Rev. 485 and in Canada, L. Boulle and K.J. Kelly, *Mediation, Principles, Process, Practice*, Canadian ed. (Toronto: Butterworths, 1998) at 59 under "Mediation and Justice". On the question of mediation of such disputes see also C. Noble, L. Dizgun and P. Emond, *Mediation Advocacy: Effective Client Representation in Mediation Proceedings* (Toronto: E. Montgomery, 1998) at 34.

[14] R. Hawkins "Negotiations" in D.P. Emond, ed., *Commercial Dispute Resolution: Alternatives to Litigation* (Aurora, Ont.: Canada Law Book, 1989).
Another respected American writer discusses similar stages as:

1. Preliminary establishment of negotiation identities and overt tone of negotiation;
2. The information stage (value creation);
3. The competitive/distributive stage (value claiming);
4. The closing stage (value solidifying).

He adds a further stage,

5. The co-operative/integrative stage (value maximizing).

1. *Setting the agenda.* The first stage involves sizing up the other side, negotiating the norms of the process such as fairness and equality, as well as how these norms will translate into agreed procedures, the physical set-up and the time lines, and exchanging information.

2. *The initial demand.* The second stage involves initial offers and explanations.

3. *The concessions — maximizing the outcome.* At the third stage, the hard bargaining occurs, and many minor issues are resolved or abandoned.

4. *The commitment.* At the final stage, the major issues are addressed, and the parties attempt to craft a settlement.

However you define or analyze the process, it is important for you not to try to bypass a stage because each builds upon the earlier one.

If, as counsel, your involvement begins part way into the negotiation, it is helpful to recognize the stage of the negotiation and determine how far things have progressed. In choosing a strategy, you will have to take any prior negotiations between the parties into account. Once you recognize how far they have gone in their negotiations, it will be much easier to choose an appropriate stratagy.

Setting the Agenda

The first stage — setting the ground rules, assessing the other side's style, *etc.* — may not take too long if you are an experienced negotiator dealing with someone who is familiar. You should beware of letting the other side keep issues that are important to you "off the table". If the other side says "That's not on the table", it is probably seeking to force you to make a concession right at the start. You could either come up with a non-negotiable item of your own, link the other side's non-negotiable item with one of its other demands and not give in on the other, or call the other side's bluff and refuse to talk further.[15]

During the process, it is also important to obtain information. If you are in litigation, and discoveries are over, subject to the continued obligation to give discovery, you may have a fair amount of information already. In mandatory mediation programs where the session is usually conducted before discovery, it is often useful to at least obtain an affadavit of documents from the other side. This disclosure, however, will be in the form of facts or documents and will not tell you much about the other side's interests or why it is seeking certain things from you. If you can investigate this, you will be better able to make principled offers which are realistic. Whether using a principled or a positional strategy, you are advised to try to obtain more information than you give at this stage (as

but only after a tentative settlement has been reached. See C.B. Craver, *Effective Legal Negotiation and Settlement*, 3rd ed. (Charlottesville, VA: Michie, 1997).

15 R. Hawkins, "Negotiation" in D.P. Emond, ed., *Commercial Dispute Resolution: Alternatives to Litigation* (Aurora, Ont.: Canada Law Book, 1989) at 66.

mentioned earlier, "cautious cooperation" is the watchword here). Also, you should be mindful of the fact that people tend to seek information which supports their view of the dispute and downgrade information which is not consistent with it.[16]

Setting the Tone

It is very important to establish the right climate for an interest-based negotiation. The intervention of a mediator can certainly help to achieve this, but there are useful ways in which to do it in an unassisted negotiation as well. The following are statements that may be helpful in setting the tone for the commencement of negotiations:

> "I would like to find a way to resolve this dispute to our mutual satisfaction."

> "I would like us to both feel good about however this negotiation turns out."

> "I think that we can work together to find a way around this problem."

> "We want to be able to develop a workable agreement for all of us, one that is justifiable to the world at large."

> "Let's devote the time necessary to explore if we can develop something that works for both of us."

> "It may seem like we are at odds with diametrically opposing positions right now, and, of course, that will be the case at trial. But let's see if we can eliminate the need for a trial and come to a settlement that takes both our needs and risks into account."

The Initial Demands and Offers

We now come to the stage of initial offers. Later in this book, we will examine offers at a mediated negotiation, the making of which often resembles a "dance", with each party taking nearly choreographed steps towards a solution. Whether you are using a principled negotiation style or a positional one, overall, you have to start somewhere.

Most literature on negotiation deals with the making of offers in positional, adversarial negotiations. In fact, the substance of the first offers may not differ

---

[16]   C. Lord *et al.*, "Biased Assimilation and Attitude Polarization: The Effects of Prior Theories on Subsequently Considered Evidence" (1979) 37 Journal of Personality and Soc. Psychol. 2098. This is partly because of "attribution". As the dispute develops, people assume they are only reacting to the other side, and they interpret what the other side does in a way that fits their perception of the dispute.

much from stated positions, depending upon which style is used. *How* the offer is presented may be the major distinction between styles at this stage.

Factors to consider when framing any offer include the following:

1. *Who goes first?* Here the "anchoring bias" principle is useful. Once a figure or position is anchored in a person's mind, he or she tends to relate all later changes to that figure or position and may not make enough adjustments in response to new information.[17] Suppose, for example, you have a settlement figure from another highly publicized case in mind. You may set your mind on it and, thus, be reluctant to recognize that your case differs from it. If the other side is at all uncertain of its position, you can set the anchor at a level you want by making the first offer. Additionally, you can prevent the other side from making an offer and committing itself to a position unfavourable to you.

   Some experts suggest that if the dispute is already in litigation, the person with the burden of proof should go first.[18] If a mediator is present, he or she may insist that the recipient of the last unassisted offer go first so that the maker of it does not feel forced to bargain against himself or herself.

2. *Reciprocity.* Another principle that is useful here is that of "reciprocity". If both sides agree on the norms of the process, and if one of these norms is that of equality, it will be reflected in a wish to reciprocate concessions made by the other side. What this means in terms of who goes first is that you can wait and make the second offer (your counteroffer) at a level that widens the bargaining range. In positional bargaining, since most cases settle near the middle of the range,[19] the use of reciprocity keeps the mid-point closer to your side's aims.

3. *Reactive devaluation.* The "fixed-pie bias" — a gain for you means a loss for me — leads negotiators to look at offers from the other side with suspicion. Negotiators will devalue them simply because they come from the other side. Therefore, it helps if you have a good relationship with the other side, something that is more common in transactional than in dispute resolution negotiations.[20]

4. *Log rolling.* Later in the negotiation, you will be able to trade off the issues which each side has valued differently. In the landlord-tenant

---

[17] See, R. Birke and C.R. Fox, "Psychological Principles in Negotiating Civil Settlements" (1999) 4 Harv. Negotiation Law Rev. 1 at 10.

[18] *Ibid.* at 40.

[19] H. Raiffa, *The Art and Science of Negotiation* (Cambridge, Mass.: Harvard University Press, 1982). On reciprocity, see R. Cialdini *et al.*, "Reciprocal Concessions Procedure for Inducing Compliance, The Door in the Face Technique" (1975) 31 J. Pers. and Social Psychol. 206.

[20] L. Ross and C. Stillinger, "Barriers to Conflict Resolution" (1991) 7 Negotiation Journal 389 at 394.

example used earlier in Chapter 2, Maria may not care about the term of the lease as much as Janine does. Janine, on the other hand, feels it is important that she receive some money up front, whereas Maria does not object enough to fight on that issue. They could trade off on these, each getting more of what she wants on the issue which she values more. This is made possible because of the Homans Principle.[21]

5. *Making the offer attractive.* As mentioned earlier, people often look at the process of negotiation more in terms of avoiding losses than in terms of making gains. This is in part because they generally are more willing to take a risk for a small gain than for a small loss. This means that when an offer is presented, it should be described in terms of the good things that it will do for them, appealing to the interests of the other side (that is, those that are being advanced). To say "I want this and you will have to lose that" is to invite rejection.[22]

6. *Social proof.* Often, people view a behaviour in a given situation as correct if they see other people doing it. When addressing a rights demand, couching it in terms of a leading case to suggest others have gone that way, or referring to a recent settlement of the same size will help.[23]

7. *Limited supply.* Things seem more valuable if they are less available. If you tell a person that something is hard to get, he or she will desire it more and try harder to get it. This may explain the rush at Christmas time to obtain that single item of little value which everyone wants. It also helps explain the effectiveness of the limited time offer and can be used in making offers, for example, by indicating that the offer will expire as of a particular date. Mentioning alternatives that you have available to you utilizes this principle as well.[24]

---

[21] G.C. Homans, *Social Behavior: Its Elementary Forms* (New York: Harcourt, Brace & World, 1961). The principle is that because people have different preferences, it is possible to increase the number of possible outcomes in any situation where differentially valued items are at stake. Clearly, the model of principled negotiation rests upon this principle.

[22] W. Samuelson and R. Zeckhauser, "Status Quo Bias in Decision Making" (1988) 1 Journal of Risk and Uncertainty 7. At the same time, while people are less willing to take a certain small loss than a gain, they may be willing to risk an uncertain large loss and go to trial. See K.J. Arrow, R. Mnookin, L. Ross, *et al.*, *Barriers to Conflict Resolution* (New York: W.W. Norton, 1995) at 17, and C. Noble, L.L. Dizgun and D.P. Emond, *Mediation Advocacy: Effective Client Representation in Mediation Proceedings* (Toronto: E. Montgomery, 1998) at 98.

[23] This is why canned laughter works; we think that if others find the material funny, we should also. See M. Smythe and R. Fuller, "Effects of Group Laughter on Response to Humorous Materials" (1972) 30 Psychol. Rep. 132.

[24] R. Birke and C.R. Fox, "Psychological Principles in Negotiating Civil Settlements" (1999) 4 Harv. Negotiation Law Rev. 1 at 56.

Most writers agree that both sides must make initial offers that are not so extreme as to be frivolous or to be taken as evidence of "bad faith".[25] Mediators often suggest making first offers that make a notable concession — to promote the continuous exchange of productive offers. In litigation, parties will often have made early offers under Rules of Court. These offers are not always realistic, particularly if made at or before the pleading stage, but they must be considered. If they are realistic, on the other hand, they should be considered as first offers, and the negotiation should move to the next stage.

After realistic opening offers are made, the bargaining range is established, and things move forward. It was suggested earlier that principled offers should be used, in which some reason is given why the offer is a valid one. Negotiating in a principled way, using the model discussed earlier, focuses on the "mutual gains" approach.[26]

The Concessions — Maximizing the Outcome

The Mutual Gains Approach

The mutual gains approach guides the resolution of disputes — through any interest-based process negotiation, facilitation or mediation. Following its elements will enable you to engage in principled negotiation and will minimize the interpersonal divides inherent in many conflicts while emphasizing the interests and areas of common ground buried in the dispute. The elements include the following:

1. Get behind the positions and focus on underlying interests.
2. Be soft on the people, hard on the problem (cognitive dissonance).
3. Invent options for mutual gain (brainstorm).
4. Use independent, respected standards of fairness.
5. Know your BATNA and WATNA, (walk-away alternatives); know the other side's BATNA and WATNA; compare and assess your alternatives; and take legitimate/lawful steps to improve your alternatives and/ or worsen the other side's alternatives.
6. Develop illustrative proposals to reach agreement (*i.e.*, make principled offers to one another).

---

[25] An interesting take on negotiating strategy is that you cannot just walk in and say "Here is my final offer, it is reasonable and non-negotiable". However realistic it is, that is not what negotiating is about. L. Boulwar, a former vice president of General Electric, used to do this until it was found that he was failing to bargain in good faith. See C.B. Craver, *Effective Legal Negotiation and Settlement*, 3rd ed. (Charlottesville, VA: Michie, 1997) at 188, who suggests that insurance companies that possess significant power in the particular negotiation may use this tactic. Even if the offer is reasonable, the tactic tends to fail because the other side resists being dictated to, or sees the tactic as unfair.

[26] This term was coined by R. Fisher, W. Ury and B. Patton, *Getting to Yes: Negotiating Agreement Without Giving In*, 2nd ed. (New York: Penguin, 1991).

Since we have already looked at getting behind the positions taken in a dispute and focusing on the parties' interests in Chapters 4 and 5 above, let us examine other elements of the mutual gains approach.

Separating the People from the Problem

...he who has never struggled with his fellow-creatures, is a stranger to half the sentiments of mankind. [27]

Being "soft on the people and hard on the problem" is an art, not a science. It involves suspending many of your natural and visceral reactions to people you may not like or respect, and who may be treating you unfairly. However, it is crucial in an interest-based negotiation to be able to do this in order to discuss settlement options maturely and to make principled offers to one another. Deep inside most peole are life learned strategies for doing this, but what follows below are some useful reminders to help you get on the right track.

1.   Listen before you talk.

2.   Build trust, respect and rapport.

3.   Consider the views of the other side (recognition). This does not mean forcing yourself to agree with the other side's perspective. It means simply attempting to see the dispute from a different point of view. Doing so may help to diffuse acrimony and even to achieve proposals which satisfy some of the other side's interests without doing damage to your own. Try to understand where the other side is coming from, and acknowledge it. Remember, understanding is not the same as agreeing. A little demonstrated empathy or understanding can go a long way in diffusing tensions.

4.   Deal with people problems directly. Do not try to solve them with substantive concessions. Attempting to improve a negotiating relationship by making such concessions can be a dangerous and slippery slope. If the other side realizes what you are doing, it may deliberately withhold improvement in order to extract further concessions from you. People and behavioural problems are best dealt with by facing the problem, drawing polite attention to it and asking for rectification — without ever involving the making of concessions. Indeed, it is better only to make concessions as a reward for a behavioural improvement (reciprocity).

5.   If the other side's perceptions are inaccurate, look for a way to educate the other side. This can be done by preparing an expert's report or using

---

[27]   Adam Ferguson in *An Essay on the History of Civil Society* (1767), Part First, "Of the General Characteristics of Human Nature", Section IV, "Of the Principles of War and Dissension".

some other independent and objective standard (see "Independent Standards" (in Chapter 6). This may also involve a level of disclosure which has not yet been made. For example, in a wrongful dismissal case, if the other side assumes that there has been no effort to mitigate and find another job, but, indeed, reasonable efforts have been made, then the full extent of those efforts should be disclosed to try to change the negative perception.

6. If emotions are running high, allow people to let off steam — let people vent.

7. Do not deduce the other side's intentions based on your fears — do not assume the worst. A common conundrum is to vilify the other side or to assume that because a path is open to it which may harm you, that it must be the other side's goal to pursue it. It may be helpful to remember a Portuguese proverb: "The worst is not always certain."

8. Try to convey as emphatically as possible those things you are willing to say that the other side would like to hear (which do not stand in the way of an agreement). This can be one of the best investments you can make as a negotiator. One tactic mediators sometimes use is to ask acrimonious parties who at one time have had a better relationship with each other to share something good that each can say about the other. This simple exercise often diffuses much tension. The danger is when one party complies, and the other does not or seems incapable of saying anything nice!

9. Look for opportunities to act inconsistently with the other side's perceptions. In psychology, this is known as "cognitive dissonance". Acting inconsistently with the other side's negative perceptions of you breaks the ice. It can pave the way for productive negotiations, and it may provoke a similar response from the other side, which can really generate momentum to settle.

   A good international example of this tendency for people to act to eliminate dissonance was Anwar Sadat's famous peace mission to Jerusalem in 1977. In one short visit, he shattered most Israelis' impressions of him. By appearing as a peacemaker, which the Israelis did not expect, and approaching the problem head on, he motivated the other side to forget about the warmongering image and to focus on the problem by working together.

10. Give the other side a stake in the outcome by ensuring it an opportunity to participate in the process. For example, the process used in Ontario to create protected wilderness areas, involves holding a hearing in the locality. All interested parties are invited to attend and express their

views, which enables concerns to be voiced and dealt with, and, at a minimum, gives people the feeling that they are part of the process.

In contrast, before apartheid in South Africa ended, white liberals in an all-white Parliament met to establish the conditions and scenarios for ending it. However, not many people of other races bought into the plan, and the well-intentioned white liberal parties did poorly in the subsequent elections.

11. Give generous credit to the other side for their ideas whenever possible — this gives it a stake in defending those ideas. Remember the quote, "There is no limit to what a person can do when they are willing to let others take the credit."[28]

12. Try to tailor your proposals to the concerns, ideas and interests revealed by the other side. Try to create ideas that might be acceptable to it. As mentioned, this means presenting the offer in terms of how it benefits the other side. Give it something to chew on. This will help it save face, increases the likelihood of securing its agreement, shortens the negotiation and calls its bluff if it backtracks. Unfortunately, this is rarely the model for many management-union negotiations. The result is often one of protracted negotiations as well as a complete breakdown for a period of time, followed by a strike.

13. Acknowledge emotions — the other side's and yours — as legitimate. Emotions are by their nature inherently "legitimate". No case is entirely about money or about the substantive issues raised. Practically every dispute, even corporate ones, have at their core some kind of interpersonal breakdown.

14. It is sometimes useful to talk about a problem in terms of its impact on you rather than what the other side has done, how and why. Not only is a statement about how you feel difficult to challenge, it also does not seem to put blame on the other side.

15. Avoid full disclosure of how flexible you are, especially too early in the negotiation. Adopt a bit of "wait and see" in order to establish the other side's good faith in making principled offers.

16. Try to build a working relationship with the other side, particularly in a protracted negotiation. An example of this was shown in a Star Trek episode in which a mediator forced the adversaries to first work together by learning his obscure language as a way to build rapport as well as a shared sense of accomplishment. This language was then to be used in

---

[28]   This quote used to appear as a desk ornament on Ronald Reagan's desk in the Oval Office.

the negotiations. Thus, the more you get to know a stranger, the easier will be the negotiation.

For another example, in 1993, Israeli and Palestinian delegates negotiated in Oslo, Norway, for several weeks and spent this time together in close proximity. In the course of carrying out everyday activities such as preparing meals together, the participants later said that they had come to relate to each other on a human level, and this led to significant substantive breakthroughs.

17. Remember that although an ongoing relationship may be nice, you do not have to like the other side to be able to reach an agreement that meets your interests. Put aside your likes and dislikes, personal preferences and aesthetic judgements. It is not necessary to be friends with the other side — you need only to be able to work out proposals that satisfy each of your set of interests. In one wrongful dismissal case, an employee had a fairly solid entitlement to a large notice period, but accepted the money equivalent of a much shorter period accompanied by the former employer becoming the "career champion" of the employee and acting like a head hunter in trying to find him another job. Despite the employee's dislike of the employer, his main interest was in securing alternate employment, and that was best accomplished with the help of the employer.

18. See the forest for the trees. No matter how objectionable the conduct or character of the other side, remember what it is you want from the negotiation and whether sufficient interests can be met as compared with the interests obtained from the best walk-away alternatives to an agreement. Keep your eye on "the prize". Too many parties, even sophisticated institutional litigants, let their negative impressions of the other side interfere with making sound judgements on the worth of specific offers and the making of principled offers to the other side. The result is that they sometimes lose out on the opportunity to achieve a settlement that would achieve their goals.

19. Help the other side to back down gracefully. If it has made threats or an ultimatum, you can diffuse the situation by doing things, such as adding a new factor and saying "That changes things, doesn't it ?", or changing the picture by linking that issue with another and dealing with the issues as a package.

Another factor to consider when negotiating is the presence of difficult people, which is almost inevitable in a hard negotiation; thus strategies must be employed in such a situation. What follows are some helpful statements in dealing with difficult people.

1. "I can see why you feel like that/why you would say that."

2. "Let me understand what you just said."

3. "I see it this way...How do you see it?"

4. "So you are saying that.../What I am hearing you say is..."

5. What is your objective in doing that/saying that/taking that position/?"

6. "How would you feel if someone did that to you/if that happened to you?"

7. "How do you see that as fair?"

8. "Why is this fair? Could you explain it please?"

9. "It's understandable why you see it that way/say that/do that. Perhaps I can explain it in a context that will shed some light on what happened/why it happened."

10. "Where is the 'high water mark' of this dispute/misunderstanding for you?"

11. "Please correct me if I am wrong".

12. "Let me show you where I have trouble following your thinking."

13. "Let me walk you through our contention."

14. Could I ask a few questions to make sure that I have this right?"

15. "One fair solution might be..."

16. "If there is an issue of credibility, then there is an issue of credibility for both of us."

17. "We cannot solve our problems with the same level of thinking we used when we created them."[29]

When dealing with difficult or unlikeable people on the other side, there can be a fear of losing face, which is extremely pronounced. That fear can impede doing things and making principled offers and concessions which might ultimately prove to be in the party's interests. As suggested by the famous quote from John F. Kennedy, "Let us never negotiate out of fear. But let us never fear

---

[29] Albert Einstein, *Out of My Later Years* (New York: Wings Books, 1956).

to negotiate", it is usually unwise to avoid making concessions simply just to keep or save face.[30]

A further problem is encountered when you have to revise a previous position, and you do not want to look foolish or inattentive. Abraham Lincoln had a perfect answer for such situations: "I reserve the right to know more now than I did in the past."

Once the parties have successfully separated personal issues from their objectives, it is much easier to explore options creatively.

Inventing Options

Creativity is at the heart of much of human endeavour, and so it is with developing settlements. In an interest-based process, the only way to dovetail shared interests, let different interests lie and work around opposing interests is to get creative and look outside the "box". Even in those rare cases which are really only about money, creativity can be applied in the making of principled offers. The crafting of the offer, and the development of the rationale behind it, can be a very creative exercise. For example, in a wrongful dismissal case, an employer felt that if it were to pay a lump sum, the employee would be obtaining a windfall if he found another job soon after, and the employer in any event felt that the former employee had not done enough to look for a job while he was still very marketable. The employer's interest was to minimize financial exposure, and it wanted the employee to "help" do just that by finding alternative employment. The former employee, on the other hand, wanted as much compensation as possible, but he also wanted to get his career back on track, and the right new job would assist with that objective. The solution finally adopted was for an agreed upon sum to be paid now, and the remainder to be paid at a discount when the employee found other comparable work. The discount was enough to give the employer a break from the agreed amount of compensation payable, but not so much as to create a disincentive to the employee to find other work. In addition, the former employer gave a great reference and became the employee's "career champion" in actively using its contacts to help find a comparable or better new job for the employee. None of this would ever have been awarded by a court, which simply would have awarded damages for wrongful dismissal and subtracted any moneys earned during the notice period following termination.

Given the benefit of creativity in making offers, how, then, can you generate such options? The following pointers may be of assistance.

1. Look for solutions only after interests have been identified. The key is to develop options which coincide or harmonize with the important interests of the parties.

2. Brainstorm options — as many as possible — jointly or privately. Invent before you judge; no criticism is allowed. Simply put, no one is committed to anything that is suggested because anything goes. Look for

---

[30] John F. Kennedy, Inaugural Address (Washington, D.C., 20 January 1961).

options that are both low cost and high benefit to both parties. Brainstorming is about enlarging the pie, not about dividing it.

Why does brainstorming tend to work? It is because the process inherently develops solutions that leave the other side satisfied as well. Further, the process essentially facilitates the development of answers for the other side. It also renders the decisions the parties have to make at the conclusion of the process easier to make —often, simply yes or no to the refined proposal is required.

Thus, shared interests, mere differences in interests and shared aversion to risk tend to make for more reconcilable negotiations.[31]

Experience suggests that brainstorming usually works best privately. The exception is with highly sophisticated parties that are motivated to settle, in a non-acrimonious dispute. Certainly, in a litigious context, this is rare. People may be shy about even suggesting options for settlement in a joint session because they fear even a residual amount of attributed committal, or they may fear raising the other side's expectations beyond a level at which they would be comfortable settling. The solution (perhaps done more efficiently by a mediator) is to brainstorm privately with the parties and to suggest and test the ideas by conveying principled illustrative proposals to the parties.

3.   Develop a shortlist of options — look for commonality — and seek options that dovetail or integrate with each other, and identify shared interests. Use any shared interests to stimulate ideas for solutions.

4.   Refine or broaden the options — make them better, more realistic.

Once you have decided to create options, how do you commence the option generation stage? The following are some useful questions to ask:

1.   "How would you solve this problem?"
2.   "Under what circumstances could you agree to...?"
3.   "Can we try to develop ideas which cater to what the other side could possibly accept?"
4.   "Can we develop a proposal that works for the other side — that meets their goals?"

An example of a high profile negotiation which involved an element of creativity was the negotiation which ensued when a newly united Germany was faced with thousands of Soviet troops in the former East Germany in the early 1990s. This was potentially an explosive situation, as the retention of these

---

[31]   Appendix III includes a number of examples from real mediations to show how creativity and option-seeking have succeeded.

troops was untenable for Germany. A hasty departure could create chaos in Russia and be perceived as some kind of a cave-in on the part of Russian hardliners, who still had the ability to effectively resist the troops' departure. This would have created a serious international sovereignty issue for Germany, and it would have heightened tensions considerably. The inventive solution was to actually pay (in hard currency) the Soviets to keep their troops stationed in the former East Germany — together with a staged and orderly withdrawal over an agreed upon period of time, the assumption perhaps being that troops paid by the country which they are occupying would be unlikely to be hostile. Thus, each party got what it wanted and saved face. Each could view it as a gain rather than a loss.

The process of inventing options and exploring interests continues until the parties are satisfied that the "pie" is as big as it is going to get. At some stage, it may become apparent that a settlement is possible. This is the point at which "Settlement DNA" will be recognized.

Settlement DNA

"Settlement DNA" is used here to denote the almost genetic-like potential of a dispute to settle. Such potential is innate within the nature of the dispute and the disputants — akin to molecular DNA (Deoxyribonucleic Acid). It can, therefore, be latent, lie dormant, require a catalyst to activate it, and it can evolve. It is very much dependent on the bundle of interests, circumstances and facts inherent in the dispute, and, in an analogous sense, is similar to the genetic potential of an organism. Our genes determine if we are to be short or tall, male or female. Our genes may even predispose us to many of our likes and dislikes, aptitudes and attitudes. It is the genetic element of predisposition (but not inevitability) which is analogous, in that if all the right stuff to constitute a settlement is present, it is still not guaranteed. There has to be the right nurturing and the right environment — in other words, a principled negotiation or mediation in which the parties' interests and their alternatives to an agreement must be canvassed and analyzed.[32]

How do you know, as a party, whether your dispute has the DNA to settle? This can be difficult for the participants who may simply be too close to it. There may be too much emotion, too much invective.

This is where a mediator can be very helpful. An experienced mediator can often spot the settlement DNA, or settlement potential in a dispute, even if the parties have trouble doing so. If there is no DNA, or if it evaporates, no amount of mediation will procure a settlement. However, even a small amount of settlement DNA, with the right kind of exploration, can evolve into meaningful settlement discussions and, very possibly, a settlement.

---

[32] For a fascinating discussion on the need for just the ideal environment and set of conditions for DNA to have evolved into complex life forms, see P.D. Ward and D. Brownlee, *Rare Earth: Why Complex Life is Uncommon in the Universe* (New York: Copernicus Books, 2000). This extraordinary series of events and conditions can be likened to the imposition of the mediation process onto the raw DNA of a seemingly intractable dispute.

What sort of factors constitute settlement DNA? It could be a strong financial incentive to settle (not necessarily with all parties); an unpalatable, likely trial outcome in a litigious context (again, not necessarily with all sides); a particular dynamic in a relevant relationship (for example, a strong interest in preserving it); the history of previous settlement offers, or the pattern of such offers developed at the negotiation/mediation; extenuating personal concerns; a desire to avert war or protracted conflict; or exhaustion.

Sometimes the DNA is not readily apparent until some negotiation process has been undergone. If you get to mediation, and you trust your mediator, let him or her ascertain the DNA — the mediator, unlike you, will have had the benefit of having spoken privately with the other side. He or she may not be able to tell you precisely why there is settlement DNA, because to do so might betray a confidence. However, this should not dissuade you from giving the mediation a chance.

While the DNA is still growing and evolving, the negotiation should probably continue. At the point at which it dies, or hits an evolutionary dead end, it should be adjourned or terminated. This may occur when a party is emphatic (as opposed to merely posturing) that it cannot make any further offers, and there is still a sizeable gap. It may occur when the party realizes that its alternatives to an agreement are genuinely better than any possible negotiated agreement. Or it may come about when a party is exhausted or rendered incapable of making a decision, for example, because it has had all it can cope with, or because it did not come with full authority to settle and has exceeded its line of authority.

An example of this would be useful here. In one long-term disability case, the claimant had a limited duration disability about which the insurer had qualms as to whether it met the requirements of the policy; in addition, the insurer alleged that the claimant had grossly misrepresented his income when he made the application and was, therefore, inappropriately insured. Indeed, the insurer's position was that the policy would never have been underwritten had the truth been known, and accordingly, the policy was void *ab initio*. The following day, by complete coincidence, a nearly identical case was mediated (though with different parties), with the same arguments, similar duration of disability and amount in issue and identical medical condition. Even some of the same doctors had given reports!

The first case settled, but the second did not. Why? In the first case, the claimant was about to requalify in his profession in a different province, and his wife was actively looking for a house in that province even as the mediation wore on. He was going to build a new career and life for himself and his family. In the second case, no such move was in the offing. The settlement DNA of the first case was accordingly higher than that of the second, culminating in the different results.

The Positional Model

The positional model, discussed in Chapter 4, makes much of the process of concession-making, using tactics which are mostly non-cooperative and based upon the use of power in the negotiation rather than on the merits or substance of the dispute. One author discusses 12 of these, including threats, warnings, promises, emotional appeals, ridicule, humour, intransigence, flattery, silence, guilt, embarrassment and indebtedness.[33] Another stresses that you start with a high initial demand, reduce it only when responding to a concession (and never by as much as was conceded by the other party) and decrease the size and frequency of your concessions as you approach the final stages.[34] He also suggests that you stay outside the bargaining range with your counteroffers as long as possible. The other side will be so happy once you have come into the range that it may reward you with a better settlement. It usually seems to be more productive to commence with smaller concessions and, in later offers, to enlarge the size or number of concessions. This "turns up the crank" and helps build a momentum towards settlement.

When making concessions, keep in mind that sometimes the fact that you are making one is as important as the content of what you are giving up. In addition, people may be more attuned to the rate of concessions (how quickly, how many) than to their substance.[35]

If you are dealing with an aggressive negotiator using a positional strategy, how do you avoid getting drawn into using the same tactics? If you are using a principled strategy and come to a stage where positional bargaining is necessary, how do you limit your stay in that arena?

The first thing to do is to recognize that even in principled negotiations, parties will use arguments that are power-based as well as those about rights and interests. Power-based means the use of some argument that may be unrelated to the merits of the particular dispute, to help get the other side to accept a position or to make a concession. For example, a threat to never deal with you in the future is not related to the dispute but may be of influence if there is a desire to maintain a commercial relationship.

Rights arguments should usually involve an appeal to some objective standard, often to a legal principle. Interest arguments go to each side's concerns, priorities and preferences — in other words, why the parties value their claims as they do.

The use of rights arguments — and those based on power (such as threats) — tends to make the negotiation more positional and to lead to a distributional agreement (dividing up the pie). As discussed earlier, interest-based arguments (principled offers) are more likely to lead to a mutually beneficial result.

A recent study looked at how parties use the three types of arguments as they cycle through the normal stages of a negotiation.[36] By audio taping 25 negotiations of simulated commercial disputes, those conducting the study were able to analyze all of the parties' statements and put them in categories which included procedural remarks (2.7 per cent overall), interests (20.8 per cent overall), rights

---

[33] C.B. Craver, *Effective Legal Negotiation and Settlement*, 3rd ed. (Charlottesville, VA: Michie, 1997) at 135-59.

[34] R. Hawkins, "Negotiation" in D.P. Emond, ed., *Commercial Dispute Resolution: Alternatives to Litigation* (Aurora, Ont.: Canada Law Book, 1989) at 74.

[35] R. Birke and C.R. Fox, "Psychological Principles in Negotiating Civil Settlements" (1999) 4 Harv. Negotiation Law Rev. 1 at 42.

[36] A. Lytle, J. Brett and D. Shapiro, "The Strategic Use of Interests, Rights and Power to Resolve Disputes" (1999) 15 Negotiation Journal 31.

(6 per cent), facts (26.2 per cent), attacks, intimidations, concessions, requests for proposals (1-2.1 per cent each) and tentative proposals (18.1 per cent).

The authors of the study found that there was a stronger focus on rights and power in the first and third quarters of the negotiation. For the first quarter, the parties were "setting up their positions as well as communicating their perceptions of their rights and their sources of power".[37] There was limited discussion about settlement proposals at this stage, as might be expected. In the second quarter there was less use of power- and of rights-based communications, and a continued focus on interests. Here the frequency of proposals (offers) increased three-fold. In the third quarter, frequency of interests, rights, power and proposal communications all increased. This suggests that the parties may have been rejecting proposals and trying to coerce or persuade the other side into making better ones. In the last quarter, interest-based communication decreased somewhat, whereas rights-based decreased greatly, as did power-based. In general, most of the communications involved the exchange of proposals.

The authors of the study discuss several ways to break the rights/power cycle of reciprocity (responding to an argument in kind) which leads to a distributional, positional outcome and how to get the other side aimed back at interests. It was suggested that a purely rights-based opening to negotiation might encourage a reciprocal response and make it difficult to move to interests. A power-based opening on the other hand might seem to escalate the conflict. Thus, opening the negotiation by asking about the other party's interests and giving some information about your own might help to move toward some interest-based offers. The key is to be strategic about information — give some in response to obtaining some, and do not reveal all. This caution is borrowed from positional bargaining strategy. To further the process from positional to principled, the authors of the study suggest responding to rights or power communications by refocusing on interests. Resist the common tendency to reciprocate. If you must reciprocate, combine your rights or power response with an interest-based one. The equivocal message gives the other side a chance to back down without losing face. Others, however, suggest recognizing or labelling the other side's tactic to show that you know what it is doing,[38] which may show that you are not fooled.

As mentioned earlier, a negotiation uses a mix of strategies. Rights- or power-based communications can be useful in getting the other side to the table, showing your teeth when there and ending impasses when all the interests have been explored and some of the pie still needs to be distributed. But another strategy for keeping a negotiation from getting stuck on power and rights, and to help turn it to interests, is to use "repetition". This is not the same as "reciprocity", which means that you respond in kind. Repetition is based upon the likelihood that you will act more cooperatively if you know that to do so will help you in the future. Knowing you will be negotiating with the same person again

---

[37]   *Ibid.* at 38.
[38]   R. Fisher, W. Ury and B. Patton, *Getting to Yes: Negotiating Agreement Without Giving In*, 2nd ed. (New York: Penguin, 1991). R. Hawkins, "Negotiation" in D.P. Emond, ed., *Commercial Dispute Resolution: Alternatives to Litigation* (Aurora, Ont.: Canada Law Book, 1989).

later, in the same or in a different negotiation, may make you less competitive and less adversarial.[39] The problem is that you do not want to be seen as overly cooperative, or you will be taken advantage of. If you can break the negotiation into parts, and settle some minor issues by cooperative behaviour, the other side may see the benefit of limited cooperation.

In a similar vein, Fisher *et al.*,[40] while discussing turning the other side from positions toward interests, suggest that you can keep coming back to interests in response. If this does not work, they recommend "negotiation jujitsu" by not pushing back. Try to identify what is behind the other side's position, what its interests are, what principles are important to it, and encourage it to discuss these. Additionally, they suggest inviting criticism and advice about your proposals to find out what the other side's concerns are. The best way to accomplish all this is to ask questions rather than make statements. Also, the tactical use of silence can trigger a new suggestion from the other side.[41]

Non-verbal communication is also important. Experienced negotiators, like experienced police officers, learn a lot from what the other side is doing, or not doing. Facial expressions and body language can both reveal how the other side is reacting as well as be used deceptively.[42] You can learn more about this from the literature that is available as well as from personal observation.

The Commitment

Once the less important issues are resolved, and each side realizes that it will have to make some major concessions, present new alternatives or admit deadlock; each side is watching for or giving clues about where it would like to go next. As time pressures mount and the court door opens, more proposals are made until a stage is reached where neither side wants to give any more, is wary of being exploited and must decide whether to accept what appears to be a final offer from the other side. Each knows that if things break down, they will need a mediator or some form of outside help or resolution. How is the deadlock to be broken?[43]

As mentioned earlier, it is often resolved through an "unprincipled" but useful move, such as an offer to split the difference. Sometimes the weight of objective criteria such as law tips the balance. Eventually, one side gives in. Sometimes the one that is less averse to risk and more willing to risk a loss will

---

[39]   D. Lax and J. Sebenius, *The Manager as Negotiator: Bargaining for Cooperation and Competitive Gain* (New York: Free Press; London: Collier Macmillan, 1986) at 156.

[40]   R. Fisher, W. Ury and B. Patton, *Getting to Yes: Negotiating Agreement Without Giving In*, 2nd ed. (New York: Penguin, 1991), c. 7.

[41]   *Ibid.*

[42]   C.B. Craver, *Effective Legal Negotiation and Settlement*, 3rd. ed. (Charlottesville, VA: Michie, 1997), c. 3. There is even a "Journal of Non Verbal Behaviour" found in the "Psychology" section of most large libraries.

[43]   This stage is discussed in many books. One of the most useful is G.R. Williams, *Legal Negotiation and Settlement* (St. Paul, Minn.: West Pub. Co., 1983) at 70-72.

prevail. The party more desirous of certainty, in wrapping things up, may concede. Often the side most willing or able to foot additional costs holds on.[44]

Several negotiators have said that once a tentative settlement is reached, by whatever means, the parties should go back and try to see if there are any additional interests which can be satisfied. This will be particularly useful if the majority of the negotiation has been positional, and less useful if the parties have already exhausted the principled bargaining approach to achieve mutual gains. The idea is to obtain the best result for both parties, and to leave both feeling that they have obtained a good deal.[45] The presence of the tentative agreement anchors and forms the basis on which to build.

The negotiation process as described in this chapter may be affected where one party is made up of a number of individuals (team bargaining) and where there are multiple parties. The peculiarities of these types of negotiations are discussed in the remainder of this chapter.

Team Bargaining

When the party to the legal dispute is a group, as opposed to an individual litigant, it negotiates as a group, or through a representative. Where the party is a corporation, or where the nominal party is acting in a representative capacity, most rules of court require that the party be represented by a solicitor. Thus, if litigation was started, the group will already have a representative. Other groups may negotiate as a team without a representative.

Interaction within the group can add a new dimension. It is unlikely that all the team members will agree on all matters of substance, strategy or tactics, just as it is unlikely that they will completely trust each other. When it comes to brainstorming, or solving problems, there is no reason why the team should not be quite successful. However, when negotiating with the other side to the dispute it is likely that the team will use a positional, aggressive strategy, particularly if the team is large. This is perhaps due to an emboldening factor achieved by large numbers, or perhaps because the team tends to generate a leader who is in that position because of his or her ability to articulate for the team. However, it is the team that assesses what it wants to hear; therefore, a more hard line spokesperson is often selected. The spokesperson may also feel he or she has to cater to the constituency within the team that is most hard line in order to maintain his or her credibility within the team.

Where the team is represented by a negotiator or by legal counsel, there exists the added complication of formulating and communicating instructions. Getting instructions from a group of beneficiaries under a trust, or from a corporation, can be difficult.

---

[44]   See, G. Gross and K. Syverud, "Getting to No: A Study of Settlement Negotiations and The Selection of Cases for Trial" (1991) 90 Mich. L. Rev. 319, and R. Mnookin, "Why Negotiations Fail" (1993) 8 Ohio State J. on Dispute Resol. 235.

[45]   C.B. Craver, *Effective Legal Negotiation and Settlement*, 3rd ed. (Charlottesville, VA: Michie, 1997) at 170. R. Hawkins, "Negotiation" in D.P. Emond, ed., *Commercial Dispute Resolution: Alternatives to Litigation* (Aurora, Ont.: Canada Law Book, 1989).

A further problem arises if a representative of the group or team is chosen for his or her expertise in the area of the dispute, as a representative would be if acting for it in litigation. You may know the other side's representative, or at least have a similar knowledge base, and both of you may be more realistic about prospects than your clients are. This puts you in the difficult position of sometimes having to negotiate with and persuade your own clients to adopt a particular tactic, or seriously consider an offer, leading your clients to wonder about your loyalty to them.[46] It may even lead you to become more aggressive with the other side, to show your loyalty to your clients, and may result in a poor settlement or a deadlock.

Another problem of negotiating with a representative, or even directly with a group, is that you are vulnerable to the "lack of authority" tactic. Negotiation against a government agency can cause serious "who has authority" problems. As well, it may be difficult to use a principled approach because bureaucrats with limited authority may be unable to come up with useful alternatives, being constrained by superiors or by legislation.[47] It is important to try to identify the individuals who have the necessary authority to make decisions, and if at all possible, have those individuals in attendance at the negotiation.

Multi-Party Negotiations

Many legal disputes involve more than two parties. You may find yourself negotiating with several entities at once. In a tort claim, there are likely to be one or more insurance companies involved, as well as more than one defendant, or third or fourth parties. Multiple plaintiffs are common, and, although in litigation all must have a common solicitor of record, they will probably have their own counsel. How does the presence of more than two parties to a negotiation change things?

The most profound change is that it makes positional negotiation very difficult, and favours principled bargaining. Each party has its own interests, which will not be the same as those of any other party. Co-defendants may cross-claim against each other. For example, it is important for parties with similar interests to meet to decide upon common strategies. Eventually, of course, each party is expected to look after its own set of interests.[48]

---

[46] See D.G. Pruitt and P.J. Carnevale, *Negotiation in Social Conflict* (Pacific Grove, Calif.: Brooks/Cole Pub. Co., 1993) at 154.

[47] See C. Menkel-Meadow, "Toward Another View of Legal Negotiation: The Structure of Problem Solving" (1984) 31 UCLA L. Rev. 754 at 833. One author suggests that there is no point in negotiating with a bureaucracy until a time pressure point approaches, such as a fiscal year end or trial date (see C.B. Craver, *Effective Legal Negotiation and Settlement*, 3rd. ed. (Charlottesville, VA: Michie, 1997) at 264).

[48] This can sometimes result in special deals, such as a *Mary Carter* agreement between one defendant and one plaintiff. In the case of *Booth v. Mary Carter Paint Co.* 202 So.2d. 8 (Fla. Dist. Ct. App. 1967), one co-defendant entered into an agreement with a plaintiff to cap its liability and had little interest in defending the case vigorously, thus putting pressure on the other defendant(s). In Ontario, the agreement's existence must be disclosed to the other parties as well as to the court. Other defendants can prevent this type of deal from occurring if all defendants sign a "joint defence agreement" in which they agree on liability apportionment in advance of settlement or adverse judgment.

A problem common to multi-party disputes is where the defendants base their offers on the extent of concessions, or on what the other defendants are doing. This can frustrate the success of an agreement by limiting concessions to the lowest common denominator. It is far more productive if the parties focus exclusively on offers compatible with their own interests, without regard to what the other parties are offering. Although there are issues specific to team bargaining and multi-party negotiations, and, in fact, each negotiation is unique in some respect, the basic path of a negotiation is as set out in this chapter. The steps along the way — "Setting the Agenda", "Initial Demands and Offers" and "Concessions — Maximizing the Outcome" — should, in most cases, lead to a successful conclusion: "The Commitment". In the next chapter, the role of lawyers as negotiators will be examined.

Chapter 8

LAWYERS AS NEGOTIATORS

There are many good reasons why lawyers should be used as advisers to parties who are negotiating, or even as representative negotiators.

Whether counsel attend the negotiation, and the extent to which they take an active part, as opposed to acting as advisors, varies greatly. In a positional negotiation which involves narrow "rights" issues, and particularly where the mediator has an evaluative role, counsel are essential.[1] In jurisdictions in which mediation of civil actions is compulsory, counsel are almost always present except in some family law cases where the issues are limited to support and access.

Just as with negotiations conducted without a mediator, the key to success is preparation.[2] It is also important that lawyers as negotiators rely upon their clients for authority and do not enter the negotiation with unlimited authority. To do otherwise is to risk making too many concessions if the other side has limited authority and can keep going back for better instructions and coming up with new demands. You will "end up bargaining against yourself".[3] Additionally, a knowledge of and facility with the processes of negotiation, and a desire to see it succeed, are essential.

In many cases, the negotiation will be the first chance for counsel to see the other side and its counsel in action.[4] Should the case move on to trial, this opportunity will be valuable.

A few of the many advantages of legal representation at a negotiation are as follows:

1. Since the dispute involves law, lawyers are in an excellent position to give advice about external objective standards, such as the law that applies.

2. Lawyers may already be on-site, if litigation has started or is contemplated, and will, therefore, have much information about the dispute already. They may also have some knowledge, and experience negotiating with counsel for the other party to the dispute, and will be able to use the

---

[1] It may be that in some areas of legal dispute, the parties prefer positional bargaining. See J. Tyrril, "Construction Industry Dispute Resolution — A Brief Overview" (1991) 3 A.D.R.J. 167.

[2] See particularly C. Moore, *The Mediation Process*, 2nd ed. (San Francisco: Jossey-Bass, 1996) at 44 and L.L. Riskin, Mediation and Lawyers" (1983) 43 Ohio St. L.J. 29.

[3] R. Hawkins, "Negotiation" in D.P. Emond, ed. *Commercial Dispute Resolution: Alternatives to Litigation* (Aurora, Ont.: Canada Law Book, 1989) at 69.

[4] This is assuming it is conducted before discoveries, as is common, especially with mandatory mediations.

legal process to obtain information and evidence relevant to settling the dispute.

3. Lawyers who are experienced and skilled negotiators will do a better job than the parties to the dispute, who may be inexperienced or unskilled negotiators.[5]

4. Legal professionals will be familiar with the processes of resolving legal disputes and, in most jurisdictions, are required to explain the alternatives, including mediation, to their clients.

5. Parties to a dispute are subject to all of the psychological factors set out earlier, such as reactive devaluation, and may be too close to it to exercise good judgement. They may also be overly affected by emotion, which is natural but can be risky. Lawyers are subject to psychological factors as well, but should be less so than their clients because they are professionals and are one step removed from the dispute.

If you are a legal professional and involved as a negotiator for someone in a legal dispute, there are many factors to consider. These include:

1. how your interests conflict with those of your client
2. use of confidential information obtained through discovery, settlement discussions and elsewhere
3. limits upon tactics imposed by codes of conduct, such as good faith and fairness

Generally, if you have been involved in litigation or in the resolution of legal disputes, you will be well aware of current ADR movements, particularly those involving compulsory mediation. Courses are offered regularly to legal professionals and to others in ADR, and law faculties are involved extensively.[6] As a result of these developments, lawyers are no longer as "rights" oriented as they were 20 years ago, and are more likely to use a principled negotiation style overall. The Code of Ethics of any of the provincial law societies or of the Canadian Bar Association (CBA) will generally require that:

---

[5]   Litigators who are too "adversarial" should consider using "settlement counsel" who are likely to be better negotiators. V. Aubert, "Competition and Dissensus: Two Types of Conflict and of Conflict Resolution" (1963) 7 J. Conflict Resol. 26. And see R. March, "Psychological Type-Theory on the Legal Profession" (1992) 24 Toledo U.L. Rev. 103.

[6]   Some recent publications also offer useful advice. See, particularly, C. Noble, L. Dizgun and D.P. Emond, *Mediation Advocacy: Effective Client Representation in Mediation Proceedings* (Toronto: Emond Montgomery, 1998); L. Boulle and K.J. Kelly, *Mediation: Principles, Process, Practice*, Canadian ed. (Toronto: Butterworths, 1998), c. 5 (at 155-62) and c. 9; G. Chornenki *The Corporate Counsel Guide to Dispute Resolution* (Aurora, Ont.: Canada Law Book, 1999); J. MacFarlane, *Dispute Resolution: Readings and Case Studies* (Toronto: Emond Montgomery, 1999) at 426; Can. Bar Assoc., 1996 Institute of Continuing Legal Education, ADR Section, *Mediation Advocacy for Litigators and Solicitors*; L.L. Riskin, "The Lawyers' Standard Philosophical Map Revisited" in L.L. Riskin and J.E. Westbrook, *Dispute Resolution and Lawyers* (St. Paul, Minn.: West Pub. Co., 1987) at 206.

1. counsel not communicate directly with a party that is represented by a solicitor;
2. counsel communicate all offers to settle to his or her own client; and
3. counsel advise his or her client of ADR alternatives and advise and encourage settlements whenever it is possible to do so on a reasonable basis.

In addition, Rules of Court will require that once you are solicitor of record in litigation, your client has an obligation to give discovery on an ongoing basis until the matter is set down for trial. The Rules may also limit the use to which this information and derivative evidence can be used, through an "implied undertaking" rule. If you are negotiating in a legal dispute in which the action has started, you will be more constrained than if it has not. While the duties and limitations imposed on counsel during the course of negotiations cannot be defined precisely, the general concepts can be explained.

CONFLICTS OF INTEREST

One of the major sources of possible conflict of interest between you and your client is financial. Once the case is settled, it is over; no fees will come your way. It has been suggested that this may tend to motivate litigators to delay settlement until just before trial. Conversely, if you are a plaintiff class action solicitor or involved in personal injury litigation, you may be bankrolling the action by carrying your fees as well as the disbursements until recovery, and may be motivated to settle early for less than the case is worth.

Another source of trouble is your relationship with the other lawyers. Is there a risk that you will recommend a settlement that is less than you might obtain if you bargained harder, because you want to continue a good working relationship with other litigators?[7] Your major duty is to your client. Does engaging in interest-based principled negotiation, in which you try to identify interests of the other side and advance these while pursuing your own interests, mean that you are improperly putting the other side's interests ahead of your client's? If a competitive-aggressive style will lead to a better result against a co-operative style on the other side, does the fact that you do not use it undermine your client's position?[8] Does "transformative" negotiation, in which you both emerge as improved people, involve undue concern for the other party? What if your professional view of how the case should resolve differs from that of your client. How hard can you push?[9]

---

[7] The CBA Code says that you should deal with other counsel with "courtesy and in good faith". It does not deal with the possibility that you may be overly solicitous except by recognizing your primary duty to your client. See generally, G. MacKenzie, *Lawyers and Ethics* 2nd ed. (Scarborough, Ont.: Carswell, 1999). This may be more likely to occur in a smaller-sized bar, such as in a smaller centre, or in a specialized bar in a large city.

[8] See "The 'Negotiator's Dilemma'", in Chapter 4.

[9] See S.B. Goldberg, F.E.A. Snider and N.H. Rogers, *Dispute Resolution: Negotiation, Mediation and Other Processes* (Boston: Little-Brown, 1992) at 72.

The more general conflicts of interests that may occur are covered in depth in numerous books and articles.[10]

CONFIDENTIALITY

The question of the use to which a lawyer may put communications he or she has received from his or her client, as well as from the other side, is effectively covered in books about privilege[11] which deal with the "without prejudice, settlement-negotiation" privilege and the "legal professional" privilege. In addition, the "implied undertaking" rules place some added limits on the use of information obtained from the other side in litigation.

Communications made during a mediation are usually also covered by a contractual cloak of confidentiality derived from a signed Agreement to Mediate, such as that included in Appendix IV.

GOOD FAITH, FAIRNESS

The most pressing problem of your duty as a lawyer negotiating with the other side is the question of how honest and fair you must be. As one author describes, "Canadian rules of professional conduct generally impose no duties on lawyers to make disclosure of that which may be detrimental to their clients, or even to refrain from misrepresentations".[12]

The tactics of positional negotiating, as developed in transactional bargaining, have a significant influence on the absence of such rules. As mentioned earlier, positional tactics don't travel well to principled negotiating.[13] It is true that the law of contract and of tort do deal with fraud, deceit, misrepresentation of various kinds and their effects upon agreements. However, while this law may place some limits on the use of "dishonest" tactics in negotiation, the duty

---

[10] G. MacKenzie *Lawyers and Ethics*, 2nd ed. (Scarborough, Ont.: Carswell, 1999), Ch 22.3; G. Sammon, "The Ethical Duties of Lawyers Who Act for Parties to a Mediation", (1993) 3 ADRJ 190; D.E. Rosenthal, *Lawyer and Client: Who's in Charge* (New York: Russell Sage Foundation 1974); A. Rubin, "A Causerie on Lawyers' Ethics in Negotiation" (1975) 35 La. L. Rev. 577. In Ontario, an interesting study was undertaken as to how, if at all, lawyers' ethics are changing. The study is described in P. Mercer, M.A. Wilkinson and T. Strong, "The Practice of Ethical Precepts: Dissecting Decision-Making by Lawyers" (1996) 9 Can. J. of Law & Juris. 141. The conclusion of the study will be published shortly, probably in 2001. An interim report is found at P. Mercer, M.A. Wilkinson and T. Strong, "Do Codes of Ethics Actually Shape Legal Practice?" (2000) 45(3) McGill L.J. 1.

[11] See R.D. Manes and M.P. Silver, *Solicitor-Client Privilege in Canadian Law* (Toronto: Butterworths, 1993) and G. MacKenzie, at Ch. 3, "Confidentiality".

[12] G. MacKenzie, *Lawyers and Ethics*, 2nd ed. (Scarborough, Ont.: Carswell, 1999) at p. 15-1. The differences between not correcting what you know to be a mistake on the other side, not offering information unless asked directly, and making incomplete statements are hard to define. Every parent of teenage children knows that unless you ask the right question, little information will be obtained. See also A. Strudler, "Moral Complexity in the Law of Non-disclosure" (1997) 45 UCLA L. Rev. 337.

[13] See Chapter 4, "Positional Versus Interest-Based (Principled) Bargaining".

of "good faith" towards other counsel seems unlikely to be sufficiently precise to place real limits on dishonest bargaining practices.

Even the American Bar Association Model Rules of Professional Conduct which prohibit lawyers from making false statements of material facts or law to others do not require that you volunteer information generally, but it recommends that you exclude estimates of price or of value about the subject matter of a transaction and statements about your intentions concerning acceptable settlement figures.[14] This means that you can be misleading, can bluff and can threaten action at will. However, none of that is covered by disclosure requirements[15] because it relates to aspirations, not to facts. Disclosure deals with facts.

In one case involving two defendants, each represented by insurers and each liable for relatively minor damages for a personal injury, the plaintiff was warned by the mediator that the defendants' consensus was coming unglued and that to push too hard in the latter rounds of bargaining could evaporate the consensus and the offers available to the plaintiff. The plaintiff had already refused to abide by a "final offer" of $20,000 and had instead counter-offered $27,000. The insurers then offered $25,000 again as a "final offer". The plaintiff had forgotten about OHIP's subrogated claim when making its previous offers, and went back, against the mediator's caution, with an offer of $26,500.

At this point, the defendants caucused privately, and one of them announced to the other that its contribution to the previous $25,000 offer was off the table. Now the defendants together had only $21,000 on the table! The other insurer was furious, as was the mediator, who could now no longer resurrect the $25,000 figure. When the plaintiff was informed of this, he offered to accept the $25,000 offer, but the hold-out insurer said, "No, that offer was rejected. Now a smaller sum is available". The hold-out insurer also refused to even go $1,500 higher (with the other insurer picking up the rest of the increase from $21,000 to $25,000). The hold-out insurer claimed that it had never been agreeable to the contribution needed to procure the $25,000 offer, which the defendants had made. Since the defendants had discussed it, the one insurer now believed the other to be lying. Even if the hold-out insurer had made an error, it refused to accept responsibility for its mistake, a responsibility which would only have cost it $1,500. Needless to say, the plaintiff felt manipulated, and the other insurer felt lied to and exploited.

---

[14] G. MacKenzie, *Lawyers and Ethics*, 2nd ed. (Scarborough, Ont.: Carswell, 1999) at p. 15-3, Rule 4-1. The ABA Model Rule also requires "fairness" in dealing with other participants in Negotiation (Rule 4-2). It is obvious that parties should not be required to reveal their intentions regarding settlement figures. In any event, were such a requirement to exist, how would it be enforced?

[15] The Law Society of Alberta's Code provides that you cannot "lie to or knowingly mislead" the other side in a negotiation. See generally L.L. Riskin and J.E. Westbrook, *Dispute Resolution and Lawyers* (St. Paul, Minn.: West Pub. Co., 1987) at 181; G. Wetlauffer, "The Ethics of Lying in Negotiations" (1990) 75 Iowa L. Rev. 1219; G. Lowenthal, "The Bar's Failure to Require Truthful Bargaining by Lawyers" (1988) 2 Geo. J.L. Ethics 411; C. Menkel-Meadow, "Ethics in Alternative Dispute Resolution: New Issues, No Answers from the Adversary, Conception of Lawyers' Responsibilities" (1997) 38 S. Texas L. Rev. 407; M. Rubin, "The Ethics of Negotiation: Are There Any?" (1995) 56 La. L. Rev. 447; D. Lax and J. Sebenius, "Three Ethical Issues in Negotiation" (1986) 2 Negot. J. 363 (of course one cannot threaten to bring criminal proceedings).

FRAUD

Allegations of fraud often surface in litigation, although rarely are they strenuously advanced at mediation, and even more rarely do they proceed. Cases involving insurance fraud, fraudulent misrepresentation and fraudulent conveyance have their entire subject matter oriented around allegations of fraud.

However, what about when the fraud concerns the manner or process by which negotiations are conducted or a settlement is reached?

Criminal law and other federal and provincial law may limit how you deal with the other side. Fraud is defined as "dishonesty" in part, and this might have a "chilling effect" upon excesses. Legislation also limits the substance of settlements. Settlements which require something illegal are ill-advised and probably not enforceable. For example, a landowner that settles a pollution dispute with a large feed-lot farmer by accepting a sum of money to compensate for ground water pollution violates provincial legislation.[16] The crux of the settlement hinges on an unlawful act.

Another example is an offer to pay money to settle a claim, and counsel and/or the mediator hears that party say that he or she may not have any intention of paying the settlement once it is signed. Problems such as this, or a settlement hinged on unlawful grounds, obviously trigger ethical responses and professional duties by both counsel and the mediator.

As we can see, trying to draw careful lines between what you can do and cannot do is a difficult thing. It is clear that your own reputation will be built upon how others perceive you. As one lawyer said, "He'll only do that once".

Most of the general concepts discussed in this chapter, with respect to the role of lawyers in negotiations, apply equally in the context of a mediated negotiation. Chapter 14 provides an in-depth look at advocacy in a mediation.

---

[16]   Raised earlier in Chapter 6, under the discussion "Opposing Interests", was the issue of whether a dispute in which one party alleges fraud could, in fact, be settled, where there is an interest advanced in making the fraud allegation.

Part II

MEDIATION

Chapter 9

INTRODUCTION TO MEDIATION

Negotiations often fail to resolve disputes. There are many reasons for this, and they are often found in the human factors at work. Impediments to settlement include lack of authority, timing, non-recognition, unrealistic demands and power imbalances. Occasionally, bad faith of the parties can also be a problem.[1] A neutral third party — the mediator — can be instrumental in minimizing these roadblocks.

Mediation is a process in which a third person assists the parties by becoming involved in their negotiation and helping them to reach a settlement. As an alternative dispute resolution process, it is the great "catch all" in the sense that it permits the use of both evaluative and facilitative methods to encourage the parties to settle. In that vein, mediation can be viewed as a "kickstart" for the parties in a dispute that would be difficult to settle through unassisted negotiation. A mediation can be relied upon to fully explore the "settlement DNA" and to establish a fair and level playing field for the conduct of negotiations. Practically anything in a mediation goes if it leads the parties towards settlement, is fair and does no harm to a party's interests.

For example, a mediator in a given dispute may play a very passive role, letting the parties make their arguments and settlement proposals to one another (sometimes even without the mediator's presence), and simply creating a forum for any venting or negotiating — all of which the parties engage in quite readily. In this situation, the mediator is more of a "master of ceremonies". Alternatively, a mediator may be very proactive, asking the parties difficult questions, creating settlement proposals on his or her own, challenging the parties on any counter-productive behaviour and/or providing his or her opinion on the merits — in essence, evaluating a party's case. Both of these passive/facilitative and active/evaluative roles can occur within the same mediation, at different times or with different parties. None of these roles are mutually exclusive, and all of them can be engaged in to varying degrees.

That is the flexibility and the beauty of mediation. It treats every dispute on its own terms. Every dispute is different — with different people involved, different sets of facts, different counsel (if there are any) and different time of occurrence. A wrongful dismissal of a clerical employee in Ontario has a different settlement context in the year 2001 than it did in 1992. The law changes, as do

---

[1] For example, a defendant's lawyer who decides in advance to use the mediation process to intimidate the other side into dropping the action, and accordingly refuses to settle even where settlement is to the defendant's advantage, is exhibiting bad faith.

the makeup of the Bench (which can be relevant in assessing litigation outcomes and alternatives) and people's appreciation of what is fair.

All this suggests that the settlement of disputes is a fluid enterprise, and mediation is the best way to grapple with that fluidity because of the flexibility afforded the mediator in his or her role of extolling the virtues of a reasonable settlement with all the parties.

A fair amount has been written in Canada about mediation, partly because of concerns about the delay and cost of litigation, and partly because of the rise of mandatory mediation. It is a flexible process and is being used in a multitude of disputes, ranging from matrimonial to public law disputes.[2] The same issues concerning private resolution of legal disputes that were raised earlier apply to the use of mediation. However, there may be some disputes that should not be resolved outside the courts. Fortunately, the reality is that most legal disputes do not result in trials — the parties often resolve them either with or without mediation assistance.

BENEFITS AND LIMITATIONS OF MEDIATION

Some of the benefits[3] and limitations of mediation are listed below:

BENEFITS	LIMITATIONS
1. Procedural flexibility	1. Added costs if mediation fails
2. Cost and time savings	2. Extra time used if mediation fails
3. Informality	3. Inability to resolve conflicts which cannot or should not be negotiated
4. Party involvement	
5. Broader range of solutions	4. Absence of regulation and possible misuse of information by the other side
6. Able to preserve relationships	
7. More predictability — less risk	
8. Looks to the future, not the past	5. Due to disclosure of information, extra ammunition available to the other side should the matter go to trial
9. Private, confidential	

BENEFITS WHEN THERE IS NO SETTLEMENT

Even if a settlement is not reached, there are some benefits to having gone through the mediation process. Failure is a relative term. It has been said that

---

[2]   A good summary appears in L. Boulle and K.J. Kelly, *Mediation: Principles, Process, Practice*, Canadian ed. (Toronto: Butterworths, 1998) at 222.

[3]   See *ibid.* at 38 for a discussion of some of these factors. See also J. Macfarlane, *Rethinking Disputes: The Mediation Alternative* (Toronto: Emond-Montgomery Publications, 1997), Ch. 2.

"success is what some people settle for when they can't think of anything noble enough to be worth failing at". A mediation which fails to settle at the session, but paves the way for more understanding about the dispute and perhaps for a settlement some time later, cannot be considered a failure.

There are a variety of ways in which you can utilize a mediation that does not settle.

Some examples are listed below:

- You may gain more information about the other side's case, perhaps doing away with the need for a discovery.
- You will have had the opportunity to test your own case with an impartial observer (the mediator) and with the other side.
- You may have been able to narrow the issues, which will simplify future litigation settlement discussions.
- You may have been able to set the stage for an arbitration or a "rights-based" pre-trial, like a session before a retired judge.
- The mediation may have been useful to let your client vent, either unloading negative emotions or conveying positive ones, such as an apology or an explanation.
- You may have been able to come to procedural and interim agreements on the conduct of the litigation.
- You may have been able to achieve partial settlements whereby certain parties are let out of the litigation or settled with.

WHEN TO MEDIATE

Clearly, there can be numerous benefits to mediation, even in cases where the mediations ultimately fail. However, not every case is appropriate for mediation. Cases involving a large public policy interest (*e.g.*, an important constitutional case) or involving a bureaucracy that is incapable of assembling settlement proposals may require an adjudicated result. Additionally, if a party is irrational or is dedicated to acting in bad faith, a mediation may not be appropriate. Fortunately, these cases are exceedingly rare. The vast majority of disputes are assisted by mediation, which is the best vehicle for assessing alternatives to settlement, exploring possible settlement options and allowing the parties to release pent-up energies that are often inherent in the dispute. The only other dispute for which mediation may not be useful is one where the money or other items in issue are so small that it does not pay to get a third party involved. In that instance, the issue is one of practicality — not process.

There are many factors to consider when determining whether mediation is appropriate. The following is a checklist of indicators — the more that apply, the more likely it is that mediation will be beneficial:

- There are ongoing or important relationships at stake.
- Communication breakdown has had a role in the dispute.

- The financial costs of litigation are high relative to the damages likely to be awarded and the costs to be ordered.
- Litigation will likely take months or years to complete.
- There is an appreciable risk in the litigation.
- The alternatives, including continued litigation, are unpalatable.
- There is not enough money to fund litigation, even if it was successful.
- The other side has misunderstood your case.
- The other side has misunderstood your resolve and determination.
- You need more information to properly assess the case, and a mediation will provide a forum for gathering it.
- You have all the information you need to assess the case, and you are ready to weigh your options.

Once you have determined that your case can benefit from mediation, you can expect the mediator to assist with the negotiation in a number of ways.

HOW DOES THE MEDIATOR ASSIST?

Specifically, what can a mediator bring to the parties' negotiation efforts? The following list may be helpful:

1. Float proposals so that the parties are able to save face and avoid reactive devaluation in making offers
2. Open up lines of communication and encourage the sharing of information relevant to settling the dispute
3. Help to generate creative solutions (either by facilitating the parties' brainstorming, or even thinking of ideas himself or herself) and get around the limitations of what a court could possibly award
4. Probe the interests of the parties (which have often never been fully thought out by them)
5. Assist the parties in reality-checking, assessing the risks of their case/position, challenge the assumptions on which it is based and play devil's advocate
6. Help assess alternatives to an agreement
7. Coordinate a large number of parties
8. Persistently keep trying to get the parties to reach agreement when they are unable to step back and see that progress is being made/have already given up/see no hope in trying
9. Utilize mutually acceptable independent standards
10. Insist on principled negotiation as much as possible
11. Put a check on bad faith, dirty tactics, lowball negotiating
12. Summarize progress to date — generate momentum
13. Float "bridging the gap" solutions at the 11th hour of a negotiation

14. Confront parties with the reality of no agreement if a final compromise is not made
15. Bring closure

As you can see, much of what a mediator does is used to help overcome some of the barriers to negotiation.[4] A mediator recognizes the many practical and psychological influences at work in negotiation and tries to bring the parties through them to settlement. Other mediators have different styles and use different techniques. The major difference between mediators is in whether they emphasize a facilitative or an evaluative approach.

---

[4]   L. Boulle and K.J. Kelly, *Mediation: Principles, Process, Practice*, Canadian ed. (Toronto: Butterworths, 1998), have an extensive chapter about "Skills and Techniques of Mediators".

Chapter 10

ATTRIBUTES TO LOOK FOR IN A MEDIATOR

A mediator is a negotiator whose interest is a good outcome for the parties.

The mediator's skill and ability is a very significant factor in whether a dispute will be resolved. How do you know what to look for in a mediator?

According to the Toronto ADR Centre evaluation, one of the things that parties and counsel liked most about the mediation process in which they engaged was the mediator. The thing that they liked the least was also the mediator! The mediator — his or her skills, ability to connect with the parties and his or her general "fit" — is, therefore, crucial.

Going through the exercise of trying to choose the right mediator or imagining what he or she might be able to do for the parties can also assist in deciding whether the case is suitable for mediation in the first place. If you cannot picture your chosen mediator being of any help, that may tell you something. Conversely, if you can imagine progress being made utilizing the style of the mediator you are selecting, then, indeed, progress may be attainable.

Since so many people profess to be mediators, a discussion of some of the important qualities to look for in a good mediator is in order.[1]

CREATIVITY

A critical quality for a mediator to have is creativity — thinking outside the box — as well as a more conventional creativity reflected in the structuring and melding of offers. The mediator may be able to bring a fresh outlook to a problem or help in crafting new offers which break the old barriers to settlement. As discussed in previous chapters, a good mediator will identify the interests of the parties, and attempt to fashion a solution that addresses these interests in non-traditional ways. A good mediator must be able to think past the type of remedies awarded by a court, such as monetary damages, and create options that address the unique interests that exist in each case.

---

[1] For other authors' views on the personal characteristics of good mediators, see Appendix I, "Choosing the Best ADR Process..." by Paul Iacono, Q.C., and L. Boulle and K.J. Kelly, *Mediation: Principles, Process, Practice*, Canadian ed. (Toronto: Butterworths, 1998) at 91-92, where they suggest that mediators should be trustworthy, non-judgemental, empathetic, creative, patient, persistent and self-reflective.

Additionally, the mediator must be able to conduct risk assessments in a creative way — to suggest new ways of looking at interests, and to provide insight into a party's problems.

Finally, creativity in picking and choosing elements from previously exchanged offers so as to create blended settlement options in an effort to bridge gaps and overcome impasses is important.

CREDIBILITY

The mediator must have credibility with the parties. While this can come about through an expertise in the subject matter of the dispute, this is, in fact, seldom necessary to properly mediate a dispute, and, interestingly, is not that often sought by the parties selecting a mediator. More important is the manner in which the mediator conducts himself or herself. Does he or she create a good climate for settlement? To do this, the mediator needs to have credibility; to establish credibility, the mediator needs people skills — the ability to put people at ease, demonstrate empathy, listen well and be a quick study on the background of the dispute. The mediator also needs to be able to use humour at the right time.[2]

Training is helpful but not crucial to the quality of a given mediator. Many experienced counsel are of the view that mediators "do not emerge from course attendance and training — individuals either have the unique mix of communication and listening skills, commercial creativity and credible 'presence' to be a successful mediator or they do not."[3]

Part of establishing credibility lies with the perceived impartiality of the mediator. From an institutional perspective, mediators who draw their experience overwhelmingly from the insurance defence bar may have a tough time establishing credibility with plaintiffs and their counsel. Similarly, mediators from the government sector may have difficulty mediating cases where one of the parties is Her Majesty the Queen. However, success is also dependent on how the mediator conducts himself or herself at the mediation. Often, what is said or not said can change the perceptions of impartiality. In one case, the plaintiff had been badly bitten by a bull terrier and sued for large damages. The insurer was incredulous, and the plaintiff asked, "Do you want to see the scars?" It was suggested that she show the group, so she lifted her shirt to expose huge red scars running almost the full length of her chest and back. The mediator expressed his

---

[2]   The author once made a regrettable gaffe in a case which involved a dismissed employee relating what a tough time he had gone through after the dismissal, and comparing it to the death of his cat from cancer. The author thought that this was said in some jest and laughed — but it was not a joke; indeed, this had been traumatic for the employee. Needless to say, the right "connection" between party and mediator was never really accomplished.

[3]   R. Pepper, "Mandatory Mediation: Court Annexed ADR" (1998) 20 Advocates' Quarterly 403 at 436. A good many people, including lawyers, are currently being trained in various negotiation and mediation skills. Many of these courses focus on "principled" bargaining, using R. Fisher, W. Ury and B. Patton, *Getting to Yes: Negotiating Agreement Without Giving In*, 2nd ed. (New York: Penguin, 1991); however, the courses all but ignore the processes of positional bargaining that are included in the book.

shock at the sight by exclaiming "Wow!" Later, in private session, the insurer expressed its concern that the mediator was not impartial because he had reacted to the scars with horror. Had this case gone to trial, it would have been in front of a jury; thus, the rhetorical question was asked, how would a jury react? The case quickly settled for a reasonable payment of general damages, in an amount larger than the insurer had initally contemplated paying. The reaction of the mediator was seen as a credible third-party assessment of what the plaintiff had gone through. The point, therefore, is that the mediator's conduct can also win or lose credibility.

One of the difficulties mediators face, as demonstrated by the above example is that while they are expected to maintain credibility with the parties by not appearing to favour one or the other, on the merits, they must also convey information and offers back and forth. A truly impartial mediator is able to do this for each side with equal vigour and enthusiasm, without appearing to favour one position over another. However, while addressing one side with the other side's proposals, he or she may be perceived as favouring these proposals. Look how vigorously he or she is putting them forward! The side being addressed may wonder about the impartiality of the mediator, who in turn may see this happening and retreat a bit, thus becoming less effective.[4]

Reading any material submitted by the parties before the mediation helps a mediator to establish credibility because it signals to the parties that the mediator cares about the facts and the parties' view of those facts. By asking pertinent questions arising from the materials, the impression is conveyed that the mediator is intelligent and cannot be fooled by specious arguments. Finally, a respected track record settling disputes is of prime importance in conveying credibility. This only comes about from experience, and it is experience which may be most sought after by parties when they select a mediator.

SELF-CONFIDENCE AND PERSISTENCE

The mediator should be self-confident, but not arrogant. He or she must have control of the process without assuming a self-importance to his or her role. Playing "traffic cop", or even, on occasion, the role of "elder statesperson", can work, but it must be tempered with a humility about his or her impact and with a sense of self-effacingness so as to relax parties that may be tense and uncomfortable.

The mediator must be able to analyze and play devil's advocate from the perspective of a proper risk analysis as well as the proffering of insight into how to solve a problem. Parties, even sophisticated ones, generally expect to be tested in their own risk analysis at a mediation. They certainly expect the mediator to

---

[4]   See J. Rifkin, J. Millen and S. Cobb, "Toward a New Discourse for Mediation" (1991) 9 Mediation Quarterly 151, who investigate a technique called "storytelling" as a way to deal with this problem. The problem that the mediator may harbour both personal and systemic bias is a separate one. As with judges, being aware of these may help him or her deal with them. See R. Delgado, "Fairness and Formality: Minimizing the Risk of Prejudice in A.D.R." (1985) Wisc. L. Rev. 1359.

do this with the *other side*! Accordingly, doing this with *all sides* is usually seen as a means of keeping the process honest and the process credible. The evaluative feedback can be put bluntly, or it can be softpeddled, but either way, a mediator should be able to move freely between evaluative and facilitative mode any number of times as the dispute dynamics require.

The mediator also needs to have the persistence and commitment to get the dispute settled. Stamina, tenacity, passion and a certain gentle bull-headedness to keep people talking and making offers to one another are viewed as prime mediator assets.

While a good mediator may not come up with or get the parties to agree to a specific dollar amount, he or she may get them reasonably close such that the parties can stare their alternatives in the face, after which some eleventh-hour intervention by the mediator may be required to bridge that final gap. A good mediator should not be afraid of barriers to settlement or of any remaining gap. He or she should be able to persist in testing that final quotient of settlement DNA in order to extract an agreement from the jaws of failure.

Finally, a mediator's skill in assessing and exploring settlement DNA (where, perhaps, even the parties might have thought none existed) implicitly recognizes the skill in knowing when to stop. You do not want your mediator to continuously "flog a dead horse". Knowing when to bring closure is no less a skill or exercise of good judgement than facilitating a negotiation. Clearly, if the parties' alternatives to a potential agreement on the table are better than the agreement could ever be, it is time to end the negotiation. Similarly, if a party has simply had enough or is incapable of deciding on the potential agreement at the mediation, then it may be time to stop.[5]

MEDIATOR'S BACKGROUND

There may be disputes in which the mediator's ethnicity, gender or specific professional background is relevant to establishing credibility or providing a proper "fit" with the parties. A mediator who shares such characteristics with the parties may have more credibility if the parties assume that the mediator will have greater insight into an issue in dispute, or a greater understanding of the context of the dispute, because of the similar backgrounds. These are generalities only — and there are more exceptions than cases which prove the rule. It is certainly possible, even sometimes advisable, to have a mediator mediate in a cultural or other context *outside* his or her own background.

---

[5] There may be perfectly good reasons for not settling. In one case, a woman had an account set up with her ex-husband into which he deposited money for child support. The financial institution was to transfer the agreed-upon sum every month into the woman's personal account. However, the transfers stopped and the institution never gave her any information. The woman sued the institution but not the ex-husband. The woman resisted suggestions that she sue the ex-husband, and much of the mediation was oriented towards ascertaining her interest in suing the institution over the "deadbeat dad". Subsequently, she revealed that she did not want her ex-husband angered as his link with the daughter was very tenuous and she did not want to jeopardize it. This, of course, was a very legitimate interest that had necessitated shutting down the mediation.

Non-Lawyer Mediators

The question often arises as to whether non-lawyer mediators should mediate in litigious cases. The quick answer is: of course — if they are good mediators.[6] The more deliberated answer is that non-lawyers may have a bit more difficulty establishing credibility with counsel in a litigious dispute, and unless they are well-versed in the mores of litigation and the law, they may have a problem assisting with a proper risk assessment. However, this can be overcome with training and experience, and there are certainly lots of specialized and adept non-lawyer mediators who routinely mediate litigious disputes with excellence. In the long run, mediators depend upon the parties' mutual acceptance, and soon develop reputations within the litigation community.

In this chapter, the important attributes of a good mediator have been canvassed. In the following chapter, mediator styles and techniques are discussed.

---

[6] On whether mediators should be lawyers, and what their duties as lawyers would be if they are, see J. Monte, "Public Values and Private Justice: A Case for Mediator Accountability" (1991) 4 Geo. J.L. Ethics 503, and G. MacKenzie, *Lawyers and Ethics*, 2nd ed. (Toronto: Carswell, 1999).

Chapter 11

MEDIATOR STYLES AND TECHNIQUES

[U.S. President Carter, Egyptian President Sadat and Israeli Prime Minister Begin talked history before signing the Camp David Peace Accords in 1979. Begin said that] the last time a treaty between the people of Israel and of Egypt had been signed was 3,000 years ago. King Solomon had made a deal with a Pharaoh. "I'll bet no one remembers the mediator," said Jimmy Carter.[1]

We have looked at some of the things that a mediator can do to help you to negotiate better, and what you should look for in a mediator. At this stage, it is appropriate to address the different styles of mediators and the kinds of techniques that mediators use in an effort to help the parties settle.

Some of what a mediator does is directed at setting the stage. Such things as providing a comfortable place for the meetings, ensuring an exchange of information between both sides beforehand and getting the people with authority to the table are important.

Other aspects of the mediator's job include chairing the meeting, making sure that all the normal steps in the negotiation process are followed, facilitating communication, creating a positive emotional climate that will defuse tension, making the parties feel that there is good reason to hope that the mediation will work and building confidence in the process and in the parties' self-perception of how they are handling the negotiation. This part of a mediator's job is strongly influenced by his or her own personality and experience. After a while, a good mediator can listen to what someone is saying and at the same time analyze it to see whether it is a power communication, a rights assertion, a comment about interests, an emotional release, *etc.* The mediator can recognize developing settlement DNA and work to encourage it to grow.

Finally, mediators employ a wide range of communication techniques. They apply their skills, training and experience, as well as their sensitivity to where the process is going at any one moment to communication techniques such as reframing, paraphrasing, summarizing, analyzing, suggesting, encouraging interactive listening through prompting, clarifying, acknowledging emotion and using various methods of questioning. Mediators will also decide when to intervene, when to caucus, what sort of caucus to suggest, when to brainstorm, how and when to float proposals, when to call time-outs, *etc.*[2]

---

[1]   Sidey, H., *Hugh Sidey's Portraits of the Presidents: Power and Personality in the Oval Office* (New York: Time Books, 2000) at 135.

[2]   These are all outlined later under "Mediation Stages" in Chapter 13. See generally, S. Silby and S. Merry, "Mediator Settlement Strategies" (1986) 8 Law and Society Policy Review 7.

How and when, and to what degree these processes are used will depend in part upon the style of a mediator. An evaluative mediator will use certain techniques more than a facilitative one, and *vice versa*. Some of the techniques mentioned above work better at one stage of a mediation than at another. Essential to the success of the process, overall, is the mediator's understanding of what the parties' negotiating history in the dispute has been.

In Chapter 7, the normal stages of a negotiation were set out, and how power, rights and interests are significant at different stages was described.[3] Your mediator must know where he or she is coming into your dispute — what offers have been made?[4] Have any doors been closed? Have enough pent-up emotions been released? It may be that litigation has been going on for some time. In that case, it may be that only formal offers pursuant to the Rules of Court have been made, and little contact may have occurred between the parties to the dispute. Here is where counsel familiar with the litigation is essential.

MEDIATOR'S RELATIONSHIP TO PARTIES — FOUR TYPES

Mediators tend to fall into four main groups differentiated by the mediator's relationship to the parties.[5] The first class is made up of mediators who are part of the same community — be it family, social grouping, coworkers — as the disputants. Because their involvement with the parties pre-dates the particular dispute, and will continue after it is resolved, they can use a reserve of trust and respect as well as a knowledge of the norms of the small community to help them.[6]

The second group is made up of mediators who have some existing authority over the parties. An example is that of an internal dispute between two department heads within an institution, such as a corporation, a government department or an academic facility. A CEO, a deputy minister or dean may act as a mediator in the dispute between subordinates. Although he or she may or may not have a particular interest in exactly how the dispute is resolved, such a mediator does have a direct interest in ending the dispute. Beyond that, depending upon the style of the mediator and his or her role in the organization, he or she may have an interest in the particulars of the agreement between the disputants, as well.

The third group is made up of vested-interest mediators who have an agenda and push it hard. Because the mediator here is not completely impartial, he or

---

[3]   See Chapter 7, "The Negotiation Process".

[4]   The author once made the error of failing to ask at the start what offers had already been made. The defendant, through the mediator, conveyed an offer which the plaintiff had rejected earlier. As soon as the plaintiff heard the offer, he interpreted it as a bad faith gesture and nearly walked out.

[5]   C.W. Moore, *The Mediation Process: Practical Strategies for Resolving Conflict*, 2nd ed. (San Francisco: Jossey-Bass Publishers, 1996) at 44-52.

[6]   A respected elder in a culturally-defined group is another example. See L. Nader, "Idealization and Power: Legality and Tradition in Native American Law" (1998) 2 Okla. City U.L. Rev. 13.

she is more akin to a third-party advocate. The example used by Moore[7] is the high-level international intermediary who tries to bring about a peaceful solution to an international conflict, such as President Clinton and his efforts to mediate between Israel and the Palestinians.

The final group, the one in which most professional mediators in litigation fit, and the focus of this book, is the independent mediator. This type of mediator is mostly used in communities that have a traditional independent judiciary, and that have a tendency to rely upon specialist professionals, such as Canada. Of course, in a multi-cultural society such as Canada, there will be many examples of communities that prefer other styles of mediation, particularly those of the first class mentioned above.

POSITIONAL BARGAINING VERSUS PRINCIPLED (INTEREST-BASED) NEGOTIATION

Whether a mediator favours a positional or principled approach to negotiation will also be important to the style of the negotiation and its likely outcome.

A mediator who favours positional negotiating will focus on the dispute as framed by the parties, and distributive bargaining will occur. A mediator who favours principled negotiating will help the parties to broaden their focus and to canvas interests rather than rights. The parties' strict legal positions will be of less importance than if the mediator favours positional negotiating.

A mediator who prefers positional negotiating will know the case well and will essentially do a risk assessment for the parties, directly assessing their cases and telling them whether they have a chance of succeeding. A mediator may push them to settle within a range and may propose rights-based compromises.

A mediator who prefers principled negotiating will focus more on the interests of the parties, but will still take an active role in pushing them in a particular direction. He or she may ask for more information or for the involvement of outside experts in this process.

FACILITATIVE VERSUS EVALUATIVE

Whether the mediator stresses a facilitative role or an evaluative one is another factor that has a major impact on the mediation. A facilitative mediator trusts that the parties know what they want better than the mediator does. The role of the facilitative mediator is to help the parties communicate with each other while keeping his or her opinions about the merits of the dispute to himself or herself. Strategies used are breaking up deadlocks, and keeping the parties talking and proceeding through the normal negotiation stages while helping them assess the pros and cons of offers in a completely impartial way.

---

[7] C.W. Moore, *The Mediation Process: Practical Strategies for Resolving Conflict*, 2nd. ed. (San Francisco: Jossey-Bass Publishers, 1996).

An evaluative mediator acts upon the premise that the parties want some direction as to how to resolve their dispute, and that he or she can provide this because of his or her education, training and distance from the dispute. The more evaluative the mediator is, the more he or she should be knowledgeable about the substance of the dispute.

The difficulty with a mediator in an evaluative role is that it seems to model a judicial role without the accountability of a publicly appointed judge.[8]

Another problem is that it is difficult for an evaluative mediator to keep the confidence of both sides to the dispute. Suggestions of lack of neutrality or of partiality in terms of the merits may cause one side to lose confidence in the process and to withdraw. Whatever the role preferred by the mediator, he or she will have some expectations about achieving settlement for various reasons, including professional reputation and personal satisfaction, and it is important that the parties not perceive this as partiality.

In most litigation contexts, external pressures such as court-imposed, case management deadlines will add to the pressure to resolve the dispute and to focus the mediation on achieving settlement. To the extent that this occurs, the ability of the process to go beyond satisfying needs and resolving a situation is limited. The "transformative" role of mediation, in which it is seen as having the capacity to transform the participants into strong and caring individuals instead of weak and selfish ones, is lost.[9]

A principled mix of facilitive and evaluative modes to be used in conjunction with each other in varying degrees where needed is probably the most effective. Mediators must often play a number of roles but cannot lose sight of the ultimate goal — settlement. The degree of intervention in the dispute has been described as a continuum: "from virtual passivity, to 'chairman', to 'enunciator', to 'prompter', to 'leader' to virtual arbitrator".[10] A mediator is the CEO of the process by which the parties are going to negotiate. Some CEOs are more laid back, and others are more assertive. However, in all cases, the mediator governs by a kind of Jeffersonian democracy.[11] It is the parties who own the dispute, the mediation, therefore, is *their* process — they own it. Accordingly, their ideas about resolution usually reign supreme, and their individual dynamics usually govern how the mediator steers the mediation and what styles of dispute resolution come to prevail at the mediation.

Having said that, however, it is not every idea or approach emanating from a party that is allowed to run its course and direct the mediation. The parties rule as long as they are directed productively towards resolution. The mediator is present to keep in check and eliminate, if possible, any displays of bad faith,

---

[8]   This perspective is further explored in the article by Gary Caplan in Appendix II. Also, see K. Kovach and L. Love, "Evaluative Mediation is an Oxymoron" (1966) 14 Alternatives to High Cost Litigation 31 (cited in J. Macfarlane, ed., Dispute Resolution (Toronto: Emond-Montgomery, 1999) at 280); and J. Alfini, "Evaluation Versus Facilitative Mediation: A Discussion" (1997) 24 Fla. S.U.L. Rev. 919.

[9]   Again, see Appendix II for a discussion of this role, and see C. Menkel-Meadow, "The Many Ways of Mediation" (1995) 11 Negotiation Journal 217.

[10] R. Pepper, "Mandatory Mediation: Court Annexed ADR" (1998) 20 Advocates' Q. 403 at 436.

[11] This refers to former U.S. President Thomas Jefferson's preference for participatory democracy.

regressive bargaining, reiterating of previously rejected offers, trading of insults and failures to communicate. Some mediators even make it a ground rule not to convey an offer they know will be interpreted by the other side as insulting and that will likely cause the mediation to collapse. If the parties own the dispute, they are at liberty to insult one another, but the utility and the credibility of the mediator is misused if merely put to that purpose.

BOUNDARIES OF MEDIATOR'S ROLE

A mediator must be seen to remain impartial with respect to the ultimate outcome, and neutral with respect to the parties.[12] It is not for the mediator to judge the worth of a particular settlement or to make value judgements about who in the dispute is right, and who is wrong. A mediator must refrain from giving legal advice or, for that matter, any kind of professional advice. This is not to say that a mediator cannot highlight aspects of a specific outcome, point out the risks associated with a particular alternative or make suggestions about given settlement options or how to refine those options. However, in the final analysis, the mediator is not a therapist, an accountant, a banker or a lawyer to the parties. The parties must be cautioned to seek their own professional advisors to deal with their questions and problems.

The often asked question is: what power do mediators have? The short answer is that mediators have no *real* power. There is nothing a mediator can do (even under mandatory mediation programs) to compel the parties to settle, to make a given offer or, in fact, to do or say anything. However, that is not to say that mediators are entirely without influence. Mediators often have a sizeable ability to affect the outcome of a mediation and to influence the behaviour of the parties. However the mediator's influence is entirely ephemeral. It is dependent on the credibility bestowed by the parties and on the manner in which the mediator conducts himself or herself.

Perhaps the largest influence a mediator has is through the ability to persuade people to act reasonably and in their own interests. A dispute has the best chance to settle and capitalize on its inherent settlement DNA if the parties are steered towards acting in their own well-assessed interests, juxtaposed with their existing or potential alternatives to an agreement. Mediators accomplish this by persuasion, risk assessment and congeniality. In many cases, the dispute has failed to settle on its own and is at mediation because there is a dysfunctional element to it. This interpersonal dysfunctionality between the parties or counsel and could be caused by myopic thinking or just plain poor communication. Whatever the reason, the mediator, because he or she is a trusted neutral, may have the opportunity to encourage the parties to abandon the dysfunctional behaviour

---

[12] Impartiality refers to the stand taken with respect to the substance of the dispute. A person who is impartial has no personal stake in the outcome, and has no wish to have it resolved in any particular way, on the merits. Neutrality, on the other hand, refers to the relationship between the mediator and the parties. A neutral does not favour one party over the other, and does not receive a benefit other than his or her fee.

or tactics and to adopt a more functional approach. This can be done by actively making suggestions for reasonable offers to settle and for reasonable counteroffers, suggesting principled basis for offers made, encouraging helpful communication and giving latitudes to the parties so that the other side does not constantly assume the worst motives or conduct.

ANALOGY BETWEEN A MEDIATOR AND A SCULPTOR

It might be helpful when analyzing the role of a mediator to draw an analogy between it and a sculptor. What do they have in common? This is a strange question, but interestingly enough, there is much that they share. One of history's best sculptors, Michelangelo, said that all of his sculptures were naturally embedded in the rock from which he sculpted. All he had to do was chip away the excess, laying bare the magnificent work of art which was always present in the rock.

In many ways, the role of the mediator is similar — all the mediator has to do is chisel away the barriers, emotional and technical, thereby exposing the settlement which has been lying latently, in the form of settlement DNA.

It is remarkable to see the number of times a settlement is achieved because of the last minute, 11th-hour change of position of a "dug in" party, which, for some seemingly miraculous reason, has a change of heart or mind during the negotiation and mediation process. The author sometimes leaves such a mediation with a satisfied sense of accomplishment, but then sits back and reflects on the humbling thought that he really had very little to do with it. The potential for a settlement was always there, and it was the parties who effectively made it happen, because in the final analysis, they wanted it to happen, and it was in their interests that it happen. In other words, the dispute had the requisite settlement DNA.

The parties are in the driver's seat. If they want a settlement to happen, then it will likely occur. This is not to say that the mediator has an insignificant role to play. The settlement may require prodding, subtlety, creativity, patience and persistence on the part of the mediator. But the skeleton, the framework of the deal, is always there; it simply remains to be discovered. That is where mediation can prove very valuable to the parties and achieve for them what would likely not have otherwise been achieved, or at least not early enough in the process to prevent substantial litigation cost.

Even Michelangelo's sculptures would remain hunks of rock were it not for his efforts. Thus, many a dispute would remain disputatious but for the interjection of the neutral. However, the essence, the makings, the soul of the final result must certainly lie with the parties, their personalities, the nature of their dispute, the constraints on their decision-making and all of the other circumstances which combine to create the context of the dispute. Just as the DNA of a fish will never materialize into a cow, the settlement DNA will in the end govern the range of potential outcomes.

Classic doctrine about mediation stresses the impartiality of the mediator and his or her role in simply leading the parties to where they ought to go anyway.

The mediator just lends a helping hand. Some of the literature available takes issue with this approach and cites evidence that the mediator actually does affect the nature and frequency of settlement. Some of the literature also advocates that the mediator take a more proactive role in helping the parties fashion a settlement. As has been stressed, much of the mediator's approach depends on the personality of the mediator, the context of the mediation and the wishes of the parties about how they want the session to proceed. Experienced mediators will recount how with some mediations they simply play the role of moderator to a constructive discussion amongst the parties. With others, the mediator is actively being creative in helping the parties understand their true interests and in brainstorming for mutually acceptable options. The mediator actively works with the parties to assess the risks of various outcomes and assists in canvassing and evaluating alternatives. In short, the job of the mediator is to extol the virtues of a reasonable settlement to all the parties.

In this sense, many cases which do not have the opportunity to mediate can appear to the mediator all the more unfortunate. The settlement DNA remains obscured (like the figure in Michelangelo's marble), by the adversarial system and by retrenchment into formalized positions from which there is, in the absence of mediation or direct negotiation, no easy way to be extricated.

Finally, a comparison with Michelangelo begs the question as to whether mediation is an art. The response is that it is certainly the art of the possible, and that in itself makes it worthwhile for the parties to undertake.

Now that the different approaches and styles of mediators have been canvassed, the next chapter will touch on some of the basics of what to expect at a mediation.

Chapter 12

WHAT TO EXPECT IN A MEDIATION

It could be said that a mediation is like a box of chocolates — you never know what you are going to get. No two mediations are alike, and the outcome is never completely predictable.[1] This is because mediations are a mixture of emotions, intellectual perspectives, vagaries of representation and legal process, and the interplay of a variety of mediation styles. Many disputes which have arrived at a mediation with no hope of settling have, in fact, settled, and the reasons for the settlement may never have been predicted beforehand.

However, there are a number of aspects that are reasonably certain to be encountered.

AGREEMENT TO MEDIATE

Usually, prior to commencing the mediation, the parties will be asked to sign a Mediation Agreement or Agreement to Mediate.[2] Some codes of professional conduct[3] assist in detailing the terms of this agreement. Mediation agreements deal with topics such as fees, submission of materials, confidentiality, the location of the mediation, liability and mediator neutrality. Mediation agreements may also commit the parties to bring people to the mediation with full authority to settle — a crucial requirement for the success of the session. There are no right or wrong agreements to mediate. They reflect the style of the mediator and sometimes the dynamics of the dispute. However, they should probably not attempt to provide a complete overview of what mediation is, or contemplate every contingency that may arise in the mediation. Agreements to mediate should be brief so that people will read them. There should be no fine print, and everything should be worded in such a manner that any literate person will be able to comprehend the contents.

Confidentiality Provision

Confidentiality is a particularly important issue to address. A full investigation of interests involves giving reasons why you are taking positions, including

---

[1] Nevertheless, the three foundation stones of mediation — impartiality/neutrality, confidentiality and involvement of the parties — are critical for any mediation to be successful.

[2] A sample Agreement to Mediate can be found in Appendix IV.

[3] See the C.B.A. Ontario Mediators' Code of Conduct at Appendix V, which is now officially the governing Code for the Ontario Mandatory Mediation Program.

personal ones. These should be protected by confidentiality, or the process will not work.[4] A provision relating to confidentiality of the communications passed at the mediation, that are not otherwise discoverable is usually included in the mediation agreement. Disclosure during a mediation of a communication or a piece of information will not confer confidential status that would not otherwise exist. Parties must, therefore, not assume that information disclosed at a mediation or in the materials submitted to the mediator and parties will attain a confidentiality it does not at law enjoy.

Note that discoverable communications are specifically omitted from the confidentiality provision because it would make no sense to cloak a communication that should otherwise be disclosed in litigation with confidentiality merely because it happened to be communicated at a mediation. If the information sought could form the answer to a proper and relevant question in the proceeding — in other words if it can be discovered upon — then the information or communication is not confidential.

Termination Provision

Agreements to mediate generally do not provide details regarding the parties' power to terminate the session. Parties have the power to withdraw and end the session whenever they want to. There is no operative compulsion that can require them to stay, even in court-annexed mandatory mediations. However, it serves no purpose to remind parties of their easy-exit ability. Whenever possible, it is preferable to allow the mediator to draw the conclusion that the session should end after milking the settlement DNA for all that it is worth.

Venue

Should a neutral location be used? Where a mediation should be held is sometimes as important to the parties as whether to hold one at all. Generally, a neutral location is most conducive to a productive mediation environment. Sessions held in one of the lawyer's offices can be problematic when one party perceives there to be a "home ice advantage" for the party in whose lawyer's office the session is being held. This may arise from that counsel's ability — because the session is happening in his or her office — to get quick legal research done, to bring in extra people for assistance or to be able to produce documents or legal accounts on the spot — all of which the other counsel is less able to do.

It can also work against the lawyer in whose office the session is held if there are interruptions to take calls on another matter, other clients show up unannounced or other counsel or staff within the same firm need a moment. This can contribute to a sense of frustration on the part of the client who is expecting undivided attention during the mediation, and may harm the solicitor-client relationship and adversely affect the mediation. Additionally, there is inevitably a

---

[4]   Parties need confidence that what they say or do in a mediation, other than what is discoverable in litigation, stays with them and the mediator. See L. Freedman and M. Prigoff, "Confidentiality in Mediation: The Need for Protection" (1986) 2 Ohio State J. Dis. Res. 37.

degree of down time in any mediation while the mediator is spending private time with the other side. During these intervals, there is a tremendous temptation for the busy lawyer in whose office the mediation is being held to do other pressing work. This can alienate the client as well. In a neutral setting, the temptation is removed.

There can also be a problem if the location does not provide enough space for the parties to effectively caucus privately, or if there is nowhere for the mediator to go when the parties wish to have a discussion in his or her absence.

None of this is to say that parties should never agree on a location associated with one of them. There may be good reason to hold the session in a particular lawyer's office (*e.g.*, both parties have had a productive meeting there before, the city in question is more convenient or the parties are very cost-sensitive). There may be reasons to hold the session at one of the parties' premises, perhaps to view a manufacturing process or to view the scene of a tort. What is essential is the parties' agreement — if it is absent, or if there is any equivocation on a venue, it is best to use a neutral location.

Authority to Settle and Mediation Ghosts

If you cannot attend a mediation session with full authority to settle, it is probably better not to have the session at all. Without full authority, the mediation will be an exercise without the right people, substantially diminishing the chances for an agreement. Full authority has been defined to mean "those persons with full knowledge of the events in issue and full authority to consider and decide upon, at the mediation, a full range of monetary and non-monetary options for settlement."[5] Arriving with a low-capped authority is often not sufficient, because it will not permit the flexibility needed to grapple with the dynamics and offers arising out of the mediation. Sometimes, when those in attendance are, in fact, subject to the will of someone not in attendance, that person who is not present is referred to as a mediation "ghost".[6] That person may not be there physically, but his or her presence is felt, and he or she rears himself or herself up, like an apparition, when it comes time to decide after much offer and counteroffering, whether a session's work will settle the dispute.

Mediation ghosts are seldom helpful because it is so easy to nix a deal, particularly on the end of a phone, without having been present to appreciate just how difficult it was to obtain. The mediation ghost does not have the benefit of having listened to the other side or to the mediator and, therefore, cannot empathize or moderate his or her position in the face of other arguments. Mediation ghosts cannot appreciate the dynamics of the offers and counteroffers that have been made, and may take for granted the attainment of any particular settlement without having a sense of how much work has been done to bring the numbers or ideas to their current level. Because they are not present, they are unable to do an alternative canvassing in the context of the ongoing negotiation, and they miss out on the subtle pressures of the mediator to champion the cause of

---

[5]   This definition was devised by the author at the Toronto ADR Centre.
[6]   This term was coined by Deborah Sword at the ADR Centre in Toronto.

settlement. Any momentum thus gained is lost on them. They are also unable to speak directly with their counsel or the mediator, and, accordingly, opportunities for persuasion are lost.

It is sometimes the case where a relatively junior lawyer will be unable to bring a relatively important client to a mediation because of his or her refusal, especially if the solicitor-client relationship is a delicate one. The lawyer can dodge this co-nundrum in a court-annexed mandatory mediation by referring the client to the Rule requiring attendance. In a private mediation, the client can be referred to the mediator's Agreement to Mediate, which requires the client's attendance. There-fore, it is not the lawyer's "fault" that the party must personally attend.

On rare occasions, attending without full authority can be justified. If a party with the authority is out of town, or if the party's presence would only inflame the discussion, the party may be advised not to attend. Also, if the party attend-ing has an unrealistic view that cannot be altered, it can help to appeal to a per-son with more authority (if that person can be reached during the mediation) who can give a more objective viewpoint.

The optimum situation, however, is to have an objective reasonable person attend with the full authority inherent in his or her position within the organiza-tion or by virtue of an express delegation. Corporations can pass resolutions authorizing a particular director or officer to make a full decision at a mediation.

PRE-MEDIATION CHECKLIST

The following is a useful checklist of things to do before conducting a mediation and to consider documenting in the Agreement to Mediate:

1. Select a neutral venue/place to hold the mediation (with ample rooms for parties to caucus privately).
2. Come to an arrangement on mediation fees with the other parties — avoid surprise.
3. Sign a confidentiality agreement (may be part of Agreement to Mediate).
4. Decide who will attend (it should be those with knowledge of the events in issue and with full authority to settle, *i.e.*, with complete discretion to decide upon a variety of monetary and non-monetary options at the mediation).
5. Cloak your client with authority (*e.g.*, have his/her board pass a resolu-tion granting authority, obtain dispensation from superiors and arrange to be able to call homebase if something unpredicted arises).
6. Have all the relevant material served on the other side, given to the mediator and brought to the mediation. *Do not arrive without it!*

In this chapter, the preliminary and logistical issues that arise before or at a mediation have been described. By knowing what to expect, you can be pre-pared — by clarifying and documenting the logistics of the mediation before-hand, in the Agreement to Mediate. In the next chapter, the structure of a mediation will be examined, and many issues regarding the mediation process will be discussed.

Chapter 13

MEDIATION STRUCTURE

While no two mediations are exactly alike, there is often a structure to a mediation, such that counsel have been seen to look at their watch and say that they were right on schedule for getting the kind of offer just received!

Matthew Certosimo, in an article for the *Law Times*,[1] has likened the sequence of fairly predictable events in a mediation to the Acts in a Shakespearean play. Act I entails introductions of the participants and the opening statements of the parties; Act II further delves into the complications which may impede a settlement; Act III is the crisis, where the parties get bogged down on specific issues which stand in the way of settlement (this usually occurs within a separate caucus); Act IV is the climax, where the parties focus on their real interests and make some important concessions to maximize their alternatives (this is the point where the parties rise to the occasion, throw away much of the baggage with which they entered the mediation, and often achieve a breakthrough); and Act V is the final Act where the breakthrough having been achieved, the parties tie up any loose ends and draft the agreement.

Regardless of the precise form which the mediation takes, the process does have a certain flow of its own which must be respected.[2] On numerous occasions at the conclusion of a mediation session, the author has wondered, "why couldn't the parties have just seen the logic of that settlement at the beginning?" "Why did we have to go through all that pulling of teeth?" The answer is that people find it hard to instantly come up with optimum solutions. There is a value to working it through. The process of arriving at the solution is in part why the solution emerges. Einstein's statement that "we cannot solve our problems with the same level of thinking we used when we created them"[3] is absolutely correct — except that it takes people awhile to achieve the new level of thinking.

For example, parties would never accept their lawyers or the mediator simply saying, "now settle for X because X makes the most sense". There is a palpable need to have struggled to get there and to really know that X was the best agreement obtainable. In this way, people feel that they have "stretched" the other side and have obtained the best deal for themselves. It is extremely rare for the parties to be able to skip this process in an interest-based mediation (as opposed to a completely rights-based process where an evaluator gives an opinion, and the parties are expected to fall in line). It happens only with the simplest of

---

[1] M. Certosimo, "All the World's a Stage" *Law Times* (22-28 February 1999) 8.

[2] See Chapter 15, written by Jim Davidson, for a discussion of the mediation "dance" — the inevitable offer and counteroffer process.

[3] Albert Einstein, *Out of My Later Years* (New York: Wings Books, 1956).

cases, where the issues have already been agreed upon, or where a party is insolvent. It may be that negotiations which have already taken place before the mediation started will have to be re-visited so that the mediator can get a feel for the stage at which the process lies.

MEDIATION STAGES

Again, while no two mediations are alike, and each one varies due to the style of the mediator and the nature of the dispute and parties, there are some broad stages through which most mediations flow. Understanding these stages assists in knowing what to expect at various points in the mediation. Different authors describe a mediation as involving four, five, seven, or twelve stages. The number, however, does not matter. What matters is that all mediations involve preliminaries, openings and presentations, identifying areas of discord and of agreement, gathering and exchanging information, searching for options and negotiating through to decision and closure. For the purpose of clarity, the "stages" as discussed in detail later in this chapter, are described briefly below:

1. Introduction of the process

At this stage, the mediator introduces the process to the parties. This involves the following:

- setting the tone
- gaining the trust of the parties
- describing the nature and structure of the process (for example, when there will be joint and separate sessions)
- laying the ground rules and clarifying issues such as confidentiality
- describing the role of the mediator, including the limits to the mediator's authority and powers
- explaining that mediation is to be interest-based

2. Initial joint session

At this stage, the parties meet for the first time in the presence of the mediator. The mediator facilitates the following interactions between the parties:

- gathering and exchanging information
- getting their positions off their chest
- communicating directly with one another and venting any emotions/feelings
- enabling the parties to assess the strengths and weaknesses of their own arguments, as well as those of the other side and to hear them juxtaposed

- enabling the parties to assess each other's credibility and talent as a witness

3. Initial separate session/caucus

At this stage, the parties first meet with the mediator separately. The mediator's objectives at this stage are the following:

- finding out more information, some of which could be confidential
- canvassing the real interests of the parties
- doing a thorough risk assessment/reality check
- canvassing alternatives — BATNA and WATNA — and comparing with the real interests identified
- determining the high water mark of the dispute
- showing empathy and allowing further venting

4. Subsequent separate sessions

At subsequent meetings between the mediator and each of the parties separately, the mediator focuses on solutions. This involves the following:

- assisting with generating creative options and principled offers
- communicating offers and counteroffers, and explaining their principled basis
- floating proposals in order to avoid reactive devaluation
- moving parties towards agreement, using single-text method[4]
- narrowing options, refining agreement and tinkering with it

5. Subsequent joint sessions

At subsequent joint sessions, the mediator's role is to assist the parties to communicate their refined positions or confirm an agreement. Specifically, the mediator may do any of the following:

---

[4] R. Fisher, W. Ury, and B. Patton, *Getting to Yes: Negotiating Agreement Without Giving In*, 2nd ed. (New York: Penguin Books, 1991) at 12 discuss procedures used by third-party neutrals such as mediators. Where parties are locked into positional bargaining, a mediator can move them to principled bargaining by:
- asking each side to identify their interests, and telling them he or she is exploring alternatives;
- preparing a separate list for each side of their interests, and having them suggest how it could be improved; or
- combining the lists and coming up with rough proposals, that accommodate as many interests from each list as possible.

This process may require several rounds of rough proposals, but may result in a settlement in which both sides have had an active part.

- allowing the parties to communicate subtle and important and/or complicated messages in person
- summarizing progress, or lack thereof, and calling the parties to action or suggesting ending the mediation
- clarifying and confirming any agreement and reducing it to writing
- acknowledging the parties and the outcome

The Mediator's Introduction

The introduction, though brief, is crucial to establishing the kind of mediation process which will ensue, and setting the tone and the ground rules for participation in that process. Introductions should not go on too long, or try to anticipate everything that can go wrong and attempt to address fixing it. What an introduction should do is give the mediator the latitude to conduct the mediation in accordance with the style of that mediator.[5] While this may seem unnecessary to many who have previously mediated, it has the benefit of consistency and of saying the right things to the uninitiated.[6]

Joint Session/Caucus

The joint caucus or session is the time when the mediator gives his or her introduction, and the parties exchange their submissions, which is usually a trading of best case positions. However, joint sessions can be useful for other reasons. They can be used to exchange relevant information that may inform a party of the relative strength or weakness of its (or the other side's) position. They provide the opportunity to meet the other party (and his or her counsel) and to assess his or her credibility and skill as a witness. Many a mediation has come to a settlement because a party was impressive, or unimpressive, in joint session.[7]

Trading Positions

It is ironic that interest-based negotiation and mediation often work best when the parties start in joint session by exchanging their positions with one another! Why is this so? It would seem to fly in the face of the earlier discussion on the utility of interest-based bargaining and the precept of the "Mutual Gains" ap-

---

[5]   The author, after spending time refining his style, now gives the same short introduction each time he mediates.

[6]   The author was once told by a counsel that he (the counsel) appreciated the repetition of the introduction because he could tell his client what to expect the mediator to say; when the mediator did, indeed, repeat it, the lawyer looked like a hero to his client!

[7]   In one case, an employer treated the case as a standard wrongful dismissal scenario, where the damages might approximate one month's pay per year of service; in that case, 12 years' or 12 months' termination pay. However, the plaintiff had alleged a pattern of sexual harassment and produced incriminating letters from the perpetrator, who had been one of her managers. The plaintiff was so convincing and sympathetic as a witness that the employer offered, for that reason and probably for others, to settle on the basis of a very high figure for Ontario — 27 months!

proach to get around the positions taken in the dispute and to come to a realization of the parties' true interests.[8]

In a litigious dispute, counsel are retained for a reason, and part of that reason is to draft pleadings and take positions. It generally helps to let the lawyers "do their thing" at the outset. Lawyers are useful, and they must appear to their clients to be useful; if this goal is met, there is a much higher likelihood of the lawyer "buying in" and a higher liklihood on the part of the client that he or she will listen to the lawyer when the lawyer recommends a given agreement. People are more likely to listen to their advocates when they have built up a level of trust and friendship with them.

Just as importantly, trading positions provides a baseline for where the parties are at in the dispute and is, therefore, instructional for the parties and the mediator. Generally, the positions represent the "Nirvana point", or best case of a party, and accordingly are platforms from which to commence negotiating. Reciting the positions also helps to articulate a party's case and to make their argument to the other parties, which is crucial for all the parties in undertaking a proper risk assessment of their own as well as the other side's case. Hearing the argument stated and refuted (if it can be effectively refuted) is informative. A proper risk assessment is in turn necessary to do the crucial alternative canvassing needed in an interest-based negotiation.[9] Thus, it runs full circle.

Exchanging Apologies

The joint caucus is also used as a venue for the parties to exchange apologies, feelings of regret or camaraderie, all of which can be vital to decreasing tensions and improving the climate for settlement. It is usually better for the parties to convey such "warm and fuzzy" feelings directly, as it has more effect. However, if a party is unable to deliver the message skilfully, notwithstanding that the sentiments may be felt, the mediator may deliver it in separate caucus.

Conveying Offers

Some mediators require the parties to resume joint sessions (after they have had a period of private caucus with the mediator) when conveying all offers that are made. This minimizes the risks of the mediator appearing to be partial. It also avoids the possibility of a mediator error in communicating the substance of the offer. By eliminating the "middleman" status of the mediator, nothing gets lost in the transmission of the offer.

Conveying offers in joint caucus tends to keep the parties "honest". Parties will be less likely to make hardball or unproductive offers face to face with the other party sitting across the table. Further, if there are any questions or comments about the offer, these can be answered directly. Finally, the mediator's

---

[8] Recall the opening stages of a negotiation as discussed in Chapter 7. This is the same process except that a mediator is there to help.

[9] The Toronto ADR Centre evaluation observed that counsel found the mediation process more satisfying when there had been a discussion of the merits and it was felt that the various arguments had been addressed.

credibility is preserved when he or she is not heard conveying offers which may have no chance of success in concluding an agreement.

Other mediators prefer to convey most of the offers themselves, without constantly bringing the parties together for that purpose. The advantages of this strategy are multifaceted: First, it prevents a game of musical chairs from developing, where parties are constantly moving up and down from their chairs and rooms, where they may have made themselves quite comfortable. This is a very real factor when dealing with a party who has an injury or disability. Second, it allows the mediator to give people latitude they would not be able to give themselves. For example, it may be that a given offer, if made directly, would be scoffed at by the other side, but when conveyed by the mediator, can be glossed and presented productively. It may be more likely to be received calmly and objectively, rather than as a personal insult. This approach has the advantage of removing much of the invective parties may relay to one another, and it allows the mediator to selectively focus on anything positive to communicate to the other side. This then helps to deal with acrimony or lack of trust, and it gives the mediator additional latitude in helping parties to craft productive offers to one another. This is an important function of mediators, perhaps more so than most parties realize. Part of the mediator's role is to diffuse tension. This is made more difficult if adversarial parties are constantly coming together to irritate one another. On the other hand, where the mediator shuttles back and forth to communicate offers with each side privately, he or she has an opportunity to insulate the parties from each other and focus their attention less on themselves and more on the problem at hand.

Where offers are quite complex or multifaceted, the mediator still has the option of bringing the parties back together for the offer to be conveyed directly. The mediator may do this if there is a risk of getting a detail wrong, or if the mediator does not understand some component of the offer, or anticipates an important question after its communication which he or she will not be able to answer. The parties can also be brought back together if there is an emotional nuance to the offer that the recipient of the offer should hear directly.[10]

There is no right or wrong way to handle joint sessions. Mediators who are a little better at insulating the parties from each other and painting things in a positive light will use joint sessions to convey offers less frequently. Indeed, a combination of both approaches can operate within the same mediation at different times or amongst different parties with different preferences. It depends on the style of the mediator and on the preferences of the parties.

Separate Session/Caucus

Separate caucus is critical for allowing the parties to do a private-interest canvassing, and to assess risks and alternatives themselves as well as with the me-

---

[10] In one case mediated by the author, one of the defendants held fast with a low offer due to his terminal illness, and due to absence of income or disability payments. The plaintiff felt that this defendant's offer was too low; thus, the plaintiff refused to settle. Accordingly, the mediator called both parties together so that the plaintiffs could hear directly the story of the defendant's illness and circumstances. This had the intended "softening" effect, and the case finally settled.

diator, all of which could be very prejudicial if conducted in the presence of the other side. Some mediators treat everything that they hear in private caucus as confidential and, therefore, do not reveal anything so learned or expressed to the other parties, unless explicitly given the go-ahead. Other mediators rely on the parties to flag what they want kept confidential, and unless this is done, what is revealed or expressed in private caucus could be disclosed to the other parties so as to assist with settlement. There is no right or wrong way about this, and, indeed, a combination could be used in the same mediation. It is a question of mediator style and of the dynamics of the dispute.

The separate caucus is the session where most of the real work gets done. This is each party's chance to really test any assumptions which are inherent in both the positions taken in the litigation and in the party's expectations as to what would constitute a reasonable outcome. Either the mediator can talk privately with the party and counsel, or the party and counsel can talk privately without the mediator. The latter is often a good idea, and, indeed, is preferred much of the time as the party, after speaking with the mediator, formulates his or her next offer in the process. For example, party and counsel may be putting on a brave face for the benefit of convincing the mediator of the case's strength or of how little room there may be to move towards resolution. This may have tactical advantages. Accordingly, counsel and party do not want the mediator to hear a discussion about just how much extra room to settle there really is or how poor the litigation prospects really are. It is not that party and counsel are deceiving the mediator, but rather that there are just some things about which, as a matter of strategy, it may be better not to disclose to the mediator. This is entirely appropriate.

Additionally, sometimes, in separate caucus, discussions about the other side are held which are best kept discreet lest they be found insulting or counter-productive by the other side. These could include assessments of credibility, hidden agendas or ulterior motives.

Although separate caucus is an indispensable part of the mediation process, it does raise some dangers. The first, which was referred to earlier, is the perception that the mediator is not impartial. This problem is alleviated in part by holding a separate meeting with the other side so that each is seen to be treated equally. Another danger is that it will be almost impossible for a mediator, while presenting offers in separate meetings, to avoid putting offers he or she thinks are better in a better light. The tendency to evaluate is a strong one.

The mediator may not always remember what information was to be kept confidential from the other side. Additionally, adding another person as a communicator of information increases the risk that the message will be garbled or incomplete. Finally, time spent in separate caucus meetings may detract from the parties' feeling that they are empowered and in control of the process.[11] However, it has also been suggested that the use of this procedure in a multi-party negotiation-mediation may be "almost essential".[12]

---

[11] L. Boulle and K.J. Kelly, *Mediation: Principles, Process, Practice*, Canadian ed. (Toronto: Butterworths, 1998) at 119, have a number of things that a mediator can do to reassure the parties.

[12] *Ibid.* at 116.

When the Mediation Should End

Absent a settlement or agreement among the parties to terminate or adjourn, there are a number of triggers that should suggest to the mediator that the session should end. These triggers operate cumulatively. However, any one of them, if significant enough, could justify terminating the process.

The first trigger is a situation in which only the mediator is making an effort; that is, the mediator is the only one suggesting new offers/counteroffers, is the only one developing any principled ideas for settlement and is generally the one person actively engaged. The second trigger is the parties simply reiterating previously rejected offers, or worse, going backward from the offers they have made. Neither of these approaches will generate any progress. The third trigger is a situation in which a party essentially "caves" and is unable to make any kind of settlement decision, through emotional collapse or by exceeding the party's capped authority to settle. The last trigger indicating the mediation should end is a scenario where the interests of one or both parties are better served by not settling. Because a settlement freely arrived at is by definition in the interests of the parties, the mediator should never push a deal that is not in the parties' interests. If it becomes clear that the parties' alternatives to an agreement are better than any agreement which may be achieved at the mediation, then it is certainly time to stop. The mediation will then have served its purpose.

If a Settlement Is Reached

Finally, if agreement is reached, it is usually a good idea to reduce it to writing (even if formal minutes of settlement are not entered into at the conclusion of the session) so as to remove any ambiguity or doubt about the terms of the agreement. One of the advantages of mediation is the reaching of durable agreements. This benefit is lost if, later, the parties cannot remember what the agreement was, or they have different versions of it.

The mediator may not play an active role in drafting the agreement; indeed, it is not good practice for the mediator to get deeply involved in drafting. Issues may arise that would compromise the neutrality of the mediator and are better left to an advocate who can recommend the inclusion of provisions in a written settlement which operate to the advantage of, or to protect a given party's interests. Additionally, mediators may not be insured for drafting agreements, as this is more in the nature of giving legal advice and, consequently, should an error occur, coverage for any liability may be in jeopardy.

However, none of this precludes a mediator (especially where parties are not represented) from writing down the terms of the agreement reached so as to encourage certainty on the part of the parties and to diminish the likelihood of a subsequent dispute over the terms of the agreement.[13]

---

[13]   Indeed, this is also in the mediator's self-interest because it can be very messy to involve the mediator in giving opinions or evidence if there is a dispute over what was agreed.

The structural components of a mediation have been identified and explained in this chapter. The next two chapters, by different authors, will expand on some of these concepts and provide additional perspectives.

Chapter 14

MEDIATION ADVOCACY

L. Leslie Dizgun[*]

In many jurisdictions, mediation has been adopted as a mandatory component of the litigation process. Crucial to this growing trend is an appreciation that the mediation rather than a trial may be the forum in which the dispute is finally resolved. Just as effective advocacy is required in trial preparation and in the advocate's performance at trial, so too is advocacy required in preparation for a mediation and at the mediation itself.

KEY ASPECTS OF MEDIATION

There are several key aspects of the mediation that impact significantly on the nature of advocacy in the context of mediation. A mediation is generally encouraged to be more informal than any court process, and the parties and their counsel are encouraged by the mediator to take a more informal relaxed approach to the problem at hand. Thus, informality is a key aspect of the mediation of disputes. Who is in attendance at a mediation is also a key aspect, which differs significantly from the trial of a proceeding. It is generally a requirement at a mediation that the principals attend, and, accordingly, counsel has the opportunity to directly persuade the principal involved or an important representative of the corporate entity involved as to your clients' position, the opportunities for settlement, the rationale for settlement and any important facts or admissions which may not have been communicated as bluntly by the opposing sides' counsel. The other noteworthy person in attendance is the mediator, who has a significant role to play in assisting or facilitating the client's negotiation and, depending on the nature of the mediation, providing some opinion with respect to the substance of the case and the litigation process. These elements make a mediation a unique phenomenon in the litigation process, and one which may be viewed by counsel as an opportunity, not as a hurdle to get past on the way to trial.

Set out below are a number of components of effective advocacy in a mediation.

---

[*] L. Leslie Dizgun is an experienced civil litigation lawyer and mediator who practises with Blustein & Pearlstein LLP in Toronto. He has written and presented on mediation and mediation advocacy topics for the CBAO and the L.S.U.C. and has participated in training sessions for the National Judicial Institute.

Preparation

Preparation is a key element of success at the mediation. Your client's ability to achieve a successful result will be affected by the degree to which you and your client are prepared. Since the mediation may result in a conclusion of the case, the degree of seriousness approximates the degree of preparation needed for trial. Although less time will be required than for trial preparation, you should carefully consider the same analysis even at this early stage.

Arrange a pre-mediation meeting with your client and explain the stages of mediation and how it differs from the litigation process. It is important for your client to have some understanding of what may be expected and the way in which it proceeds.

It is also important to explain that the mediator will listen to all parties and is required to act in a neutral and disinterested fashion in hearing out their intentions and in probing the basis of the parties' positions.

The next step in the pre-mediation is to review with your client the strengths and weakness of your client's case and the strengths and weakness of the opposing parties' cases. Test out positions with your client, as well as the objective in pursuing litigation. After reviewing the strengths and weakness of your client's case, and your client's position in litigation, probe with your client what your client's interests are. Clearly, your client's interests should be directly related to the objective to be achieved, whether through the litigation process or otherwise. It is always important — and no doubt, your client will do so — to raise the matter of the further costs to be expended in pursuing litigation. In Ontario, as in other jurisdictions, consideration should also be given to an explanation of the costs consequences of offers to settle. If there have been any other settlement offers made, then review them with your client and provide a candid assessment of how close these offers are to the objectives set out by your client.

Opening Statement

Unlike a court proceeding, the mediation offers a unique opportunity for your client to speak directly to the opposing party. This is obviously an opportunity which may have drawbacks if you do not prepare your client well in advance and allocate roles to both yourself and your client during the mediation. It is often very effective for the client rather than counsel to make the opening statement. This may encourage the opposing party to come forward and be more forthright, and to possibly engage in creative problem-solving. There is nothing inappropriate with going so far as to rehearse with your client the opening statement, the timing of the conciliatory gesture or other components in the mediation.

The opening statements of parties are quite influential to both the mediator and the opposing party. This may be the first and last time you have an opportunity to directly influence the client on the other side of the case in an atmosphere that is informal and relaxed, and where, accordingly, that client may be more open to influence. A recitation, which repeats the statement of claim or presents like a statement of fact and law, will not likely be successful in influencing the other side. In fact, it may simply encourage the other side to respond similarly, maintaining fixed positions. The opening statement is an opportunity to disarm the other side. Choose the material facts that you wish to emphasize, and present your case more like a story rather than a legal argument. What is the ultimate impression you want to leave on the other side and on the mediator? In order to leave any impression, you must choose an overriding theme. Is the overriding theme the repair and maintenance of the continuing business relationship? Is it fair compensation for a long-term devoted employee? Remember that an opening statement should also provide clues both to the mediator and to the other side as to what is necessary to settle the case, that is, what is necessary from an emotional perspective, from a psychological perspective and in stark monetary terms. The mediator will also recognize that it is important for the client to "vent". This is the clients' opportunity to be heard. It is quite likely that if the client says little during the opening statement, the mediator will ask questions of the client in order to illicit responses, simply to conclude that necessary process.

Another important factor in the conduct of the mediation is the timing of concessions. You may choose to make a concession in the opening statement in order to inspire the other side to make responding concessions. You may choose to maintain a firm position, particularly if you believe that the opposing side has an unreasonable view of their chances of success in the matter. You may also wait for the time when the mediator meets with the parties privately in order to make the first concession. This demonstrates to the other side that the mediator is able to influence the process, and it may encourage a dynamic leading to a successful resolution.

Documents

In Ontario, the mandatory rule provides that the opposing parties are to submit documents which are key to their case. Review all documentation provided by your client and determine which documents you are prepared to disclose in the mediation, and whether there are any documents you are prepared to disclose to the mediator only. Also, in light of the rules with respect to early mediation, it may be very prudent to require that all parties to the mediation provide sworn affidavits of documents and all relevant productions or those requested by counsel.

Demonstrative Evidence

In a complex matter, it may be appropriate to arrange for the presentation of demonstrative evidence, the provision of organizational charts, charts of corporate structure, engineering diagrams, *etc.* Counsel also make use of experts in a number of mediations. Business valuators or forensic accountants for the parties may be of assistance both as advisors in structuring an appropriate settlement or by providing a sufficiently disinterested analysis to assist in resolving the matter. For example, it may be that the mediator may ask the accounting experts to meet with each other and come up with a joint mutual proposal which may be acceptable to the parties. Due to the informality of the mediation, the scope of possible creative ways to resolve a dispute is greater, and the roles of the parties, counsel or experts can be shifted in a way which allows for more constructive and creative participation in the process.

The Caucus

In most mediations, the mediator will caucus with each of the parties privately. You can anticipate that this will occur and can prepare in advance for what you want to communicate to the mediator in the caucus as well as whether you want those communications to be disclosed to the other side. You may also wish to explain to the mediator what the important or key interests of your client are, and assess where you believe the other side is and where they may have an unrealistic view of their position or their interests. If you intend for the mediator to communicate an offer to the other side, then ensure that the mediator fully understands the rationale of that offer. You should take full advantage of the mediator and the skills he or she brings to the mediation. Do not be reluctant to use the mediator to assist in persuading the other side as to its worst alternative to a negotiated settlement. You may also need to have the mediator assist you with your client in explaining the alternatives to the negotiated settlement. Typically, both parties are prepared to accept the neutral third party as impartial, as someone who acts in good faith and is genuinely interested in assisting them to achieve a settlement.

THE MEDIATION MAP

It is important to develop a strategy with your client for the mediation, one which may also incorporate a number of tactical gambits in light of anticipated positions of the opposing party. What are the ranges of possible settlement options? Is the only settlement to be achieved a monetary one, or are there other non-monetary components that are desirable? For example, would your client accept an apology? Is there a structuring of the settlement that your client would prefer, from a tax-planning point of view? Is there an ongoing business relationship to be preserved? Indeed, is there further business to be obtained if the relationship with the opposing party can be repaired? These factors are necessary to canvass in terms of developing a step-by-step approach to the negotiation of the settlement. It is almost certainly better to prepare your client to have a range of settlement possibilities in mind rather than a bottom line. In many cases, actual communication between the parties and the facilitation of the mediator may shift both parties' positions and move parties from the bottom line, and may still achieve a satisfactory settlement. It is also important to appreciate that parties will more likely achieve a settlement where their interests are acknowledged and, if possible, satisfied.

BARRIERS TO SETTLEMENT

Perhaps the most important aspect of the facilitated negotiation process is recognizing the barriers to settlement and developing techniques to overcome these barriers. These may include rigid positions, a perception of significant power imbalance, lack of preparedness on the part of one of the parties, cultural differences, cognitive differences, *etc.*

Suspending Reactions

When faced with a barrier to the settlement, it is important to suspend a reaction because it is very easy for counsel or clients to react. Often, reaction is exactly what the opposing side wants when it raises a barrier to the settlement. The best response in that circumstance is to suspend that natural reaction. Develop the ability to consciously recognize these negative tactics. It may be necessary for the other side to vent, so let them. Do not lose sight of your own client's objectives in the mediation. If your client's objectives are met, in what way does it matter that the other side has "pushed your buttons"?

There are two often useful ways to deal with this negativity. One is to respond with silence. Do not respond immediately. Another is to reframe the position. This is often done by asking open-ended questions and inquiring into the other side's rationale for any position that it has proposed. This will expose the fact that there may be no rationale, and that a principled negotiation may not be possible in these circumstances.

Sometimes, actually attempting to satisfy the other side's interest may be an effective way to respond to a barrier to settlement. This does not mean that you should just sit there while the other side makes threats or is absolutely rigid in its position. Know when it is appropriate to advise the other side that there is no further point in engaging in negotiation when that party is not prepared to move away from its position or elucidate a clear rationale for it. Above all, you are there to advocate on behalf of your client, and if attempts at conciliation are not responded to, do not be afraid to call an end to what may be an unproductive negotiation.

Being creative and developing non-monetary options is often very useful in mediation. However, it may be necessary, in the appropriate case, to discourage a mediator from suggesting creative options to both sides, as to do so would be disadvantageous to your client or would represent an unnecessary and awkward precedent for your client in respect of other negotiations in the future.

Another practical tip is to never let the mediation be used for an inappropriate purpose. The mediation is not an examination or cross-examination of your client, and any inquiries by counsel that are not directly or indirectly related to achieving a settlement should not be answered. Any attempt by opposing counsel to intimidate, to display a contemptuous attitude or to behave inappropriately should be dealt with immediately and directly.

Part of any negotiation or mediation is both counsel's and the mediator's recognition of the solicitor-client relationship. Clients expect their counsel to protect them, and this should be recognized by all parties to a mediation. Furthermore, counsel are involved in maintaining an ongoing relationship with the client, which has an impact on counsel's ability to move his or her client towards settlement. One of the key features of a mediation is that a mediator can often suggest a reasonable settlement which both sides may find acceptable, but which neither side would have offered to the other.

DOCUMENT THE SETTLEMENT

Finally, never leave the mediation without documenting the settlement. Even if full minutes of settlement are not prepared by the parties, ensure that a document which sets out key terms of the settlement exists, and that it is signed by both the parties and their counsel. It is important to avoid the situation where the client later expresses "remorse" at having resolved the case in such a fashion. The best way to deal with this remorse is to ensure that a written reflection of the settlement exists, and that it is executed by all relevant parties and counsel.

There is no doubt that mediation is becoming an integral and important part of the litigation process and, as such, requires the same effective advocacy that is found in other aspects of the litigation process.

Chapter 15

THE MEDIATION DANCE

James B. Davidson[*]

INTRODUCTION

An opening offer is rarely accepted. While this statement can apply to any negotiation process, it rings particularly true in the context of formal mediation. In fact, conventional wisdom holds that a first offer is never made with the expectation that the other party will accept it, rather, it is viewed as a step necessary to begin the process. This *process*, in the context of mediation, refers to the inevitable exchange of multiple offers between the parties which is usually necessary before a settlement can be reached. What makes mediation unique in this regard is not so much the fact that multiple offers occur within the process, but rather that mediation incorporates this ritual-like *dance* back and forth between the parties as a formal component of the very structure of the process itself. Parties attend mediation fully expecting there to be a multiple exchange of offers, and, as the following discussion will suggest, this procedure is just as important in reaching settlement as the substance of the offers themselves.

In this regard, the focus of this chapter will be on the importance of the exchange of multiple offers within the mediation process. This will involve a very practical stage-by-stage analysis of the process, with special emphasis on the incremental role each stage plays in bringing the parties closer together. It is intended that such an analysis will illustrate why this aspect of mediation is not only important, but perhaps even necessary to a successful outcome.

Much of this discussion will be based on observation and anecdotal evidence gathered from regular participants of mediation, particularly from the lawyers who represent the disputants. In addition, it is important to give some indication as to the scope of this chapter. In this regard, it has been said that there are very few disputes that cannot be mediated. However, the nature of a particular dispute will have an extremely significant effect on the structure and form of the mediation process. This chapter intends to go no further than examining the typical mediation that is commonly employed in a civil lawsuit, particularly a lawsuit involving a claim for monetary relief.

---

[*]   James B. Davidson practises with the Toronto law firm MacMillan Rooke Boeckle, in the insurance fraud and insurance litigation areas. He holds a Masters Degree in Dispute Resolution from the University of Sydney in Australia. He also assists in teaching Ryerson Polytechnic University's dispute resolution course.

STAGE ONE — THE MEDIATION BRIEF

The mediation process begins not with the opening statement but with the exchange of mediation briefs. Typically, a mediation brief sets out each party's strongest arguments and best case scenario. Under such circumstances, it is not uncommon for a defendant to suggest that a case is worth very little. Likewise, it is not uncommon for a plaintiff to indicate that its case is worth a figure much higher than the reality of the situation. While part of this serves as simple posturing, it also serves to desensitize the other side as to what it may expect from the first offer. This paves the way for the creation of the proper environment for the actual mediation itself. This is because a mediation brief will always identify the parties' outer limits. From this point, the parties will naturally move closer together. Therefore, when the actual first offer is better than the hardline positions taken in the mediation brief, as is normally the case, there is an immediate perception of compromise and progress. This perception is extremely important, as this is what creates the necessary "positive" environment in which meaningful negotiations can take place. Without the mediation brief, the opening offer, instead of being viewed as a progressive step, could very well be viewed as extreme and, perhaps, even offensive. Accordingly, the mediation brief operates to effectively extract those elements from the negotiation process that might otherwise alienate the parties. This first stage of the mediation process serves as an excellent example as to the importance of the actual procedure itself in bringing the parties together.

STAGE TWO — AUTHORITY TO SETTLE

Another important preliminary step in the process is the requirement that participants have authority to settle. If there is no one at the mediation with authority to settle, one can almost be guaranteed that the mediation will be less successful than if that person had been present. As a second-rate alternative, it is possible to attend a mediation with someone with limited authority, provided that someone else with full authority is constantly available by telephone. However, there are many drawbacks to such a situation. The most notable is the fact that mediation creates a certain environment, as alluded to above. Those in the environment have experienced the "give and take" of the negotiations and have seen the other side at its best. To a certain extent, they have been "won over" by the other side and have lost some of the barriers to settlement that existed prior to the mediation. By then picking up the telephone and calling someone in another office who has been spending the day doing something completely different defeats the purpose of creating a mediation environment and eliminates the benefit of all that has been gained by the personal interaction of the parties. Insofar as the mediation process generally requires that the participants have authority to settle, and that they personally interact, at least to some degree, there is little risk that outside influences can derail the process in this regard.

STAGE THREE — OPENING STATEMENT

The opening statement is often just an oral presentation of the contents of the mediation brief and, to that extent, has no independent value in bringing about a resolution. However, the opening statement is an important aspect in the mediation process and often serves to bring the parties closer together for reasons other than its substantive content.

In this regard, an opening statement may differ slightly from the mediation brief for a number of reasons. One of these reasons may be that there may have been further developments between the parties from the time that the mediation brief was drafted to the time that the opening statement is given. Under such circumstances, the opening statement can be used to highlight progress made to date and, therefore, further contribute to the positive environment.

On the other hand, the opening statement may also trigger negative feelings. This is because the opening statement requires that the parties now engage each other face to face (for perhaps the first time), and this can give rise to feelings of awkwardness, anxiety and tension. However, this too can bring the parties closer together. In this regard, it is important that the parties start to invest time, energy and emotion into the actual process as soon as possible. This investment will act as an additional incentive for settlement. This is likely because people by nature want value for their efforts. No one wants to spend a long day at a difficult mediation only to see it fail. Logically speaking, the more effort that the participants must expend, the greater the desire to see a successful settlement. This is why the mediation process itself is so important. The process requires effort to be expended on the part of the participants, thereby creating a reason for settlement above and beyond the substantive aspects of the case. The opening statement is where this investment begins.

STAGE FOUR — THE OPENING OFFER

How Offers Are Presented

Before discussing the opening offer, it is necessary to make some comment on how such offers should be presented. There are essentially two schools of thought in this regard. The first is that offers should always be made face to face. This requires the two parties to sit down together and to experience the difficult task of putting a number on each other's case. It is essentially a comment as to how you value the other person's case. If you value it low, you can expect some emotion and confrontation. This is unpleasant and something that most people do not wish to undergo unless they have to. Making people give offers face to face reduces the chance that people will be frivolous with their figures. It serves as a reality check and ensures an element of reasonableness.

The other school of thought is that offers are best made and presented by the mediator who acts as a special envoy between the two parties who have retired to their individual caucus rooms. Some feel that this is a better method because it allows the mediator to put the best possible spin on the offer and also eliminates any personal antagonism that may exist between the parties. It also allows the mediator to help the party to craft a productive offer.

There is no right answer as to which method is better. Like many things, it will probably depend on the specific circumstances of each individual mediation or on the strengths and style of the mediator. It is probably useful for each party to enquire of the mediator as to which method the mediator thinks would work best. Quite often, the mediator may have a more objective view of what is going on between the parties at the mediation and is probably in a better position to make the call.

The Actual Offer

As previously stated, most participants in a mediation assume that a party's opening offer is not its last. The fact that the opening offer will not be the last does not mean that it is not important. In fact, it is the offer that will set the stage for all further offers, making it an extremely important part of the process. Moreover, an opening offer will often take into consideration what has been said in the opening statements and generally will offer some concession from the original positions set out in the mediation briefs. This, as discussed earlier, can often create the perception of compromise and goodwill, which will be crucial later on if there is to be any hope for success.

However, the most important aspect of the opening offer, from a procedural point of view, is in the fact that it represents a shift in the direction in which the parties have been moving. In this regard, prior to the making of the opening offer, the parties have been working against each other. The mediation brief and the opening statement, while laying the groundwork for future co-operation, are essentially efforts to "stake" the parties' individual claims. These stages revolve around best case scenarios as well as the strengths and weaknesses of each party's case. There is no effort made during these stages at compromise or at bridging differences. By making their opening offers, the parties now turn their attention to the goal of settlement which will inevitably require movement from their original positions. In this regard, while the opening offer seldom results in settlement and, in fact, seldom represents even real progress, it does represent a shift in the parties' focus from the individual positions to a mutually acceptable settlement. The fact that the mediation process requires at least one offer from each side forces the parties to start to work together in this respect. Without this procedure, the parties would run the risk of continuing to focus only on their positions as opposed to focusing on the goal of settlement.

STAGE FIVE — SUBSEQUENT OFFERS

It may be that the exchange of subsequent offers is more important than the opening offer, as it gives some insight as to the direction of each party. A large drop from the plaintiff's side may indicate that the opening offer was simple posturing. Similarly, minor movement from either side may indicate that the parties are close to a final offer and simply do not have much more room to move.

It is during this stage where the parties either become inspired by progress and work towards the goal of settlement or become frustrated with the process simply because there has been no substantial progress. While this frustration can be unpleasant, it can also, as discussed earlier, be useful. It may force the parties to communicate on a more sincere level. It also allows the parties to blow off the steam regarding ancillary issues that may be preventing compromise.

It is also at this point that the participants really start to invest effort and emotion into the mediation. The participants feel that they have put substantial effort into the process and that it would be a shame if something positive did not result. At this stage, the parties start to see the goal as settlement as opposed to simply getting what they wanted at the outset of the mediation. Moreover, the emotional costs that start to accumulate at this point and continue to accumulate with each new offer act as an incentive to avoid having to go through a similar process in the future. This is true whether it be an additional mediation or the actual trial. After all, if one day of mediation, where the parties are supposedly working together, is emotionally draining, one can only imagine what a long and involved trial would be like when the parties are actually working against each other.

These thoughts and emotions continue to mount and become increasingly more important as each new offer is exchanged. As each side concedes a little more, its opponents see progress and feel that they have achieved something. They have made the other side move from its original position and, perhaps, even see the issue from their point of view. This can often be as important as the money that is involved. However, without a structure in place, such as is imposed by mediation and which requires the parties to continue to make subsequent offers, and without the parties' acceptance of that structure, it is likely that such progress would never be made, or certainly not made in one day.

STAGE SIX — THE FINAL OFFER

There are two types of final offers worth mentioning. One is where one or both parties offer to split the difference between the penultimate offers. Splitting the difference can be a useful solution founded on economics and can, therefore, be a face-saving suggestion. In addition, it is used so commonly in mediation that it is to be expected at some point and, again, operates as a face-saving solution. It is also effective because both sides give equally under this technique. If the parties are close enough, they may relish the easy opportunity to close the deal that splitting the difference provides.

The other type of final offer is the one where parties are extremely far apart, and each party essentially "lays its final cards on the table". Such a strategy can backfire if the offers remain far apart. Essentially, at that point, both parties have indicated that they will not move any further, and to do so would be an admission of defeat. When final offers of this nature do not work, the mediation usually breaks down. However, quite often, such final offers are made with the legitimate purpose of trying to make some progress. They are made at the end of the day when the parties are tired and fearful that they may have wasted their time in attending the mediation. These factors often combine to make parties offer large concessions. If they are really close, they can often then move to the split-the-difference strategy. The importance of the "dance" process in this situation is that without the back-and-forth movement of multiple offers, major concessions of this nature would likely never be made. If parties were asked to give their final offer at the beginning, and such offers were far from a settlement, as would likely be the case, there would be nowhere else to go without a capitulation by one side or the other. Moreover, if such final offers were made at the beginning, the parties would have invested very little time and energy — and likely little emotion —and would, therefore, not have that "investment" operating to motivate them further. In this regard, it is often only when one party sees the other side conceding that it too begins to concede. It is unlikely that major concessions will be made in one offer; it usually takes several offers to get the ball rolling. Each new offer is a further concession, and as the concessions start to add up, the parties start to feel a spirit of cooperation, and a common goal develops. Without these incremental offers being made back and forth, there would be little in the way of momentum, and, therefore, the risk of the negotiations breaking down would naturally increase.

CONCLUSION

Mediation over the past decade has become an extremely popular method of dispute resolution. This is particularly true in the civil litigation context, where the use of mediation has been generally viewed as extremely successful in settling lawsuits. This discussion has suggested that part of the reason for this success is based upon the process itself, particularly the requirement for an exchange of multiple offers. Parties attend mediation, knowing that they will engage in an almost ritualistic-like *dance* back and forth with their opponent as they move closer and closer towards settlement. Once involved in this *dance*, the parties often begin to view settlement itself as the measure of success as opposed to the original positions taken in the dispute.

This is because mediation requires that the actual participants invest their individual time, effort and emotion into the process. This creates a further incentive above and beyond the merits or economics of the specific dispute. Without this investment, the participants may not see a breakdown in the negotiations as a shameful waste of their own personal energy. In order to receive some return on their investment, participants will often make concessions to save a deal or achieve the goal of settlement.

In addition, the mediation process is designed so that compromise is made incrementally with each new offer. Not only is it easier to make concessions on an incremental basis, but such movement can generate, at the very least, the perception of progress which creates momentum and inspires further movement. It is this environment that is crucial to settlement and that is a direct product of the process of mediation itself. And while there will be many reasons why a case may settle, there is one reason that remains constant, and that is that at a certain point, the parties shift their focus from working against each other to working with each other. The very process of mediation provides parties with a number of reasons to do so.

Chapter 16

THE FOUR FACTORS IN A
DIFFICULT NEGOTIATION AND
HOW A MEDIATOR CAN HELP

It is apparent that there are cases which do not settle, despite the presence of seemingly rational parties and good "settlement DNA": These mediations/negotiations have all the right stuff; there are people in attendance with authority to settle; a proper interest canvassing, risk assessment and alternative comparison is undertaken; the timing of the negotiations is good — the parties are prepared and able to assert their best case, and there has been enough litigation that the parties have a sense of the time it takes and the costs incurred, but the parties' funds have not been drained to the extent that that is an impediment to settlement — and there are no obvious flaws to the mediation. Why then would these cases not settle?

There are four factors which can arise in a difficult negotiation which are the cause of most such cases not settling. They are potentially present in any negotiation, and, depending on the strength of their presence, either singly or in conjunction with one another, they can debilitate any negotiation if left unchecked.

FACTOR #1 — PERCEPTION OF UNFAIRNESS

People will not agree to something, even if it is in their interests to do so, if they perceive it to be unfair. Despite the worst WATNAs and BATNAs, and the most thorough canvassing of interests, if a person perceives a proposal to be unfair, agreement is unlikely because to agree would countenance the unfairness. People do not like to be neutral in the face of unfair treatment, particularly when it is aimed in their direction.

Accordingly, with disputes involving very poor BATNAs, it may be that practically every settlement option has an element of unfairness. How do you work around this structural impediment? The only way is to characterize the agreement as a victory, at a level meaningful to the party. This is very difficult for a party to do because of the degree of objectivity it requires. It is nearly impossible for the other side to accomplish because of the inevitable devaluation of the other side's viewpoint (see Factor #2 below). A neutral, such as a mediator respected by the parties, is in the best position to present such a prospective agreement with a positive gloss.

A mediator may be able to bring the party around to see the result as a vindication of some sort, or as a positive statement relating to its self esteem. Perhaps the party can be brought to see the closure of a final agreement as a benefit in itself. Perhaps the party can be made to feel that it "out negotiated" the other side and can feel good about its handling of the dispute, or perhaps the party's attention can be drawn towards some positive end to which the money will be put. Whatever the case, those involved in the dispute must find a way around the feelings of unfairness to ensure that these feelings do not predominate and scuttle a good agreement.

For example, an agreement on general damages (those awarded for pain and suffering) in a personal injury case can be tricky because of the relatively low levels of compensation awarded by Canadian courts (comprising a relatively unattractive BATNA).[1] Court-awarded damages seldom match the level of pain and suffering the claimant perceives to have suffered. In many cases, the claimant may be right. Weeks or months of pain, fear and several surgeries over an extended period and the prospect of diminished function may only be worth several tens of thousands of dollars. What then can be done to prevent the party from feeling that the result is inherently unfair and from rejecting a settlement that is within the range awarded by the courts (and, therefore, as good or better than the BATNA)? A mediator may be able to work with the party, usually in separate session, in determining whether a given settlement is a better alternative to litigation. A mediator may be able to assist the party in realizing that it has not been a pushover, and that it is getting a reasonable resolution. The party may also appreciate that the settlement brings closure and ceases the cascading effect of the injury into every aspect of the party's ongoing life.

FACTOR #2 — REACTIVE DEVALUATION

"Reactive devaluation" happens when the reasonableness of a party's proposal is discounted solely because of the low esteem in which the recipient holds the proposer. When one or more parties automatically devalue the reasonableness of anything that emanates from the other party, this can prove fatal to a negotiation. There is an almost instinctive negative reaction to anything that the other side suggests, such as a fact, an offer or an idea. If it is good for the other side, it must be bad for us. Otherwise, why would the other side suggest it? The result is that parties refuse to believe what the other side says and dismiss any facts it asserts or offers it makes. This, of course, is especially true in acrimonious disputes where there is little trust. If left unchecked, the parties can get deadlocked into an inability to trade any offers at all, or get stuck trading unproductive, unprincipled offers which do little to narrow the gap and may even be insulting. It is the "if you give an inch they will take a mile" syndrome. At the very least,

---

[1]   Unlike American courts where juries can award millions of dollars, general damages in Canada are limited by the decision of the Supreme Court of Canada in *Andrews v. Grand & Toy Alberta Ltd.*, [1978] 2 S.C.R. 229, and are currently capped at about $275,000.

reactive devaluation can encourage the making of hardball offers which make a negotiation longer and less efficient.

Without a mediator, it can be very difficult to combat this phenomenon. The best approach is to simply strive to make principled offers notwithstanding what the other party may be doing.[2] For example, develop offers that are, in fact, reasonable, even if such offers leave you less room to move. Indicate that the offers are being made in an effort to jump-start the negotiation and to skip a number of unnecessary negotiation steps. Indicate that you are, in fact, near "the edge of your envelope". This will give the other side a choice: play its offer the same way — or react extremely, and watch you shut down the negotiations. The other side will either come back to the table, or, if not, you will have quickly found out (rather than after a drawn out, futile negotiation) that a satisfactory deal was not possible.

A mediator can be instrumental in countering the effects of reactive devaluation by helping the parties to structure productive principled offers to one another. Having the mediator present proposals may also assist in having the proposals delivered and received objectively. Settlement options can be generated with less devaluation when they have not emanated from the other side.

This strategy was used by the mediator in a fatal motor vehicle accident case, where emotions were running high. The parties were completely unwilling to make offers other than those that had already been rejected. Instead of deeming the mediation at an end, the mediator caucused with the parties separately and got a sense of what might be seen as acceptable. Emotions were running high because it was a fatal motor-vehicle accident case. The mediator was able to propose ideas to each, and gradually gained acceptance to compromises that resulted in an agreement.

A mediator can also emphasize the positive and minimize the negative. When a party devalues the other side's offer, the mediator can explain how it, in fact, is a principled offer, and that although further negotiation is required, the offer goes part way in resolving the dispute. By relaying the party's regrets concerning the issues involved in the dispute, or anything positive about the party, the mediator may diminish the acrimony and generate positive feelings. By encouraging the parties to make reasonable, principled and productive offers to one another, the mediator is inherently controlling reactive devaluation by reducing opportunities for it to occur.

Mediators may take a different approach where reactive devaluation is not too severe. Most difficult negotiations entail at least some reactive devaluation. A mediator's strategy in some cases may be to let it "play out" for a while. The mediator does this when allowing the parties to trade offers back and forth for a while, even if the offers are not very productive. It is almost as if people need to get the reactive element out of their systems. It has often been observed that people like to negotiate — witness an outdoor market — and it is probably because of the anticipation of reactive devaluation that this is so. People think they need to make offers that have little chance of acceptance because they anticipate that the other side will devalue their offers regardless of how reasonable they

---

[2] See the discussion on the Type C negotiator in Chapter 3.

are. Therefore, they might as well make offers that leave sufficient wiggle room for the other side's devaluing. So many settlements, after they are arrived at, seem obvious. And maybe they were obvious from the beginning, but the parties could never have agreed without the ritualistic dance involving offer, devaluation, counteroffer, devaluation, *etc.*[3]

FACTOR #3 — FEAR OF MAKING THE FIRST OFFER

Seldom does a party want to be the first to suggest an idea for settlement or for a settlement discussion, lest they be perceived by the other side as being weak. This reluctance to "be the first" can have a debilitating effect when trying to solicit the first offer or concession. The parties view making a substantive move much like a hot potato, and they can waste an entire negotiation session taking baby steps or not promoting offers between each other at all. If not dealt with, this phenomenon can stall or even halt negotiations.

The solution can be advanced with the assistance of a mediator, but it requires the cooperation of the parties. A mediator can help convince a party that making the first move can help it to set the agenda or "flag its range", which might be an advantage. Making a first offer may also be a useful way to at least generate an offered compromise from the other side when it is certain that future negotiations will have to take place. In this way, the stage has been set to begin the future bargaining from a more compromised position.

Alternatively, if the history of the dispute has involved previous offers of any kind, the party that last made such an overture should *not* be required to make the first offer at the mediation, otherwise the party will be perceived as bargaining against itself. Instead, the other party should be convinced to take a turn and move towards settlement. The mediator's role is essentially to create an environment in which the making of a first offer makes sense, or, at least, in which the party has fewer misgivings about making some sort of compromise.

FACTOR #4 — RATIONALIZATION OF BEHAVIOUR

People sometimes rationalize or justify their behaviour after the fact, rather than face up to the possibility that they may have made a mistake. This can cloud a party's judgement and interfere with its risk assessment and canvassing of interests and alternatives that are necessary to properly evaluate settlement proposals. This phenomenon was evident in 1960, when John F. Kennedy won the American presidential election with only 128,000 more votes than Richard Nixon, out of over 68,000,000 votes cast, and a poll conducted two years later indicated that 66 per cent of Americans said that they had voted for Kennedy. This, of course, was a mathematical impossibility — many of the poll respondents either were mistaken or were lying. But why?

---

[3]   For further discussion on this point, see Chapter 15.

In 1962, Kennedy was popular and trendy, and was perceived to be doing a good job. Nixon had lost the California governor's race and had faded into obscurity. Many people could not come to terms with their actual vote in 1960 and, therefore, rationalized a different scenario.

People do this all the time without really knowing that they are distorting the truth. It is not because people are evil or conniving. It is often done quite innocently in an effort to save face or explain one's inexplicable, wrong-headed or questionable behaviour. Parties can convince themselves of the truth of their position because it makes sense in their world to do so.

This factor poses obvious hazards in an interest-based negotiation where an honest risk assessment and canvassing of alternatives to an agreement is required. The mediator can help in a number of ways. With the right combination of empathy and "tough love", he or she may succeed in shaking the mistaken belief. A transformative event will have occurred, and a breakthrough will be possible.

More commonly, however, the mediator will not be able to shake the mistaken perspective entirely. The only way around this lingering problem is to somehow find a settlement that allows the mistaken version to coexist with the reality. For example, an employer who really believes its own trumped up "cause" argument[4] as to why the employee was dismissed may never admit to the precipitousness with which the firing took place. However, if the employer can become comfortable with the operational necessity of the firing from a business perspective — albeit knowing with the wisdom of hindsight that the deficiencies of the employee fall short of just cause — then the employer might agree to pay damages notwithstanding the significant after-the-fact justification. The positive characterization needed for the mistaken belief to coexist with the reality is a subtle transformation, and it can usually only come about with the assistance of a mediator.

To conclude, the mediator's input into these four factors is among the highlights of the "value added" provided by the mediator. These interventions are amongst the key reasons why dysfunctional disputes which have failed to settle often do settle at a mediation. In the next chapter, common issues, situations and problems that arise at mediations will be explored.

---

[4]   "Just cause" is needed to fire an employee without the obligation to give reasonable notice or payment in lieu of notice.

Chapter 17

PARTICULAR ISSUES IN MEDIATION

In the last chapter, the four factors that commonly occur in a difficult mediation were addressed. In this chapter, other issues and problems that frequently arise are explored, and possible solutions are presented.

NEGOTIATING THE AGENDA

In the section on negotiation, the utility of meeting with the other side to see if there is any agreement about the norms of the process was stressed. Where counsel are involved, it can be very useful to call the other side's counsel and talk about the case in general terms. This does not mean discussion of offers to settle, but determining whether factors necessary to make the mediation succeed are present.

An example of a case where this initial step was unfortunately omitted was a wrongful dismissal case in which the employer had a fairly weak case for "just cause". The employer's counsel had arranged the mediation. However, he came to the session unprepared to make a meaningful offer. Instead, he reiterated an already rejected offer and told the mediator that the former employee faced criminal charges which were not related to the employment, thinking that this would intimidate the former employee into capitulating. The employee, who had a good defence to the charges and was aware that the employer also knew that, was very upset and dug in his heels. This set the process of settlement back significantly.

PRE-SCREENING

Earlier, we examined the factors (such as extreme power imbalances, strong public interest issues, *etc*.)[1] which, if present, suggest that negotiations should probably not take place.

It is sometimes suggested, particularly with cases that are required to be mediated as opposed to those in which the parties choose mediation, that some pre-screening take place. Issues such as whether the case is a proper one for mediation and whether it is within the competence of the mediator (particularly if he or she uses an evaluative style) can be addressed. Most private mediators do not

---

[1]   See Chapter 9, under "When to Mediate".

have elaborate pre-screening procedures and can assess fairly quickly when discussing it with counsel whether a case has a chance of settling through mediation.

An important finding of the ADR Centre in Toronto was that the likelihood that a case would settle was not generally impacted by the subject matter, number of parties or dollar amounts at stake in the dispute. The exception to this was wrongful dismissal cases which were generally more likely to settle than other cases, probably because the law on termination payments is fairly certain.

THE USE OF APOLOGIES

A meaningful apology offered freely and accepted without reservation has been said to be one of the most profound interactions between civilized people.[2]

Part of the effectiveness of mediation for resolving disputes is that it enables the parties to face one another and to evaluate each other's credibility as well as the efficacy of each other's arguments. Mediation also enables the sharing of thoughts and feelings in a dynamic process of mutual persuasion and empathy. Ultimately, where mediation is successful in facilitating agreement, it is because the alternatives to an agreement have been canvassed, and the core interests of the parties have been met. Because most disputes, even those solely between corporate or government entities, involve some element of interpersonal breakdown, an apology or an important admission can be a useful device in breaking down barriers, meeting emotional needs and increasing receptivity to proposals. An admission can also be effective, even though it is not always associated with remorse or a quest for forgiveness.

Regrettably, very few people seem to know instinctively how to apologize, or have an instinctive appreciation of its value in the mediation context. Mediators can recount the numerous times in joint sessions where they have wished that a party had the good sense to perceive the cry for recognition and acknowledgement coming from the other side and to apologize. It costs nothing[3] and can go a long way towards reducing tension and increasing trust.

It takes courage to make an apology an explicit recognition of having done something wrong. The main impediment to making an effective apology is the feeling that it is a sign of weakness. Unfortunately, ego often gets in the way. A sincere apology that names the offence or that demonstrates some shame and an understanding of the extent of the wrongdoing can often work wonders to heal and even restore a relationship. The value in promoting the relationship can translate directly into a better settlement. This can have the effect of saving money and avoiding needless litigation.

---

[2]   A. Lazare, "Go Ahead, Say You're Sorry" (January/February 1995) Psychology Today 40.
[3]   In most mediation contexts, the proceeding is completely confidential and without prejudice; any apology really is "free" in the sense that it cannot be used to haunt the maker as any kind of admission of liability.

Elements of an Effective Apology

There is also such a thing as a botched or ineffective apology. A classic example is the apology offered by the Premier of Alberta, Ralph Klein, for that province's forced sterilizations between 1928 and 1972, which had been a blight on Alberta's record for decades. The Klein government had introduced legislation to cap claims at a low amount and had sought to use the "Notwithstanding Clause" in the *Canadian Charter of Rights and Freedoms* to keep victims from challenging the limit in court.

After a settlement with the victims was finally reached, Premier Klein was absent from the news conference announcing the settlement. Instead of apologizing directly, he told reporters, "We extend regrets for the actions of another government in another period of time."

Contrast this with the apology given by President Bill Clinton in 1997 for the U.S. government's role in the 1940s for failing to treat African Americans in Tuskegee, Alabama, who had contracted syphilis and who had sought medical help, but were not, in fact, treated, as part of an experiment to see whether treatment was effective. Portions of the speech were as follows:

> The eight men who are survivors of the syphilis study at Tuskegee are a living link to a time not so very long ago that many Americans would prefer not to remember, but we dare not forget. It was a time when our nation failed to live up to its ideals, when our nation broke the trust with our people that is the very foundation of our democracy...without remembering it we cannot make amends and we cannot go forward...

> Men who were poor and African American...they believed they had found hope when they were offered free medical care by the United States Public Health Service. They were betrayed...even once a cure was discovered, they were denied help and they were lied to by their government...

> The United States government did something that was wrong – deeply, profoundly, morally wrong. It was an outrage to our commitment to integrity and equality for all our citizens...

> The American people are sorry – for the loss, for the years of hurt. You did nothing wrong, but you were grievously wronged. I apologize and I am sorry that this apology has been so long in coming...I am sorry that your federal government orchestrated a study so clearly racist. That can never be allowed to happen again. It is against everything our country stands for...We cannot be one America when a whole segment of our nation has no trust in America. An apology is the first step, and we take it with a commitment to rebuild that broken trust...

> The people who ran the study at Tuskegee...forgot their pledge to heal and repair. They had the power to heal...and they did not. Today all we can do is apologize. But you have the power, for only you Mr. Shaw, and the others who are here, the family members who are with us in Tuskegee – only you have the power to forgive. Your presence here shows that you have chosen a better path than our

government did so long ago. You have not withheld the power to forgive. I hope today and tomorrow every American will remember your lesson and live by it.[4]

Note that there was no mention in Clinton's speech of past governments and past periods of time. Responsibility for the atrocity was taken by the current government for the failed duty owed to American citizens.

In one complex financial case which the author mediated, it became clear after each party's diatribe in the joint session that everyone had lost money and that no one had really intended to harm anyone else. Yet each party had done things which had set off the other parties. Consequently, each party was asked to think carefully about what it was that it regretted having done to the other, and to apologize for it in a way that the party would find sincere if it were the one receiving the apology. When everyone had done this, tempers cooled, and the atmosphere in the room became conducive to collaborative and creative problem-solving. The case settled, thus avoiding years of litigation.

Acceptance of the Apology

Acceptance of the apology is also crucial. A rejected apology will do little to further the objective of settlement and may even reinforce anger. Like the making of the apology itself, the acceptance can be effective or counterproductive. Where there is a genuine, heartfelt acceptance, there is what has been described as a "re-humanizing of the enemy ... Understanding what has driven the perpetrator, discovering similarities through basic common needs, separating the evil from the actor who committed it, are part of a process of intensive healing for a victim."[5] By sacrificing the desire for revenge and seeing offenders as human after they have made a genuine apology or similar expression of remorse or regret, victims are freed from anger and can begin to forgive and move on with their lives. "By asserting their need to communicate their suffering to the offender through forgiveness rather than anger, and motivated by the need to complete the healing, victims break the pattern of the victim/aggressor relationship."[6] By eliciting a genuine expression of remorse from the offender, the desire for punishment is thus satisfied. The apology is, therefore, the "punishment" because it is accompanied by the pain of shame. The focus then changes from the past to the future.[7]

Apologizing Not Always Appropriate

It should be stated that an apology may not be useful in every case. For example, in one wrongful dismissal case, mutual apologies for bizarre conduct seemed like a good idea — a way to calm the parties down before breaking into separate

---

[4]   Remarks by the President in Apology for Study Done in Tuskegee, May 16, 1997, The East Room, The White House, Office of the Press Secretary (obtained from the Internet).

[5]   Centre for Conflict Management, M. Landrum, *The Stages of Processing Victimhood and the Role of Mediation*, Issue 2, Winter 1999.

[6]   *Ibid.*

[7]   *Ibid.*

sessions. Fortunately, the lawyer for the employer knew her client better than the author did and indicated that if her client had to pay *and* make an apology, her client would become infuriated and never agree to settle. The apology idea was neatly buried, and we proceeded to talk solely about settlement figures, which eventually led to a mediated settlement.

The key to using an apology as an effective relationship-building tool is to be able to discern where and when an apology might break down barriers and assist in meeting certain emotional needs of the parties. When these needs are met, the parties derive a sense of satisfaction that paves the way for settlement.

Apology Not Always Possible

What happens when a party cannot bring itself to apologize, and the refusal blocks the other side from considering a settlement? In one case, a doctor had sexually harassed a patient over a period of years of treatment. The patient desperately wanted an admission of guilt or an apology. The doctor, who was in partial denial, could not bring himself to do either. His refusal impeded the patient from making a concrete offer, which, if it were in the range being discussed with the mediator, would probably have been accepted by the doctor and would have represented good compensation to her. The breakthrough occurred when she was asked, "What kind of man would have done this to you, what kind of man would have defended the claim and what kind of man have we seen at the mediation today?" It was pointed out that the character flaws which led him to behave as he had done were now rendering him incapable of admitting or apologizing. He could do neither because he was so flawed, and she had known that about him for some time now. Drunks cannot be expected to act sober. Thus, the patient then took pity on the doctor, dropped her demand for an admission and focused on the compensatory aspects of the case, which did settle.

Though it is useful, an apology will not always materialize. If a party feels the need for an apology from the other side, and it is not forthcoming, this issue must be addressed in some way before the mediation can move forward.

WHEN TO DISCLOSE AND WHEN NOT TO DISCLOSE

When considering whether to disclose at a mediation or not, it is generally better to opt in favour of disclosure because this opens the lines of communication and advances the parties towards an understanding and a settlement. It also may serve to destroy any negative notions of the other side that a party may have, which are getting in the way of a settlement. Further, if the information is helpful to your view of the dispute, why would it be better to hold it back if it might alter the other side's view of what the case is worth? Mediators will usually favour disclosure because it helps bring things at the mediation to a head and assists with settlement. Accordingly, disclosure should be the general rule.

While disclosure should be the general rule, it is not advisable in all situations. A party may be better off resisting disclosure if:

- the other side has refused reasonable requests for disclosure, leaving you in a position where you do not know enough to be able to recommend a settlement (accordingly, any disclosure on your part would be one way and could prejudice you);[8]
- you are certain the matter cannot settle, and to disclose a particular item might ruin a future important cross-examination;
- the disclosure requested is clearly irrelevant to the information needed to be able to recommend a settlement proposal;
- to provide the requested disclosure will only reinforce the other side's negative impression of you, will not particularly assist with information needed to recommend a settlement and will generally throw into the negotiation a "hot potato," making a settlement in your interests less likely; or
- the other side is using a positional, adversarial style of negotiating, and you want to bring it back to a principled style.

The following case is a good example for this rationale. In a long-term disability case worth millions of dollars over the following 26 years (the monthly benefit was very high), the main issue was whether the claimant could do the essential duties of her specific job, which was argued by the plaintiff to include a small but very important amount of time at job sites. The plaintiff claimed to be unable to walk properly, and she also claimed a pathological fear of the job sites themselves. However, the insurer had extensive surveillance of the plaintiff walking without difficulty and attending at various job sites with zeal. Rather than disclose this at the mediation, the insurer kept it confidential because it wanted to continue its discovery of the plaintiff and have her make admissions on the record that could then be contradicted with the surveillance. The insurer was certain it was being lied to, and any settlement would have involved substantial money that would have been misapplied if the plaintiff were lying. To confront the plaintiff with the lie, considering how good a liar she was, would only have given her the opportunity to reframe her story and minimize its effect at trial. Further, if she were capable of such a lie (she had been lying about her abilities for over seven years), revealing the evidence at the mediation would not have affected her view of her case — she simply would have lied around it. Pride would never have allowed her to own up to it, and the case would likely not have settled notwithstanding the disclosure.

The importance of disclosure can be illustrated by this true story of the Canadian Security Intelligence Service (CSIS) staff members who grieved a number of things, including salary, working conditions, hours and job requirements. Under the staff members' collective agreement, the grievances came before an arbitrator who was forced to rule against them. Why? Because their jobs were secret, and they could not reveal anything about their salary, working conditions, hours or job requirements!

---

[8] A solution would be to have the mediator develop a disclosure process to be followed.

WHEN TO DEFER, AND WHEN TO "SET THE MEDIATOR STRAIGHT"

The following are some useful tips about dealing with mediators in a mediation.

Deferring

The most important time to defer to a mediator is at the eleventh hour, when the mediator floats a proposal meant to combine some of the core interests of the parties. This occurs when the parties have come as far as they can with principled negotiation and are at an impasse. The mediator tries to reflect a balance and shape an agreement that all sides can live with, but it is not certain that any side will agree.

It is advisable to listen and consider the proposed agreement — do not reject it out of hand. If you can live with it, accept it; if you need time, wait to see if the other side accepts it. The other side's acceptance may be what you need to accept it too.

As was discussed in Chapter 16, allowing the mediator to be the person who floats proposals to the other parties can be useful for combatting reactive devaluation. Because the proposals will be seen to be coming from the mediator, they will not have a stigma attached to them and may be considered more seriously. Relying on the mediator as messenger may also let you off the hook. You are less likely to be seen as caving in, or if a proposal is negatively received, you are less likely to be blamed — because it was the mediator who presented the proposal, not you.

The mediator will likely have a good idea of the settlement DNA. Defer to the mediator's judgement about whether to continue the mediation. The most valuable commodity which the mediator adds in obtaining a reasonable settlement is third-party persistence — being able to push the envelope further than the parties could do on their own.

Follow the mediator's advice, especially in the first rounds of the negotiation — make principled offers, and do not reiterate previously rejected offers. The mediator will have had the opportunity to caucus with the other parties and will have insights into their interests. If the mediator tells you that a particular offer/approach will infuriate the other side, he or she is probably correct.

Do not pressure the mediator, for example, telling him or her to "make it snappy — as I have to leave". If the other side senses that the mediator is pandering to the time schedule of one party, the mediator could lose credibility. No one party should be seen to be dictating the pace of the negotiation.

If the mediator provides an insight into your case, or gives a perspective which is helpful, do not play it down. Use the mediator for some objective analysis of your case.

"Setting the Mediator Straight"

If you find that you know more about the relevant law than the mediator does, do not be afraid to politely educate him or her. If the mediator suggests making a proposal which is out of line with your client's substantive rights (and there is nothing to be gained by making such a proposal), inform the mediator and develop a new proposal. The party knows its business, and counsel may also be fairly well-educated about it; therefore, if the mediator suggests a business approach that will not work or is not advantageous, say so. If you hear the mediator recite back to you an offer or other communication for disclosure to the other side, and you hear something wrong or unclear, straighten it out immediately.

Counsel know their clients better than anyone else in attendance. If you know that a particular approach or proposal will be counterproductive with your client, inform the mediator immediately (sometimes a private chat is most effective and least embarrassing to your client). Similarly, if your client is particularity bullheaded or cantankerous, discreetly inform the mediator. You may have to work together to form a joint strategy for dealing with the client.

THE ROLE OF EXPERTS

Expert reports are crucial to an evaluation of the merits, and, generally, notwithstanding many mandatory mediation rules' timelines, a mediation should not start until both sides have sufficient expert reports such that any relevant opinion can coincide with their theory of the case. Expert reports are, therefore, just as critical to an interest-based mediation as they are to a trial. In fact, it has been said that the war of experts may be the last gasp of the adversarial process in the evolution of how we handle disputes from a litigation mode to mediation mode. This is not likely to change anytime soon. Very rarely can the parties agree on a common expert and, therefore, usually retain their own expert. It is incredible how experts can differ so widely on the relevant issues. Often, they cannot both be right, which implies that one of them is wrong. This ought to give a party that is at all averse to risk cause for concern. It could be that the party's whole stand in the dispute and all that is riding on it will boil down to how a given expert testifies and stands up to cross-examination. That test may, in fact, have little or nothing to do with the essential correctness of the expert's opinion. Developing a good opinion and performing on the witness stand are two different talents.

It is also important that the expert's report is truly helpful in advancing your position. Sometimes an expert opinion is submitted out of knee-jerk reaction and represents a double-edged sword. In one fire loss case, two experts had completely different opinions as to how the fire started. The only thing that they could agree on was that the fire had started in an appliance. However, even if the defendant's opinion on the cause was correct, the corollary was that there was still a design defect in the appliance, regardless of what sort. Indeed, if the defendant was right, the defect was of a far more serious and frightening nature than that suggested by the plaintiff. It was odd, however, that the defendant thought that this report would be helpful!

In a long-term disability case, the insurer's independent medical reports (upon which it had relied in cutting off the plaintiff's benefit) referred to the plaintiff's susceptibility to stress, and that it was difficult for her to work. A second independent report also concluded that the plaintiff could never be a nurse again. Although these reports had concluded that the plaintiff could work at gainful employment, the test in the policy was "employment for which the insured is reasonably capable by reason of training, education and experience". The plaintiff had only been trained and had only ever worked as a nurse for over 25 years. Accordingly, the report's conclusion was of little value, and some of its content could actually assist the plaintiff. Based on the defendant insurer's reports, the case settled for a reinstatement of the monthly benefit.

MANIPULATION

"A White Lie: A person may tell a white lie for the sake of peace." Great is peace, for even the Tribal ancestors resorted to a fabrication in order to make peace between Joseph and themselves.[9]

There is no question that manipulation, subtle and not so subtle, is present in just about every mediation conducted. Clients, counsel and the mediator will necessarily be selective in what, when and how information is revealed.

The word "manipulation" has a negative connotation, but in reality its presence in a mediation is not altogether negative, and indeed, it can even be constructive. It is, in effect, one of the devices used to de-intensify acrimony and produce a positive climate for negotiation. The use of humour, analogy, metaphor and historical references all fall into this camp. The "bluffing" about bottom lines and where a party would be prepared to see the dispute resolve are all efforts to manipulate the outcome and get the best deal. Making the most of one's own arguments so as to seemingly worsen the other side's alternatives to an agreement is another form of this manipulation. Counsel in joint session hardly ever say, "Here are my arguments, and now here is why they are weak!"

This is illustrated by what a lawyer who appeared in a difficult product liability case with the author relayed about his client. A hard-fought settlement was reached, but, given the communication and body language the lawyer received from his client, it appeared that the client was quite unhappy with the result, and, perhaps, blamed him for it. The lawyer became worried that he would lose the client. After they had left the building and were on the street, the insurer client told him how happy the insurer was with the outcome and what a great deal it was. What happened here? Clearly, the client had been manipulating the lawyer!

Counsel and their clients, of course, are good at manipulating the mediator, and the mediator can even get in on the game and utilize some subtle manipulation as well. For example, when the mediator is faced with an immovable party who is resisting compromise, the mediator may start asking, "why would you want to settle this case, anyway?" "You are probably right that this is a case that you could win, so what is in it for you to make any concessions?" *etc.* It is amazing how this spurs the party into revealing its exposure, and why, indeed, it

---

[9]   W. Gunther Plaut, "Gleanings" in *The Torah: A Modern Commentary* (New York: Union of American Hebrew Congregations, 1981) at 318, quoting from the Talmud.

desires a settlement. The mediator can also selectively control the flow of information. For example, if in separate caucus the mediator hears all sorts of derogatory things about the other party, it is usually not productive to repeat them to the other side. On the other hand, something said which is conciliatory, or an expression of regret, or anything else upon which a positive gloss can be put, probably does bear repeating.

Much of the manipulation is by counsel because they are the primary advocates for the client and usually take the upper hand in deciding what offers to make. Keeping in mind that the objective to any negotiation is to get what your client wants, here are some of the stratagems counsel have successfully employed (remember, counsel are their client's advocate — do not stop advocating!):

- The mediator will likely try to get each side to make principled offers to one another. Follow his or her suggestion. However, do not be afraid to attempt to persuade the mediator of the merits of your case and to make principled offers which reflect those merits. Stick to your guns.
- You will have to impress your client, especially if he or she is irritable or "on the edge". The mediator may come to you with a fairly reasonable offer from the other side, or one which clearly shows some progress. *The experienced mediator will know this; you do not have to articulate it. Do not be afraid to "dump" on the offer to show solidarity with the client. (Just wink at the mediator!)*
- Nixon used to say of the Soviets that "where there is mush, they proceed, and where there is a wall, they stop". In other words, do not hesitate to delineate your "lines in the sand", and do not be afraid to attempt to set the tone by showing the other side where you are not prepared to go.
- As the mediation draws to a close, do not be afraid to appear to dig in your heels. An experienced mediator — if you and the other side are at all close (or have even made progress) — will not let it fall apart without attempting to save it. You can rely on the experienced mediator to attempt a rescue, which may let you and/or your client off the hook.
- Using some well-placed humour (especially self-deprecating) can sometimes get you a lot from the other side. It costs nothing, but can soften up the other side.[10]
- You do not have to tell the mediator your bottom line, at least not until the very end. To do so may plant an unwanted seed in the mediator's head.
- If you think that you would like the mediation to begin with an offer from the other side, serve a settlement proposal the night before the mediation. The other side will likely not have time to respond to it, which means that you will be going into the mediation with an unanswered offer. A good mediator will never encourage a party to bargain against itself and will likely caucus with the other side first to procure an offer in response to yours.

---

[10]   The author usually brings home-baked chocolate chip cookies to mediations. Each batch is different from the last, and many jokes and comments, which tend to diffuse tensions, result.

SATISFYING AT-HOME CONSTITUENCIES — GHOSTS

This problem of satisfying at-home constituencies derives from the absence from the mediation of the person with full authority to settle. (See Chapter 12 for a discussion of "mediation ghosts".) Since we do not live in a perfect world, there are going to be occasions when, despite all the pre-mediation preparation and agreements to mediate, a mediation "ghost" will exist. This ghost will very often undo the progress made at the session by overriding the decisions and concessions made by the delegate who is attending the mediation on the ghost's behalf.

There are a number of strategies to cope with the problem. The most commonly used is one in which, rather than make a phone call and incur the risk of the ghost rejecting the deal over the phone, the people present come to an agreement, which the party with the ghost then takes back and pledges to recommend to the absent constituent (ghost). While no agreement is produced at the session, this can often work better than a quick phone call (as it is much easier to reject anything over the phone). The party, therefore, has a few days in which to respond, and the personal presence of the party or counsel recommending the deal usually secures an agreement a few days later.

Another method that can work is where a party agrees that if a particular offer were to materialize, it would be given every consideration with a view towards accepting it. This is a kind of "nudge, nudge, wink, wink" play, where a party for one reason or another has come to the mediation with an unrealistic capped authority, and the people in attendance, during the course of the mediation, have come to realize the cap's lack of realism. This often occurs with insurers. The party goes home to its ghosts (usually someone higher up the chain of command) and seeks to obtain a new "bottom line" or a new offer, which, unknown to the ghost, has been previously worked out with the other side to be accepted, or barely modified.

Finally, there is always the solution of requiring the ghost to attend. In the very first mediation the author ever conducted, it became clear in the first half hour that certain people situated in Kingston, Ontario, were critical to approving any settlement. The mediation was being held in Toronto, about a three-hour drive from Kingston, and it had commenced at 10:00 a.m. It was eventually decided to put the session on hold to allow the parties to drive to the mediation which was to recommence at 2:00 p.m. This worked, and the first mediated case at the Toronto ADR Centre settled later that evening.

ATTACHMENT TO THE DISPUTE

Generally speaking, parties can become "committed" to a course of action, even if it is not in their best interests. While many people are resilient enough to recover from an emotional trauma, sudden change-of-life circumstances and even significant personal injury, some seem unable to depart emotionally from their problem. They seem to almost thrive on the continued existence of their dispute, and their life becomes oriented around their pain. Counsel are familiar with clients who swear they will mortgage their house, their retirement and even their children's future to be able to continue with litigation, even when they are told that litigation outcomes are far from certain, and that they could face financial ruin. Rarely do such client sentiments seem rational to an outside observer, and from a mediation perspective, such people who are unable or unwilling to let go of their hurt pose real difficulties.

Experience suggests that only in rare cases are such people truly incapable of ever letting go. However, occasionally such behaviour may be a symptom of a psychiatric illness or a serious emotional disturbance going far beyond the events that led to the litigation, and it is not reasonable to expect the mediator or counsel to play the role of therapist.

Most litigants simply need time to be able to talk and work through it with a sympathetic listener — not so much sympathetic in the "I agree with you" sense, but more in the "ok, I can be a sounding board and will give you back, empathetically, what you dish out" sense. In a real sense, such people need their counsel and the mediator to listen and then respond with objective comments about where their interests may really lie. This may take awhile, and the arguments back and forth may take many forms. The client's ideas about "justice" and right and wrong, even the meaning of his or her life — or, at least, the meaning which they would like to ascribe to it — could all come out. Counsel and the mediator have to work together on this. Both must have built the trust of the client.

Fundamentally, the client must come to understand that a compromise which satisfies some of his or her important interests can be a vindication of his or her cause célèbre in the universal sense. Through a negotiated agreement, the client has stood firm against the "oppressor", maintained his or her dignity, got at least some of what he or she wanted and prevented any major loss. Through such an agreement, the client can be cleansed of the burning passion to right the wrong. Only then can the client get on with life.

Finally, much of a party's attachment to a given dispute may be based on fear. The mediation can help the party confront the fear and thus "accommodate the loss". In this way, the party can focus on building a post-trauma future rather than perpetually reliving the past.[11] Where clients (generally plaintiffs) undergo this change from debilitating hurt to dignified accomplishment, mediation can, in fact, be truly transformative.[12]

MEDIATOR BIAS

Mediation, of course, does not involve any findings of fact or conclusions of law on the part of the mediator. It is up to the disputants to determine whether or not they will reach a settlement, and even whether the mediation should continue. Nevertheless, it is of crucial importance that the mediator be neutral and not

---

[11]   Centre for Conflict Management, M. Landrum, *The Stages of Processing Victimhood and the Role of Mediation*, Issue 2, Winter 1999.

[12]   See Appendix II.

display any bias towards a party or its position. Without complete independence and neutrality, the mediator loses all credibility, and simply becomes a dupe for the agenda of one party over the interests of the others.

However, the mediator also has to marshall the parties to explore their interests and alternatives, and often encourages parties to look outside the level of thinking which got them embroiled in the dispute (or which has failed to resolve it for them). The mediator must be impartial with respect to the outcome, but not with respect to the process. The process is the domain of the mediator (subject, of course, to any limitations on how to conduct the session imposed expressly by the parties).

It goes without saying that a mediator in a conflict of interest or with a bias must disclose it. Under these circumstances, the mediator must withdraw from the mediation, unless the parties expressly state that they want the mediator to continue).[13] It follows further that if a party perceives a mediator to have a bias or a conflict, the party should raise it with the mediator and clear the air or bring the issue to a head.

However, what about systemic bias? Can a mediator remain neutral when settlement is an overriding objective? Mediators explain that a trial is expensive, risky and emotionally draining — in other words, by reviewing the BATNAs and WATNAs, mediators put fear into the heads of risk-averse parties. By encouraging settlement, are mediators pressuring parties to do things that they do not perceive to be in their interests? In a relatively one-sided case, is settlement facilitated only because the mediator has effectively adopted one side's view of the chances and impressed that view on the other side?

These are good questions for which there is an easy answer: There are plenty of other litigation processes in which to engage, and in which settlement plays scarcely a role (*e.g.*, discoveries, motions and even pre-trials). Mediation is the only process that is unashamedly pro-settlement. That is why it is effective. There is nothing a mediator can do, nor should there ever be, *to force* a settlement. To a far greater extent than in any other litigation process, the disputants are in the driver's seat and are masters of the proceeding. A mediator champions the cause of settlement in order to elicit all the possible settlement options, all the possible best and worst case alternatives, and in so doing facilitates the parties' arrival at their own informed decisions. If there is a bias towards settlement, there should be no apologies for it.

WHAT CAN BE DONE IF THE OTHER SIDE WILL NOT AGREE TO A MEDIATION ?

On numerous occasions, one or more parties desire a mediation, but another party does not. Outside of the mandatory referral process connected with a court-annexed program, there is nothing you can do to force a mediation. However,

---

[13] Virtually all Mediation Codes of Conduct are of one mind on this subject. For example, see the CBAO Mediators' Code of Conduct, Parts IV and V (see Appendix V), as well as the Ontario Mandatory Mediation Program Code of Conduct.

there are some good arguments which can be used to persuade the other side of its utility:

- "Counsel can bang heads all they want, but a mediation is a chance for a neutral third party to extol the virtues of a reasonable settlement with all sides. Without a mediation, this will never happen in the litigation."
- "Despite your client's seemingly firm instructions to you, he may not be that sure of what he wants. A good mediator will thoroughly canvass this and help your client to see all sides of the problem and ascertain his real interests."
- "You haven't heard everything there is to hear from my client yet, and you won't until we get before a mediator and we can communicate it in a controlled and completely confidential environment."
- "My client needs help formulating where he wants to go with this — I think that a mediator will be helpful in focusing my client's thinking, which, with any luck, could translate into some concrete proposals."

CASES JUST ABOUT MONEY

The answer to the question about the effectiveness of interest-based mediation of cases that are only about money lies with the question of why people negotiate. People negotiate because other means of resolution, such as litigation, are unpredictable as to outcome. Negotiating can be more predictable than going to court because if the negotiation is successful, the party will, at least, win something. If the negotiation does not succeed, the party is not bound to accept its outcome. Negotiations also occur when there is some urgency to reach a decision and the court process would take too long.

Further inherent in most conflicts is some level of interpersonal breakdown. It could be a question of credibility, a misunderstanding or something more malevolent. Strong emotions, feelings and psychological factors sharply affect a person's ability or willingness to negotiate. While many commercial cases may on their face seem to be only about money, they are in fact often about a good number of other things, such as a failed relationship, failed expectations, a misunderstanding, a failure to communicate or even a desire for revenge.

Finally, assessing the alternatives to an agreement has the effect of placing the mediator in the position of extolling the virtues of a reasonable settlement with *both sides*. Interest-based bargaining also requires all bargaining to be principled. This means that every offer made is based on some rational principle (as opposed to being arbitrary), which tends to create momentum towards settlement.

The interest-based process addresses these and other issues, and, accordingly, when the parties do not wish a third-party neutral to simply make a ruling for them, interest-based bargaining for "money cases" is highly effective.

Cases primarily about money, into which most insurance litigation falls — including medical malpractice cases — are readily mediated using an interest-based model. Money offers are made on a principled basis, by using an evaluation of the merits to model the offer, or on some other rational basis for calculation. As the negotiation continues, frameworks from previous offers made by each side are combined into illustrative proposals which lessen the gaps between the parties. If the negotiation is eventually successful, enough "good stuff" is present for both sides to sign on.

If settlement is desirable, an effort should be made to cater your own offers somewhat to the other side's needs and arguments. This does not mean capitulating to the other side's monetary demands. It does mean, however, that something of what the other side is asking for should be included in the offers you make, so as to flag the desire to make progress.

DO YOU HAVE TO INTEND TO SETTLE WHEN APPEARING AT A MEDIATION ?

The short answer to the above question is: of course not. The purpose of mediation is to enable the parties to identify their interests and work towards maximizing them. It is possible to have legitimate reasons for not settling, either at that stage in the proceeding, or, more rarely, at all. However, a good mediator will assertively question your client's interests and options, and ensure that they are making a fully-informed decision.

What if your client is sophisticated, and you, as counsel, have discussed the utility of settlement but have rejected any such prospect prior to the mediation? Is the mediation then a waste of time? The short answer here is probably not.

First, you may gain, even ephemerally, from the opportunity to meet the other side, attempt to persuade them and assess their credibility and skills as a witness. You may gain by finding out some concrete information, or about the other side's lack of it. You may learn in a kind of dress rehearsal how best to respond (or not to respond) to the other side's arguments.

You may, of course, also benefit from the interest canvassing and risk assessment done with the mediator, because no matter how sophisticated the client, it is sometimes easier to have a neutral third party ask the probing questions than to achieve the same dialogue with yourself introspectively.

Finally, if you are at a mediation, you have not settled yet. The mediator can, therefore, be of use to you by floating settlement options which you might have been afraid to suggest, perhaps because of fears that your case might appear weak or unreasonable. The mediator can explore options with the other side and run them by you. This may be the first time you will hear something meaningful from the other side, and it may change your strategy and even your desired outcome.

It is a frequent occurrence where a party or parties attend with no intention or with little hope of settling, only to be proven wrong by the dynamics of what goes on in the mediation. Turn these opportunities to your advantage by "going with the flow" for a while and seeing if anything significant develops.

The important issues and problems that can arise before or during a mediation were identified and explained in both this and the previous chapters. Solutions and strategies for dealing with them were suggested. Most of these problems, as was discussed, are surmountable. The one problem that may not always be overcome is getting a reluctant party to a mediation in the first place. If reasoned arguments, some of which were canvassed in this chapter, are insufficient, mandatory mediation may be the answer. In the next and final chapter of this book, the pros and cons of mandatory mediation are investigated.

Chapter 18

THE ADVENT OF MANDATORY MEDIATION

In several provinces, mandatory mediation of civil actions is required. The requirement is often limited to certain types of cases or to certain regions of the province, but the practice is spreading. The issue of whether requiring mediation is a good thing or a bad thing is in all probability being generally resolved in favour of the requirement to mediate, provided that the program is well structured. The fact that parties must use mediation is often a positive factor. It gets them to focus on settlement early in the litigation, it gets their attention and it brings them together.[1]

Is the content of settlements affected by the mandatory nature of the process? If the parties realize that they are required only to try, not to succeed, it is hard to see how that could be. The danger is not that the content of a settlement is affected, but that the attitudes of the parties might be; their willingness to take part in a meaningful way might be compromised.[2] There might also be a danger of the mediator feeling pressure to obtain settlement and, as a result, moving from stressing facilitation to becoming more evaluative.

Nevertheless, it seems clear that once having used the process, whether voluntarily or by mandate, most parties rate mediation highly.[3] The success of the ADR Pilot Projects in Toronto (where the model was a staff-run centre) and Ottawa (where the model was based on selection from a roster of private mediators) have led to a revolution in the Ontario litigation culture whereby mediation is not only accepted, but it is a desired form of dispute resolution. Adding substance to form are the mandatory mediation projects that are coming into existence, most notably in Ontario where the Early Mediation Program (EMP) is based on a system of early mandatory referral. Parties can select a mediator from a roster of mediators maintained by the court, or can select someone else if they prefer. Roster mediators are required to charge a below-market rate for the first hour of preparation time and for three hours of attendance time. Higher-market

---

[1] W.F. Coyne Jr., "Using Settlement Counsel for Early Dispute Resolution" (1999) 15 Negotiation J. 10, suggests that a "settlement event" such as a mandatory mediation or pre-trial conference is very useful in promoting early settlement.

[2] J. Alfini, "What Happens When Mediation is Institutionalized?" (1994) 9 Ohio S.J. Disp. Resol. 307; C. Menkel-Meadow, "Pursuing Settlement in an Adversary Culture: A Tale of Innovation Co-opted or 'The Law of ADR'" (1991) 19 Fla. St. L. Rev. 1, and G. Smith, "Unwilling Actors: Why Voluntary Mediation Works, Why Mandatory Mediation Might Not" (1998) 36 Osgoode Hall L.J. 846.

[3] C.M. McEwan and T. Milburn, "Explaining a Paradox of Mediation" (1993) 9 Negotiation J. 23. See also R. Ingleby, "Court Sponsored Mediation: The Case Against Mandatory Participation" (1993) 56 Mod. L. Rev. 441.

rates are chargeable after those initial time frames if it is cleared in advance with the parties. The EMP won the 1998 Achievement Award from the American Center for Public Resources. The award recognized the EMP as well as the consensus created to approve it.[4] The granting of the award singled out the EMP as a model to be used elsewhere. Other jurisdictions across the United States, the United Kingdom, Hong Kong and Singapore are adopting various kinds of programs with support of the local bar and judiciary.

THE MACFARLANE REPORT

Why is there such a rapid acceptance and implementation of mediation protocols? The answer lies in part with the findings of the Toronto ADR pilot project formal evaluation. The Macfarlane report authored by Dr. Julie Macfarlane, reviewed questionnaire responses from lawyers and parties that had attended a mediation at the Toronto ADR Centre. Interviews were also conducted, and a control group outside the ADR Centre was utilized. Data from the 1,460 cases mediated by the ADR Centre during the first nine months of 1995 were measured against a control group of equal size that had not participated in mediation. Some of the key findings are set out below:

- The mean time for mediated cases to settle was 124–129 days (depending on case type), whereas the mean time for non-mediated cases was more than twice as long, that is, 203–404 days (depending on case type).
- According to 70.4 per cent of lawyers, the mediation resulted in cost savings to their client as compared to the costs without a mediation. Of these, 43.7 per cent saved $1,000–5,000, 29.6 per cent saved $5,000–10,000, 8.5 per cent saved $10,000–15,000 and 18.2 per cent saved in excess of $15,000.
- The skill of the mediator was critical in determining a party's perception of the value of the process. A majority were satisfied with the mediator's services, but there were concerns about mediator bias or improper pressure to settle. Accordingly, Dr. Macfarlane recommended that parties be allowed to choose their mediator — something that the ADR Centre did not allow.
- Consistent with American studies, the most common reason for opting out or adjourning the first session was that the referral came too early.
- For those cases which did settle at the ADR Centre, the following factors were reported by the parties to be the most significant advantages:[5] 88.9 per cent of respondents reported cost savings, 77.8 per cent reported time savings, 66.7 per cent reported good rapport between lawyers and 55.6 per cent reported that the skill of the mediator was instrumental.

---

[4]   See the CBAO ADR Section Newsletter of February 1999 in an article by Elana Fleischman (Ontario was the first Canadian recipient of the award).
[5]   R.A. Pepper, "Mandatory Mediation: Ontario's Unfortunate Experiment in Court-Annexed ADR" (1998) 20 Advocates' Q. 403 at 428-29.

Clearly, there are settlement advantages to a mediation program. But why mandatory mediation?

THE MANDATORY ONTARIO "EARLY MEDIATION PROGRAM" (EMP)

A great deal has been written about the advent of mandatory mediation, but little has been expressed about the procedural framework in which a mandatory mediation regime can thrive. Having been one of the two full-time mediators at the Toronto ADR Centre from its inception in September 1994 to June 1997, the author had the opportunity to observe in over 1,000 mandatory mediation sessions what works and what does not. The author also had the opportunity to observe the logistical realities of private mediation. While the dye for the Early Mediation Program may have been cast, no doubt it will continue to be refined as problems are encountered and weeded out.

The Pros

American voluntary programs have a low rate of usage, despite high levels of client and lawyer satisfaction.[6] Suggested reasons for this include the bar's unfamiliarity with the mediation process. However, this argument loses currency over time. A second proposed reason is that more settlements result in fewer billable hours for lawyers; therefore, they are reluctant to mediate their cases voluntarily. However, a rapid turnaround of cases can result in an expanded client base, and it is becoming generally accepted that lawyers are entitled to charge a premium if they settle a case quickly and advantageously. A more likely fundamental reason for this, then, is that with voluntary programs, there is a fear that the party which suggests mediation will be perceived as being weak. It is clear that this factor is of real concern in an adversarial system. Interestingly, the Macfarlane report did not find any significant opposition amongst lawyers or parties to the mandatory nature of the mediation referral.[7] Indeed, the author has observed that many counsel welcome the mandatory referral, because it lets them off the hook in cases where they really wanted to mediate but do not want to give the impression that their case is weak by having suggested it.

Mandatory mediation improves the quality of justice. It gives disputants a structured forum for communication, a reality check and the opportunity for an interest canvassing in which their alternatives to an agreement are reviewed. Power imbalances are often addressed, creativity is employed, and relationship factors are given weight, which the court's strict adherence to the law does not permit. Mandatory referral eliminates any perception that those who suggest ADR are weak. It also provides a neutral setting in which to jump start dialogue, explore settlement possibilities and have a third-party neutral extol the virtues of a reasonable settlement with all parties. The high user satisfaction revealed

---

[6] *Ibid.*

[7] *Ibid.*

through evaluations by the Toronto ADR Centre and through the Ottawa pilot project speaks for itself.

It seems obvious that no single development in our civil litigation system could be more beneficial or more radical in terms of differing from traditional litigation practice. It is welcome, and long overdue.

The Cons

As presently constituted, the Attorney General's EMP will likely foster some of the problems it hopes to alleviate. Mediation works when it treats every case on its own terms. If a mediation program treats every case in the same manner, some of the benefits are lost.

The early referral in the EMP, while helpful in small, simpler cases, will render many mediations for complex cases irrelevant or impossible. Injuries need time to mature, and counsel need time to assess their client and their case, retain experts, do an accounting, conduct discoveries, *etc.* There is little utility to a mediation if the parties are not prepared. The danger is that many cases will be required to attend a mediation far too early, and the process itself will suffer. If that happens, the EMP could be seen as just another litigation hurdle to overcome; and many people's first exposure to ADR will be negative, clouding support for the process. For the EMP to improve the administration of justice, it must be as effective with complex cases as with simple ones. Otherwise respect for the program and its relevance may suffer.

It should not be necessary to obtain a court order to opt out of mediation. The Toronto ADR Centre Practice Direction stipulated that if one party wanted to go to mediation, then the case proceeded, but if all parties consented to opt out; no court order was required. This system made sense because it built into it an internal "settlement DNA" check.[8] Clearly, if none of the parties wanted to proceed, there would be little "settlement DNA", and a mediation would likely waste time. However, if even one party wanted to proceed, there would be something with which the mediator could work. Then the case would not be held hostage to the most recalcitrant party, and the "settlement DNA" could be explored. Again, the goal should be to maximize the utility of that first session.

It is disappointing that there is no mention in the EMP of the possibility of having a sitting judge perform neutral evaluations on a legal point which has created an impasse in the mediation. This was a tool available for use in the first year of the ADR Centre; while bringing in a judge to give an opinion never settled a case, it always helped, and the cases that received neutral evaluation and continued with further mediation almost always settled. In a court-annexed program, the mediators could access willing judges to perform this useful though rarely used function.

It is difficult to see why the EMP was restricted to case management cases, to the exclusion of estates cases, bankruptcy matters or class actions. All of these areas are ripe for mediation and almost always benefit from the process. Estate cases are usually about relationship issues and a fixed set of assets — ideal for

---

[8]   For a discussion of settlement DNA, see Chapter 7.

mediation. Bankruptcy cases present stark alternatives to both debtors and creditors and mediation is almost always useful where the parties are risk-averse. Class actions also can be rendered more efficient and cost effective through the implementation of a mediation procedure within the order establishing the class action, as has recently been done in some noteworthy instances.[9] Indeed, but for administrative arguments, it is hard to see why the program should be limited to case management. There is certainly nothing singular about case management that would make it more suited to mediation.

Implications of Ontario Mandatory Early Mediation Program Statistics[10]

According to these statistics, most cases (55.9 per cent)[11] that attend a mandatory mediation end with a positive result, in that some level of settlement has been achieved. This statistic does not rate any benefit derived from narrowing issues, exchanging information, assessing credibility or agreeing on procedural items.

---

[9]   Examples are the successful ADR regimes established by Ontario court orders in the Sillcorp layoffs and with respect to the Inco chemical leak in Sudbury.

[10]   Below are some interesting statistics valid as of March 1, 2001.

    A. Mediations Concluded: 3,713
        Settled (within 10 days of the mediation): 1,464 (39.4 per cent) (Toronto 895; Ottawa 569)
        Partially Settled: 612 (16.5 per cent) (Toronto 472; Ottawa 140)
        Not Settled: 1,637 (44.1 per cent) (Toronto 998; Ottawa 639)

    B. Total Applications for the Court Roster Received to Date: 647
        Toronto: 391
        Ottawa: 80
        Both: 176

        Total Applications Approved: 368
        Toronto: 203
        Ottawa: 47
        Both: 118

        Total Applications Rejected: 192
        Toronto: 125
        Ottawa: 25
        Both: 42

    C. Total Number of Cases in which Roster Mediators Selected: 3,383
        Toronto: 1,482
        Ottawa: 1,901

        Total Number of Cases in which Roster Mediators Assigned: 2,821
        Toronto: 1,955
        Ottawa: 866

[11]   The 55.9 per cent figure includes cases that completely settled (39.4 per cent) and those that partially settled (16.5 per cent). It includes cases in both Toronto and Ottawa.

Mediating Too Early

The settlement rate is somewhat lower than that achieved at the Toronto ADR Centre and the Ottawa Pilot Project (which also mediated cases on a mandatory basis). This may be because many cases at the ADR Centre and with the Ottawa Project did not come for a mediation so early in the litigation. Many cases came on consent after discoveries were conducted and documents exchanged. Some cases arrived as a result of a pre-trial conference, and some came just before trial. The more optimum timing for some cases may have improved the mediation outcome. The main criticism from counsel and mediators of the mandatory program is that many cases are referred too early. This often puts the parties and the mediators through hoops to adjourn or to extend the time for a mediation.

Quality of Mediators on Roster

In Toronto, approximately one-third of all applicants to the court roster are rejected. This does inspire some confidence that the placement process is not a rubber stamp, and that those who are placed on the roster have qualifications. However, parties and counsel should not assume that placement on the roster means that a given mediator will be adequate for a given case. Counsel should make informed decisions when selecting mediators.

Agreeing on a Mediator

Finally, especially in Toronto, counsel seem to have a fair bit of trouble agreeing on a mediator. For quite a few cases, a mediator must be assigned because counsel are unable to select one. The opposite is true in Ottawa. This may be because Ottawa has a smaller bar and has had more experience with a private mediator roster. Counsel are more familiar with the reputations of the mediators and can more readily choose. It is doubtful that it is because the cadre of mediators in Ottawa is better than that in Toronto.

There is an alarming trend in Toronto which finds lawyer-mediators beginning to decline to mediate mandatory cases because of the tariff rate, which prescribes a below-market fee for the first hour of preparation and for three hours of attendance ($150 in a two-party case — which is lower than the amount at which many Toronto articling students bill!). Because qualified lawyer-mediators are opting out, the pool from which to select good mediators in Toronto is reduced, perhaps making it more difficult to make an appropriate selection.

THE "SIGNED DECLARATION APPROACH"

As explained on the preceding pages, mediation tends to be more successful when the parties have more control over the process — such as when to mediate and what mediator to choose. When a mediation system starts to treat every case the same, some of the benefits of mediation are inevitably lost. An approach that has been considered but not yet tried is to make mediation mandatory; however it should be left to the parties to determine when and how to mediate. A rule of practice could be created that would require mediation as a prerequisite to setting a court date for a trial in the Superior Court of Ontario. The parties would be required to file a signed declaration by a mediator listed on an approved court roster that the parties had attempted to settle their dispute before that person at an ADR session.

This would allow the parties to select when to mediate and what type of ADR service to utilize. Parties could elect to have the session after discoveries, after a pre-trial conference or after pleadings. Counsel usually have a feel for when they are ready to mediate and their judgement should be trusted. There would be no tariff, parties could select who they wanted, and market forces would determine fees. Discounts and waivers would be available for parties in need.

While the new EMP has some defects, to quote again a Portuguese proverb "the worst is not always certain". It is hoped that either systemic changes will be made or practical solutions found so that Ontario can lead the way towards a modern and effective civil justice system.

PRIVATE MEDIATION — HIGHER SETTLEMENT RATE

Settlement rates in private mediation exceed those in state sanctioned/institutionalized mandatory programs. Although settlement rates in mandatory mediation regimes (such as those of the ADR Centre in Toronto or the Ottawa private mediation project) are very respectable — hovering at over 50 per cent, rates of settlement in a private context are always higher. Why is this so?

There are a number of factors. First, with private mediation, the cases are, to a large extent, self-selecting. The parties decide amongst themselves to try mediation and to pay for a mediator; therefore, they are already at least somewhat amenable to the process and to the concept of settlement. With mandatory regimes, many participating parties would not have chosen to attend, and settlement may not have been contemplated. The parties may not be enthusiastic about mediation.

On the other hand, this factor is tempered to the extent that cases in which private mediation is selected are often more substantively or emotionally difficult. That may be why the parties have elected for a mediation — all their bilateral negotiations, pre-trials and litigation processes have failed to produce anything conclusive.

The greater degree to which the parties are able to have control of the process with private mediation is also an important factor in its favour. The mediator does not have to rush the parties or the process, and the parties always select the mediator. At the Toronto ADR Centre, there was a strict three-hour time limit, which meant that the parties and counsel had to be either less expressive or not expressive at all. The ADR Centre evaluation revealed that parties and counsel were more satisfied with the process when they felt that the merits and issues had been discussed. This requires sufficient time — especially in multi-party cases. The mandatory time limits at the ADR Centre resulted in many adjournments, which, while useful for keeping the parties talking, may also have reduced the settlement momentum generated at the session.

In a private mediation, the parties always select the mediator. This may account for a greater mediation success rate in those cases that make it to mediation. All the evaluations conducted by the ADR Centre revealed that the single thing which parties liked best, or least, about their mediation, *was the mediator*. The mediator can make all the difference. If parties are able to select someone who they think will be competent enough to mediate *their* case, they will have more trust in that person, and that person's effectiveness will be enhanced.

Private mediation also provides for sufficient time for the mediator to read the parties' material — to "know the case" and to be able to prepare for what might transpire. At the ADR Centre, mediators were often given the file the morning of the mediation, and there was very little time to prepare. The mediators did their best but often went into the situation "cold". Private sessions provide the luxury of submitting material early so that the mediator can be well-versed with the facts and legal arguments in advance, saving considerable time and enabling the discussion to be directed to interest-canvassing more quickly.

Finally, people have a greater stake in things in which they have participated. By paying for a mediation, there is a built-in incentive to maximize the process. By selecting a mediator and scheduling the session (sometimes a task unto itself), the parties will have had some participation and, accordingly, a greater stake in the outcome.

Interestingly, one is left to speculate whether the greater participatory elements inherent in a private mediation (which account for the higher private settlement rate versus the EMP rate) in some way contribute to a greater will to settle. The topic of motivation has deliberately been left to the end of this book and will be dealt with in the conclusion, which follows.

Chapter 19

CONCLUSION

We live in an era in which many problems seem unsolvable and intractable. For example, as this book was being written, the Mid-East peace process went from a period of intense and hopeful negotiations mediated by the Unites States to a complete absence of negotiation, ongoing uprising and terrorism, and an absence of U.S. involvement. Positions have hardened, and the players have changed.

For years, the world scientific community has known about global warming caused by human activities. The 1997 Kyoto Protocol was entered into, and at the time of writing, Canada had not met its agreed upon carbon dioxide emissions reductions. Indeed, at a follow-up to that conference in Montreal, Canada was an obstacle to the implementation of the agreement. The United States, the world's largest single polluter, has not implemented the agreement either, and now it has an administration that has just concluded that it will not regulate carbon dioxide emissions at all![1]

The above two examples typify major problems that clearly pose a threat and require a solution, and over which there had been years of discussion, but about which little has changed and nothing has been accomplished.

The point here is that no matter how good the resolution process, no matter how much authority or leadership the players have, there must be the will, the motivation to solve the problem, the willingness to sometimes make uncomfortable sacrifices and to change one's behaviour. People must have the desire and the will to find and then implement the solution. History is full of examples of willpower overtaking all obstacles and producing results that only a short time earlier were thought impossible. Witness landing a man on the moon in less than eight years. Witness the mediations that do settle where no one thought a settlement possible.

Mediators can also recount cases where the settlement of a dispute was apparent, even glaringly obvious, but it did not happen because the parties did not want it to happen. This book has been about achieving a better process in order to realize resolutions, but it has not addressed the larger question of the motivation, or lack thereof, to solve problems.

That larger question is at the root of all conflict and of our inability to solve it and make a better world. Einstein said that the chief issue our society faces is that our technological progress "has outstripped our moral advancement".[2]

With better resolution techniques, we are half way there — but humanity's lack of will to solve its conflicts and dilemmas, at both the levels of the individual and

---

[1]   "World Report" *The Globe & Mail* (15 March 2001) H11.

[2]   Albert Einstein, *Out of My Later Years* (New York: Wings Books, 1956).

society, is the other half. Nevertheless, there is always hope — Pandora managed to close the box in time to keep hope alive.

> Our problems are manmade — therefore, they can be solved by man. And man can be as big as he wants. No problem of human destiny is beyond human beings. Man's reason and spirit have often solved the seemingly unsolvable — and we believe they can do it again. [3]

---

[3] J.F. Kennedy, commencement address (American University, Washington, D.C., 10 June 1963).

Appendix I

CHOOSING THE BEST ADR PROCESS FOR YOUR DISPUTE AND MAXIMIZING THE CHANCES OF SUCCESS AT THE MEDIATION

Paul M. Iacono, Q.C.[*]

As the process of Alternative Dispute Resolution evolves, it appears to be developing many hybrids and variations. What is happening is that creative counsel are redefining the process for each individual case to suit the purposes of that particular dispute. The choice of the dispute resolution mechanism will be premised upon the type of dispute involved, and sometimes upon the litigants themselves.

RIGHTS-BASED DISPUTES — LEGAL ISSUES

Certain kinds of disputes do not lend themselves to mediation. These disputes would be those involving disagreements over "rights". Disputes over titled property must be settled in a clear and unambiguous way. There is no grey area. Disputes where one party alleges that his or her constitutional or statutory rights have been denied cannot be mediated. A classic example would be guilt or innocence in a criminal case, or custody of children in a matrimonial matter. These types of disputes must be settled either by arbitration or by traditional judicial fact-finding. They must be based on evidence subject to the usual scrutiny and cannot simply be negotiated.

In arbitration, the more difficult decision that has to be made is whether or not the arbitration should be binding or subject to judicial review. Ultimately, the decision depends on the desire for finality.

---

[*] Paul M. Iacono, Q.C. is a partner of the Toronto law firm Iacono Brown and has practised insurance litigation since 1972. He is a mediator for YorkStreet Insurance Dispute Resolutions and Canadian Dispute Resolution Corporation. He is also a member of the Arbitration and Mediation Institute of Ontario.

GREY-AREA ISSUES

When thinking about the mediation process, one cannot help but be reminded of the words of Mr. Justice Edson Haines, who once stated that "a lawsuit is not a scientific search for the truth but merely the resolution of a dispute".[1] It is those grey-area issues, such as quantum of damages in a personal injury case or the value of certain assets or property, that best lend themselves to a mediation. These are areas where there is no clear right or wrong. It is a matter of working out a compromise that both parties can live with. In the area of motor vehicle litigation, perhaps the largest "grey area" is credibility. This latter aspect of any lawsuit can affect the ultimate result of both liability and damages and can create a very wide negotiating spectrum.

OTHER FORUMS

It is sometimes possible to combine both arbitration and mediation. This process can be used when certain findings of fact are necessary, perhaps on a side issue or on an issue such as liability in a car accident, and once those findings of fact are made and a decision on that part of the dispute given, the quantum of damages can be mediated in the traditional way.

Some disputes can best be solved by a combination of a pre-trial conference (neutral evaluation) followed by mediation, or mediation followed by a pre-trial conference where the mediation does not resolve all of the issues. The kinds of cases that would fit into this category are those where one or both of the parties require some individual, in whom both have confidence, to express an opinion on the likelihood of the disposition of the dispute if it were to be conducted by the court. In those types of situations where you are asking a third party to make findings of fact, some caution must be exercised. The person conducting the fact-finding process may become very involved and may have to sell a certain scenario to one of the litigants. It may sometimes be difficult for a "fact finder" to then become a mediator, so you may require two different people. It is absolutely essential for a mediator to be perceived as neutral. The *Arbitration Act, 1991* in Ontario,[2] in fact, has a section that does not allow an arbitrator to become a mediator once the arbitration has commenced.

Those using the mediation process today are sometimes resorting to binding mediation. That is, if a mediation proves to be unsuccessful, the person acting as mediator will make a decision the results of which will be implemented in the form of a judgment, which is final and not subject to appeal. This process obviously has certain risks, and you must be very sure of your case and of the person you choose to resolve it.

---

[1]   Historical interview with The Honourable Mr. Justice E.L. Haines, Supreme Court of Ontario, Osgoode Society (Archives Historical Interview Compendium, Osgoode Hall, Toronto, Ontario, 1987).

[2]   S.O. 1991, c. 17.

MEDIATION AS DISPUTE RESOLUTION —
THE STYLE OF THE MEDIATOR

One of the advantages of mediation is that the parties can select the individual whom they wish to use as a facilitator. Under these circumstances, it is very important to know the style of the mediator you have chosen. Some mediators will not deviate from the traditional role even if requested to do so. You should know this in advance. In a true mediation, the mediator is a facilitator who helps the parties arrive at a mutually acceptable settlement and does not express opinions about any of the issues. However, this is not always the case.

Sometimes, going into a mediation, you will be aware that your opponent is taking a position that cannot be substantiated in law. In that type of situation, you will want the facilitator at some stage to be able to make a statement to the other side, pointing out the deficiencies of its position. There are certain mediators who will conduct a mediation on that basis. It is important that you know who they are. They will do this automatically — they will not have to be asked. It is simply their *"modus operandi"*.

Another important ingredient in the style of the mediation is the persistence of the mediator. Certain mediators will simply not conclude the mediation until a settlement has been achieved, regardless of how long it takes or how difficult it is to keep the parties talking. Other mediators will conclude the mediation when significant resistance is met. Once again, this is an aspect of the mediation style, and it is important for you to know the style of the mediator you have selected. Another factor that should be considered is your own style of negotiating in the sense that if you perceive yourself to be an aggressive negotiator, you may want a mediator who is aggressive, or *vice versa*.

The importance of selecting the best person for resolving the dispute can be illustrated by the simple statement that, as lawyers, we have all wished that we could pick the trial judge we wanted for each and every case. In the alternate dispute resolution process, you have that luxury available to you. It is important that you take full advantage of it. Ordinarily, when you are preparing a case for trial, you attempt to ascertain as much information as possible about the judge who will be hearing the case; the same applies to the ADR process. This information is essential, and it is available simply by speaking to other colleagues, just as you would discuss the known preferences of a prospective trial judge.

THE DYNAMICS OF THE PROCESS

The Alternate Dispute Resolution process can easily be described as a "catharsis". This means that it is very important for the disputants to have an opportunity to tell their story. In many personal injury situations, particularly those involving alleged psychological problems, this can be extremely important. Of course, this will affect the choice of the mediator. In this type of mediation, it is more important to have as a facilitator someone who will be able to establish empathy with the plaintiff and will assist in eliciting the victim's story in such a way that all of the issues will come out and be addressed. Some mediators are

better at this than others. In some cases it is this listening process which is the
key to the resolution; financial issues are really secondary. That is another reason why you should promote dialogue between the litigants during the ADR
process — it facilitates the "catharsis". A striking example of this would be a
situation that has sometimes occurred in medical malpractice litigation. A simple apology properly phrased by the doctor has been the single most important
factor in resolving the case.

With careful planning and preparation, and by thinking about how the mediation will evolve, you will be able to ensure that the "catharsis" will take place
sooner rather than later. Once that takes place, it is more than likely the parties
will resolve the dispute.

The most important aspect of mediation is that the parties themselves control
the ebb and flow of what happens. It is the parties themselves that ultimately
have control over the resolution of the dispute. This is why the parties' participation is so important. As part of counsel's preparation for the mediation, it is
almost certainly very good practice to have the victim and/or the insurance representative prepared to say a few words. The statements that are made by the
parties themselves — that is, the "decision makers" — tend to have more impact
on the other side than any comments made by counsel. The reality is that everyone in the room knows that the lawyers are paid to make arguments, but the
comments from the "civilians" usually come from the heart.

ADVOCACY STYLES AT MEDIATION

Even though ADR and, in particular, the mediation process are designed to facilitate a settlement, counsel who represent clients in the ADR process are still
advocates. It is just a different kind of advocacy. It is still persuasion, although
of a different kind — it is persuasion, directed to the litigants themselves. Your
advocacy plan, therefore, must be tailored to the audience that will receive it.

Perhaps the most important part of the mediation from an advocacy stand-
point is the opening statement. These statements should last no more than 20
minutes. If you are a defendant, you should, in some way, attempt to demonstrate empathy towards the plaintiff. Counsel for the plaintiff, on the other hand,
will be attempting to persuade the insurance representative in a personal injury
case as to just how serious his or her client's injuries are and how dramatically
the client's life has been altered. Therefore, make sure that in your opening
statement you highlight all of the issues that are in dispute, and give cogent logical reasons why they should be resolved in your favour.

Sometimes personalities play a key role in the success of a mediation. In a
case where credibility issues are significant, you may need to decide in advance
whether counsel or the client will produce the iron fist. In these kinds of disputes, this is extremely appropriate. If the insurer is taking the position that the
claim is specious, that message must be delivered. It must be supported by ad-
missible logical evidence, not by suspicion. An important part of your preparation will be to determine who will deliver that message. If it is done by the
lawyer, the client still has some room to develop empathy with the plaintiff. The

worst thing a defendant can do at a mediation is make unfounded allegations against a plaintiff.

A great deal of consideration must be given to the nature of your presentation and to the timing of when to produce certain evidence. A defendant intending to produce surveillance, for example, should do so at a moment when the plaintiff makes a statement which can be easily contradicted by that evidence. This makes a plaintiff vulnerable and more amenable to accepting a conservative settlement.

Remember that in considering your selection of mediator, you should take negotiating styles into consideration and select a mediator who suits your own style of negotiating. The ADR process is full of surprises; thus, during the course of the mediation, you may have to adjust your mediating style to deal with the ebb and flow of the process as it occurs. Some of these things cannot be thought out in advance because you cannot anticipate every possibility. Nevertheless, as part of your preparation, you should try to anticipate at least some of the possible surprises that may occur.

EFFECTIVE STRATEGIES

As mentioned above, what takes place at a mediation cannot be predicted. Therefore, it is very important to encourage your client representative to speak up whenever he or she has a thought appropriate to the proceedings. In the pre-mediation preparation session, these proceedings are entirely "without prejudice", and there is nothing your client can do or say to hurt the case. From a defence point of view, a few key words made by the insurer's representative at the right time may be crucial in bringing about the resolution of a case.

For example, in one case during a mediation, there were extensive caucuses between the mediator and counsel as well as the clients. The mediator chose this strategy because there were some very sensitive issues that either one of the parties might have taken personally. The end result was that the parties were left alone together in the main meeting room, and during counsel's long absences, the insurance company's representative — quite a gregarious outgoing sort — became quite friendly with the plaintiff. The insurer's representative consequently established lines of communication with the plaintiff that were ultimately instrumental in resolving the case.

Another example that is worth mentioning is that on some difficult mediations, particularly those involving multi-parties, the mediator, probably as a result of frustration due to the group's impasse on many different issues, will try to caucus different combinations of people together. In one case, a situation arose where each of the lawyers for two defendants and the plaintiff's lawyer came to a resolution of the matter that everyone seemed prepared to live with. Unfortunately, the plaintiff's counsel could not obtain instructions from his client. At this point, the mediator tried various methods of combinations: a group session; a private caucus with the plaintiff, plaintiff's counsel and the plaintiff; and a caucus with the mediator, plaintiff and defence counsel. Ultimately, it was a caucus with the plaintiff and the insurer's representatives that brought about a resolution of the case. The conclusion to be drawn from this is that you should not give up at a mediation; when different combinations of caucusing do not work, keep trying others.

Sometimes you will encounter a situation where the chemistry between either the parties or their lawyers is very charged with emotion. When this occurs, if at all possible, warn the mediator privately in advance of the session. In these kinds of situations, while it is important that the parties listen carefully to opening positions, it may be necessary for the mediator to keep the parties in caucus for much of the time while the mediator "shuttles" back and forth, bringing the parties together as they gradually reach consensus, and, finally, of course, when resolution is achieved. This method should eliminate emotional confrontations that could derail the mediation.

Whether or not the trial lawyer needs to attend the mediation depends on the particular case. There is a place for hard-nosed litigators in ADR as well as in litigation. They will, however, have to wear a different hat. Hard-nosed litigators must learn that mediation is the antithesis of the adversary system. Mediation is about compromise, and it is a process by which opponents in a lawsuit explore mutually acceptable creative solutions to resolve their dispute. In the mediation process, the parties explore each other's strengths and weaknesses, and assess the risks of proceeding. At a mediation, the parties make the decision to solve their own lawsuit, as opposed to having a court make that determination for them. The trial lawyer, on the other hand, is programmed to fight to the death. This latter type of individual should not be turned loose in a mediation setting unless accompanied by a capable facilitator who has control over the process. As a matter of fact, as part of the mediation process which requires the exploration of the strengths and weaknesses of the opposing parties, having the "bad cop" at the mediation table can prove to be an interesting stratagem. It brings to mind the old adage that "in order to make peace you must be able to wage war". If the trial lawyer does too much posturing, and the mediator fails to cut it off, there is little likelihood of achieving resolution.

CONCLUSION

As always, the facts of the case and the personalities of the key protagonists will determine how you should tailor the process to each particular situation, keeping in mind that all of the foregoing factors have to be considered. The desired result, after all, is to resolve the dispute and there are many routes you can take to achieve the goal.

Appendix II

OF PROMISE AND DESPAIR: TRANSFORMATION IN LAW AND MEDIATION

Gary M. Caplan[*]

INTRODUCTION

> ... disputes can be viewed not as problems at all, but as opportunity for moral growth and transformation ... This different view is the transformative orientation of conflict.[1]

And, with that apostolic nostrum, Bush and Folger proclaim mediation's potential to change people who find themselves in the midst of conflict. The basic tenet of Bush and Folger's manifesto is that the employment of mediator techniques which engender empowerment and recognition can transform disputants to "a higher vision of self and society, one based on moral development and interpersonal relations rather than on satisfaction and individual autonomy".[2] They suggest that mediation can elevate parties to a dispute to some higher plane of moral consciousness and can create the basis of a paradigm shift from individualism to some form of relationalism. The social implications for mediation are wide-ranging, they say, and they can take us beyond the individualistic ethics of modern western culture and give us a new synthesis of individual freedom and social conscience in a revised social order.

The messianic vision of transformative mediation contemplated by Bush and Folger sees the individual or self as the primary engine for change. Although Bush and Folger acknowledge that moral development will likely lead to changes in social institutions, the essence of transformation is a refinement of the consciousness and character of human beings. Individuals will, in turn, impact social structures and thereby change society.[3]

---

[*] Gary M. Caplan is a commercial litigator and ADR practitioner with the Toronto law firm Weir-Foulds LLP. He has lectured and taught ADR at Osgoode Hall Law School and to professional groups.

[1] R.A.B. Bush and J.P. Folger, *The Promise of Mediation: Responding to Conflict Through Empowerment and Recognition* (San Francisco: Jossey-Bass, 1994) at 81.

[2] *Ibid.* at 3.

[3] *Ibid.* For comment, see C. Menkel-Meadow, "The Many Ways of Mediation: The Transformation of Traditions, Ideologies, Paradigms and Practices" (1995) 11 Negotiation J. 217, and N. Milner, "Mediation and Political Theory: A Critique of Bush and Folger" (1996) 21 L. & Soc. Inquiry 737.

The transformative process, according to Bush, takes place in two ways.[4] First, empowerment can encourage individuals to better appreciate the cause and dimensions of their problems, and recognition will encourage them to identify the larger issues facing them, which will, in turn, precipitate the formation of coalitions which can better lobby and bargain for social change.

Second, the recognition process will encourage parties to a dispute to develop a more positive view of other disputants, and this will infect other members in the social network. Eventually, this will result in a reciprocal multiplier effect on both the personal and group levels, yielding a greater receptivity and tolerance for diversity.

To suggest that concepts such as empowerment and recognition can induce both individual and social transformation appears jejune. Is the enhancement of moral development necessarily the consequence of empowerment? Are the powerful and recognized necessarily more morally developed? If the powerful and morally conscious derive their power and consciousness from what others may see as exploitive and hegemonic practices, can it be said that they are morally or ethically more developed than those they exploit?

Moreover, to view transformation as a "bottom up" process, which, in turn, would affect social structures and institutions, runs contrary to one of the major themes of twentieth century legal and philosophic critique. Institutions and bureaucratic processes have long been viewed as tools of domination and exploitation, and it would appear counter-intuitive to suggest that moral growth can take place in isolation of fundamental institutional restructuring.

Finally, the conception of transformative mediation proffered by Bush and Folger is curiously detached from notions of social justice. In describing their various "stories" of mediation, they distinguish the Transformation Story from the Justice Story.[5] To separate social justice from transformation, at least for analytic purposes, seems artificial and, indeed, dangerous. Transformation without a concomitant adherence to social justice would appear to be regressive and empty of promise.

Of course, mediation is not the only enterprise concerned with transformation in the context of conflict. Law, politics and philosophy each offer their own promise of transformation to effect human betterment, and they each carry within them their own constraints and limitations in achieving it. To better appreciate the promise of transformation in mediation, it is helpful to examine, compare and contrast these other conceptions of transformation and determine whether they can illuminate better our understanding of individual and social change in mediation.

This article seeks to explore the transformative potential of mediation and compare it to law. It presupposes that mediation is more than a value neutral process and that it can have social and political implications that transcend mere

---

[4] R.A.B. Bush, "The Unexplored Possibilities of Community Mediation: A Comment on Merry and Milner" (1996) 21 L. & Soc. Inquiry 715.

[5] R.A.B. Bush and J.P. Folger, *The Promise of Mediation: Responding to Conflict Through Empowerment and Recognition* (San Francisco: Jossey-Bass, 1994) at 18-21.

problem-solving.[6] Although there exists a rich literature with respect to the nature and contours of disputing, conflict resolution and mediation techniques, this literature is not the central focus of this article. Instead, the transformative potential of mediation in regard to a synthesis of notions of the self and theories of law and social change is examined.

LAW AND MEDIATION AS TRANSFORMATIVE LANGUAGE

Conversation is a game of circles.[7]

Charles Fried has written that law should be viewed as something of which we only catch a glimpse as it rushes past us. Legal scholarship, he suggests, should be engaged in devising not so much theories of law, but rather theories of legal change.[8] How and why law and legal analysis change, and how and why this transforms the "speaker" and "listener" lies at the heart of what law is all about.

We might say the same of mediation, lying in law's shadow, as some say it does.[9] Mediation can and should be seen as a transformative and transforming agent for those individuals who participate in it.

***

Let us first examine "law". To be sure, theories of law and legal analysis have undergone significant change over time. Our views of what law is and what it should be have been transformed and continue to do so.

Contemporary liberal legal theory is centred on the notion of a "rule of law". Individuals seeking to maximize their self-interest and maximizing the "good" must be granted conditions which encourage or, at least, do not hinder that pursuit. Hence, individuals are armed with rights and are granted these entitlements to protect them from state interference and the promotion of the invasive self-interest of others. Also, under liberal notions of law, rules are seen as emancipating rather than constraining, and legal theories seek to determine how these emancipatory rules can be found or discovered.

As well, the classical juridical model which informs our current legal culture is premised on the notion that power is centred in the state. This arises because, although power was a natural right held by individuals, individuals ceded or delegated that power to central authority in order to create the modern nation

---

[6] This article does not attempt to distinguish the various models of mediation (facilitative, evaluative, community, bureaucratic, *etc.*) and contrast their "transformative" potential. See the discussion in C. Menkel-Meadow, "The Many Ways of Mediation: The Transformation of Traditions, Ideologies, Paradigms and Practices" (1995) 11 Negotiation J. 217 at 219.

[7] Ralph Waldo Emerson, "Circles" in B. Atkinson, ed., *Complete Essays and Other Writings* (New York: Modern Library, 1940) at 284.

[8] C. Fried, "The Laws of Change: The Cunning of Reason in Moral and Legal History" (1980) 9 J. of Leg. Studies 335.

[9] R. Mnookin and L. Kornhauser, "Bargaining in the Shadow of the Law" (1979) 88 Yale L.J. 950.

state. This social contract model has thus given rise to our current notion that the source of oppressive power is the state, and only the rule of law can patrol the precarious borderline between state interference and individual autonomy.[10]

Moreover, the state must remain neutral in its treatment of citizens. It must treat individuals equally and with equal respect because to do otherwise would be to impose a conception of the good and thereby trespass upon the sanctity of individual autonomy. Hence, equality means legal neutrality, for it compromises the tension between majoritarianism and individual rights.

This classical juridical paradigm is reflected in the caselaw. In *R. v. Morgentaler*, the Supreme Court of Canada, per Wilson J., said the following:[11]

> The Charter is predicated on a particular conception of the place of the individual in society. An individual is not a totally independent entity disconnected from the society in which he or she lives. Neither, however, is the individual a mere cog in an impersonal machine in which his or her values, goals and aspirations are subordinated to those of the collectivity. The individual is a bit of both. The Charter reflects this reality by leaving a wide range of activities and decisions open to legitimate government control while at the same time placing limits on the proper scope of that control. Thus, the rights guaranteed in the Charter erect around each individual, metaphorically speaking, an invisible fence over which the state will not be allowed to trespass. The role of the courts is to map out, piece by piece, the parameters of the fence.

But how are legal rules found and legitimated? How are we to know which rules are right and which are wrong?

Legal formalism, or "legal science", which was popular in the last century, saw law as a matrix of rules arising from cases and statutes.[12] The formalist project was to "discover" these principles and rules in caselaw as well as statutes and, hence, there arose the notion that there was no need to resort to social context, or to social, moral or political values. The correct result, the formalists argued, was arrived at in each case when the decision-maker or judge reasoned logically and applied the "discovered" rule dispassionately. Leane notes the following:

> This legal formalism is self defining and self referential — substantive justice is not considered in contradiction to it because there is no contradiction. One follows from the other. The mechanical application of the rules is presumed to produce an optimally "just" outcome, and substantive justice is not so much assumed as not considered, in that one does not look beyond the rules to the consequences of their application ... The judicial gaze is (in theory) averted from social context and consequences, and from moral, political and ideological values.[13]

---

10   D. Litowitz, "Foucault on Law: Modernity as a Negative Utopia" (1995) 21 Queen's L.J. 1 at 18.

11   (1988), 44 D.L.R. (4th) 385 at 485 (S.C.C.).

12   G.W.G. Leane, "Testing Some Theories About Law: Can We Find Substantive Justice Within Law's Rule?" (1994) 19 Melb. U.L. Rev. 924. See also S.M. Feldman, "Diagnosing Power: Postmodernism in Legal Scholarship and Judicial Practice (With an Emphasis on the Teague Rule Against New Rules in Habeas Corpus Cases)" (1994) 88 NW. U.L. Rev. 1046 at 1081.

13   G.W.G. Leane, "Testing Some Theories About Law: Can We Find Substantive Justice Within Law's Rule?" (1994) 19 Melb. U.L. Rev. 924 at 928.

Hence, even today we have echoes of formalistic thinking. In the interpretation of statutes or private contracts, the courts will apply "interpretative rules" and will seek to find, for example, the "plain" or literal meaning. In trying to "discover" what the draftsman or the legislature may have intended, the courts will use a number of interpretative techniques, all of which are intended to achieve an interpretation which is the result of the application of interpretative "rules".[14] For the formalist, therefore, the act of interpretation, be it a statute, caselaw, or contract, is limited to the act of understanding the text, precedent or case, searching out mechanically some interpretative rule or device or precedent, and applying it to the text or issue at hand, thereby achieving the "right" result.

Formalism in time gave way to legal realism, which challenged the notion that the determination and application of a choice of rules was unconnected to moral, ethical or political values.[15] Legal realists acknowledged that rules were, indeed, indeterminate and capable of varying and conflicting interpretations. Realists sought to tie the choice of rules to the social effect of their application. For the realist, law was consequentialist and should be made to operate within the social, economic and political setting in which the rule was applied. The judge's role, therefore, was not to "discover" the rule or law in existing precedents or statutes, but rather to *choose* the appropriate rule from a constellation of competing and contradictory rules. The appropriate choice was that which not only responded to the case at hand, but also conformed to some policy or some perceived social outcome.

Yet, although law was now seen as attached to some rationalism tied to social purpose, the realists failed to define how to choose among competing rules. Although there was certainly an ostensible move away from dogma toward a relativism based on social need, the reality of choice of rules remained. Despite stripping away the formalist claim to consistency and predictability, the realists could offer nothing by way of organizing or by way of analytic principles, which could provide the appropriate guide to the choice of rules.

Idealists attempted to find some meta-theory of law and society that could provide law with guidelines for choosing between competing rules.[16] For example, some theorists looked at political and community morality as providing that neutral background which could inform legal decision-making. But, how were the courts to discover or perceive that political and communitarian morality? There was always the risk that in making a choice among competing rules, law would simply reinforce the will of the majority to the detriment of minority interests. Other theorists suggested that the courts were granted the institutional power to discover and expose the deeper background tied to communal morality, and, given this institutional licence, only the courts could trump legislative and political action. Politics was seen as the product of the moment or the whim of the executive; law, on the other hand, could serve to correct the community's

---

[14] See the discussion in P. Perell, "Plain Meaning for Judges, Scholars and Practitioners" (1998) 20 Advocates' Q. 24, and T.A.O. Endicott, "Linguistic Indeterminacy" (1996) 16 Oxford J. of Legal Studies 667.

[15] G.W.G. Leane, "Testing Some Theories About Law: Can We Find Substantive Justice Within Law's Rule?" (1994) 19 Melb. U.L. Rev. 924 at 929.

[16] *Ibid.*

imperfect understanding of its own morality and reset, as it were, the communitarian mechanism which served to inform the social good.[17]

In the end, however, one is left with perhaps the unanswerable: what is this morality, and where is it to be found? Is there not a risk that morality may, in the end, be simply a function of majority rule? And, perhaps, most fundamentally, how are we to find those transcendental principles of right which can serve to trump the passion of the moment? In the final analysis, is it not a matter of the privileged and the powerful exerting their notions of morality over the weak and dispossessed?

Critical legal theorists answered these questions by arguing that in the end, that which informs law and legal decision-making is, in fact, the ideology of the powerful. Law is the instrumental tool of those who exert power, and the game is to legitimate the current social structure which serves, of course, to promote the domination of certain groups over others. Law is not the search for interpretative truth and is certainly not the search for some basis of a deeper realism which can transcend and guide the moment.

> ... Critical legal theorists would say that it is the morality of the dominant class, the class of property, wealth and power who people the legislature, the Courts, the legal profession and the business sector. In that case, it is no morality at all other than a legitimating one which conceals unjust inequality and hierarchy. Without some reasonable approximation of distributive justice, going to the distribution of goods, wealth, and life opportunities generally in society, we cannot realistically aspire to corrective justice, which aspires to correcting the vagaries of legal rules applied to hard cases.[18]

Hence, for at least some critical legal theorists, law cannot be seen as a means of social and distributive justice. Instead, law is an insidious tool which blinds the exploited and the weak to the ways of liberation and emancipatory thought.

To be sure, whatever we perceive the purpose of law to be, we want law to be seen, at least, as rational, that is, logically connected in some way to perceived reality and to our experience. Moreover, we do not want law to be arbitrary or to be the function of the whim of the decision-maker, be it the executive, judge or bureaucrat. [19]

In addition to rationality, we demand that law be coherent and understandable, and this, it is argued, permits us to predict social outcomes. We are led to believe that law can give us ordering principles which can in turn inform social order and guide us to the correct action. Hence, we demand that law's rules be internally consistent and predictable.

---

[17]   *Ibid.* See also, E.L. Rubin, "The New Legal Process, The Synthesis of Discourse and the Micro-analysis of Institutions" (1996) 109 Harv. L. Rev. 1393.

[18]   G.W.G. Leane, "Testing Some Theories About Law: Can We Find Substantive Justice Within Law's Rule?" (1994) 19 Melb. U.L. Rev. 924 at 937. See also William H. Simon, "Legal Informality and Redistributive Politics" (1985-86) 19 Clearinghouse Rev. 348, and for the application of critical theory to legal education see P. Goldfarb, "Beyond Cut Flowers: Developing a Clinical Perspective on Critical Legal Theory" (April 1992) 43 Hastings L.J. 717.

[19]   See the discussion in G.W.G. Leane, "Testing Some Theories About Law: Can We Find Substantive Justice Within Law's Rule?" (1994) 19 Melb. U.L. Rev. 924 at 930.

We also expect law's rules to be *applied* consistently; hence, we strive to develop procedural and substantive rules which in the end can be no better than the rough generalizations which capture the rationality, coherence and social ordering we want.[20]

On the other hand, law's rules cannot be too rigid or inflexible. We do not want rules to be applied mechanically without regard to their social context. Just as equity grew to soften the harshness of the inflexible application of common law, we expect law to tailor its rules to our intrinsic notions of fairness.

Caught in this dilemma between formalism and substantive justice, between the need to develop universal, internally consistent and rational rules and to apply them to varying and different specific contexts, law has developed as a binary system of countervailing rules and analysis.[21] Hence, the doctrine of unequal bargaining power or duress balances rules of contract formation; individual rights granted or protected by the Charter are to be determined against the State's interests; rules of foreseeability and remoteness offset duty and responsibility in the law of tort.

At once, we can see that this binary system espoused by law is unstable. Countervailing rules permit both construction and deconstruction of rules at the same time. Because law's binary system and focus on rights protects the illusion of choice and promotes the myth of autonomy, law in many ways promotes or aids and abets a social structure characterized by unequal distribution of opportunities and resources.

Law's only response to this inequality is to extend rights and to widen the canopy of juridical persons and juridical entitlements. Hence, law creates categories of "legal persons", be they human or social constructions, and chooses to grant them the right to speak.[22] Hence, a corporation, a legal fiction, is granted the right to "commercial speech"; however, a fetus may be considered not to be a human being and, therefore, may have no right to a voice in juridical discourse.

Moreover, law creates classifications of demands.[23] Some of these demands will be classified as rights and will, therefore, be treated with the protection afforded by law. Other demands will not be seen as rights, notwithstanding the importance or value of that demand.

Law not only creates classifications of demands, but ranks them when such rights come into conflict with each other. For example, in constitutional law,

---

[20] For the most part, we require that when rules are applied, reasons for their application should be elucidated. On the requirement for judicial reasons, see R.J. Allen and G.T.G. Seniuk, "Two Puzzles of Juridical Proof" (1997) 76 Can. Bar Rev. 65. See also the discussion of rights as reason-dependent demands in A. Harel, "What Demands are Rights? An Investigation into the Relation Between Rights and Reasons" (1997) 17 Oxford J. of Legal Studies 101; and see also B. Chapman, "More Easily Done than Said: Rules, Reasons and Rational Social Choice" (1998) 18 Oxford J. of Legal Studies 293 at 294.

[21] R.M. Unger, "Legal Analysis as Institutional Imagination" (1996) 59 Mod. L. Rev. 1.

[22] For a review of the ideas of Jacques Derrida concerning the relationship between deconstruction and justice, see J.M. Balkin, "Transcendental Deconstruction, Transcendent Justice" (1994) 92 Mich. L. Rev. 1132 at 1142.

[23] A. Harel, "What Demands are Right? An Investigation into the Relation Between Rights and Reasons" (1997) 17 Oxford J. of Legal Studies 101.

political speech may be more valuable than commercial speech. Hence, the interests of the state will sometimes override or trump the rights of an individual. The hierarchy of rights and the constant friction that is generated each time such rights come into conflict produce a never-ending cycle of categorization and hierarchy. Law's obsession with classification (which is the subject of justice, and whose demands are juridical) serves to create conflict, and so, non-rights holders press for recognition as subjects of justice, and rights holders seek juridical recognition for their demands. And, to mediate these conflicts, law must in turn create further classifications and nuances of difference. Law thus creates a cascade of communities and demand, all of which shift and change in time. Hence, the extension of rights can only serve to in turn create and exacerbate conflict. Giving legal voice and recognition to "communities" ironically serves to bring them into juridical conflict, and law must then develop methods of mediating and containing the very conflict created by rights. Law mediates these conflicts by arranging rights in hierarchies, permitting some rights to trump others (*e.g.*, political speech is of a higher priority than commercial speech). Law creates categories of juridical persons and may or may not grant them preferential treatment.[24] Again, all of this serves to promote conflict rather than dissipate it; the juridical self is caught up in a stylized web of conflict created by law which simultaneously purports to mediate and manage it.

And so, we see law as containing both promise and despair. Law purports to be the product of the balancing of competing or conflicting pluralisms, as well as the embodiment of the good and the right. By focusing on rights, law and legal analysis rarely challenge institutions and the modes of social and economic distribution that they promote. Power is perceived as state-derived, and rights are seen as the product of a social contract designed to protect individuals from the manifestation of state power. Law celebrates a vocabulary which pretends to neutrality, rationality, coherence and substantive justice, but ultimately, law cannot or will not transform the unequal distribution of social and economic goods, or challenge our institutional arrangements.

Postmodernism suggests a different orientation and asks us to conceive of law as a "language", that is, as a reified force which attempts to connect experience with reality.[25] In the postmodern eye, law, as a form of language is, like all language, incapable of fixed or stable meaning. Each time we speak or read a text, we are already interpreting it, and our interpretations are in themselves constantly transforming. If we accept the postmodern assumption that the self is created and recreated by discourse, and if we come to look upon law as a vocabulary or language, we can develop the notion that the self is transformed or can be transformed through the act of interpretation that is the law.

---

[24] D. Kropp, "'Categorical' Failure: Canada's Equality Jurisprudence — Changing Notions of Identity and the Legal Subject" (1997) 23 Queen's L.J. 201. See also G. Rose, *Mourning Becomes the Law: Philosophy and Representation* (Cambridge, Mass.: University of Cambridge Press, 1996) at 4-7.

[25] See S.M. Feldman, "The New Metaphysics: The Interpretive Turn in Jurisprudence" (1991) 76 Iowa L. Rev. 661; J.M. Balkin, "Transcendental Deconstruction, Transcendent Justice" (1994) 92 Mich. L. Rev. 1132; D. Patterson, "The Poverty of Interpretive Universalism: Toward the Reconstruction of Legal Theory" (1993) 72 Tex. L. Rev. 1.

For postmodern theory, there are no foundational principles or meanings.[26] Experience and understanding are interpretative acts, and there can be no source of meaning standing outside the text. The essence of the dialectic of understanding is not the interplay between the subject and the object. Rather, the individual comes to develop an understanding of the text out of his or her own prejudices and interests. The individual, in the postmodern conception, lives in an interpretative community which is itself a matrix of cultural practices. It is from this very community that we as individuals come to shape and form our understanding of the world around us. Hence, the text, the rule, the communication, is not an object in some foundational sense, as the formalists would argue; indeed, there are no interpretative rules which can be mechanically applied to permit us to understand the link between experience and reality. Instead, the text reveals new meaning and new insights each time we read, analyze, interpret, question and rethink it.

The self is an historical and contingent construction. It follows that the self is in a constant state of reconstruction and transformation. For postmodernism, this reconstructive process takes place through "discourse", that is each time we think, speak or act:

> First, post-moderns argue that knowledge is not acquired through the abstraction of an autonomous subject from a separate object but, rather, that knowledge, along with subjects and objects, is constituted collectively through forms of discourse. Second, they challenge the notion that there is only one, true method by which knowledge is acquired. Instead, they define knowledge as plural and heterogeneous; there are "truths" not Truth.[27]

Hence, for postmodernists, there are no foundational principles, no pretense to any "true" knowledge of reality because in the end, all knowledge is belief. It follows, then, that when we engage in discourse, creating and recreating ourselves, our language cannot correspond to any transcendental sense of reality because our language and the ways of thinking behind it are simply the product of our culture and social situation.[28]

Because ethical and moral action cannot be founded on any sense of reason, or on any conception of the good, such action must be the product of some spontaneous response to the uniqueness of the moment and our place relative to

---

[26] See the discussion in F. Ankersmit, "Experience, Transcendentalism and the Limits of Interpretation" (1997), online: Rice University <http://www.ruf.rice.edu/-culture/papers/Ankersmit. html>, and S.M. Feldman, "The Politics of Postmodern Jurisprudence" (1996) 95 Mich. L. Rev. 66 at 173-84.

[27] S.J. Hekman, *Gender and Knowledge: Elements of a Postmodern Feminism* (Cambridge: Polity Press, 1990) at 63, quoted in D. Kropp, "'Categorical' Failure: Canada's Equality Jurisprudence — Changing Notions of Identity and the Legal Subject" (1997) 23 Queen's L.J. 201 at 210. See also the discussion and definitions of postmodernism in S.M. Feldman, "Diagnosing Power: Postmodernism in Legal Scholarship and Judicial Practice (with an Emphasis on the Teague Rule Against New Rules in Habeas Corpus Cases)" (1994) 88 Northwestern U.L. Rev. 1045.

[28] S.M. Feldman, "The Politics of Postmodern Jurisprudence" (1996) 95 Mich. Law Rev. 166. See also A. Hunt, "The Big Fear: Law Confronts Postmodernism" (1990) 35 McGill L.J. 507. See also A. Heller, "The Contingent Person and the Existential Choice" in *Hermeneutics and Critical Theory in Ethics and Politics*, M. Kelly, ed. (Cambridge: MIT Press, 1991) at 53.

others. It is this relationship with the "Other" that gives rise to a discourse which may determine ethical action.

> ... the Other is not my alter ego. The Other and I are singular, unique and incommensurable human beings. The Other deserves respect for what (s)he is, and not because we are equal partners in a common human nature ... Consequently, the Other cannot be subsumed under a unifying category of the mind or of legal language.[29]

For postmodernism, the relative position of the Other is what drives us to notions of what is just, and there is no need to resort to the search for universal principles of morality or ethics. For postmodern thinkers, the quest for universal and transcendental principles of justice should be abandoned in favour of a search for localized cultural practice.

For postmodernism, the interpretative act is not the result of mere caprice, whim or subjectivity.[30] Nor is the interpretive process unconstrained and free roaming. The reader, or the interpreter, is embedded in the interpretative community and can only read, understand and interpret the text based on a practice or tradition which reflects the prejudices and interests of that community. In this way, these practices or traditions both constrain and enable our understanding of our world. Our interpretative community, as well as our prejudices and interests, forms the horizon which feeds our sense of understanding.

With the foregoing in mind, we come to understand how law can be conceived of as a language or vocabulary which both constrains and creates our understanding. Although legal rules spring from our communal prejudices and interests, the very act of "interpreting" and applying rules means that we are, in effect, creating and recreating our practice of legal rule use. As previously noted, legal rules are not stable, nor are they founded upon any universal principle; rather, they reflect our contemporary conditions and interests. Hence, precedents can come to no longer be seen as old rules, and contemporary caselaw should not be seen as new rules. In effect, legal rules simply reflect our communal traditions. Hence, we should dispense with any pretense of objectivity, neutral values and devices such as plain meanings.

But the language of the law adheres stubbornly to a vocabulary which must speak in objective, neutral, rational and objective terms. Law must be pronounced in both general terms, so as to have wide applications, and in specific terms, so as to do justice to the parties in adjudication. Thus, law speaks in a manner that ignores the uniqueness of the individuals involved or of the conflict in which they are involved.[31] Law then becomes an imperfect representation of the actors and of their dispute. Speaking as it does in the third person, law, therefore, fails to communicate the richness of the human experience and the tragedy that feeds it.

---

[29] C.M. Stamatis, "Justice Without Law: A Postmodernist Paradox" (1994) 5 Law and Critique 265 at 266.

[30] S.M. Feldman, "The Politics of Postmodern Jurisprudence" (1996) 95 Mich. L. Rev. 66 at 180.

[31] See the discussion in J.M. Balkin, "Transcendental Deconstruction, Transcendent Justice" (1994) 92 Mich. L. Rev. 1132 at 1158.

And so, law simultaneously creates and alienates the self. Law speaks a language of a symbolic order which can only be an imperfect representation of shared experience. By expressing itself in the third person as well as in a voice of neutral general rules, law depreciates the uniqueness of the Other. The self is locked in a gap, in a form of suspended animation, floating somewhere between perceived reality and experience and the language of law. Law seems to offer us the promise of voice and entitlement, but ultimately, we are trapped in a web of ever-widening and deepening conflict. Transformation is, therefore, an arrested process for both the self and the social institutions and arrangements that give rise to communal experience.

The postmodern response to this critique is varied. Balkin argues that justice can be deconstructed in a way that shows that our yearning for a better and more perfect justice is a value that transcends all human culture.[32] The source of this yearning, he suggests, is not culture or its manifestations, but rather the "well springs of the human soul".[33] For Balkin, this yearning for justice comes before culture, and it is culture which serves to articulate and express the way we put justice into practice. Balkin argues that there is a gap between our infinite demand for justice and the cultural and social institutions that we create to deliver and administer justice because such institutions can only deliver an imperfect form of justice. Culture is the vehicle which turns our inchoate sense of justice into concrete and articulated forms. Because there may be different ways of constructing institutions, cultural constructions which seek to articulate our urge for justice can never be perfect. Hence, we live in a constant state of deconstruction and reconstruction (or what Balkin calls rectification) of our cultural manifestations of our search for justice.

Feldman criticizes Balkin's premise that the individual's yearning for justice has priority over culture.[34] Moreover, Feldman disagrees with Balkin's view that justice is a human value that transcends all human culture. Feldman suggests that by positing a "precultural human soul", Balkin betrays the postmodern notion that we have always stood within communal traditions and cannot stand outside that which constitutes us.

Hence, from Feldman's perspective, our meanings of justice shift and are reshaped as we move into new cultural contexts. Our insatiable yearning for justice arises from and is tied to the shifts and transformations inherent in our culture, which are bound by traditions which themselves are neither fixed nor stable, but are in a constant state of transformation.

---

[32] *Ibid.* See the critique of postmodern thought in E. Blumenson, "Mapping the Limits of Skepticism in Law and Morals" (1996) 74 Tex. L. Rev. 523, who argues that certain legal and social constructions such as "corporations" can be easily deconstructed, but human rights claims cannot. See also D. Patterson, "The Poverty of Interpretive Universalism: Toward the Reconstruction of Legal Theory" (1993) 72 Tex. L. Rev. 1, who warns that postmodern theory leads us to analytic and interpretive nihilism.

[33] J.M. Balkin, "Transcendental Deconstruction, Transcendent Justice" (1994) 92 Mich. L. Rev. 1132 at 1156.

[34] S.M. Feldman, "The Politics of Postmodern Jurisprudence" (1996) 95 Mich. L. Rev. 66 at 195-96.

Hence, as we strive to attain a more perfect justice, we must continue to create and recreate that which is just and unjust. As Feldman says, justice can never be fulfilled; it is always displaced and redefined. Each time we identify an event or action as just, we also identify that which is unjust, and in each act, there is a trace of the Other lurking in the margins of our understanding.[35]

Thus, if we conceive of our drive to achieve an ever more perfect justice as part of the transformative ethic inherent in our traditions and cultural practices, and if we come to see that each act of justice also brings us into a relation with injustice, one might be tempted to conclude that we have arrived back at the very question that legal and political theory asks: What are the appropriate principles by which "justice" can be ordered? Must we create classifications and categories on the subjects of justice and their demands in order to avoid chaos and nihilism? Must we create hierarchies between the dominant and the marginalized in order to mediate the conflict? Have we merely returned to the notion that law is a binarism which merely reflects the fact that conflict is our perpetual predicament and paradox? Have we travelled to nowhere?

The postmodern project is to develop deconstructive practices that can overcome binarism and difference without opposition.[36] Binary opposites and conceptual hierarchies are the product of language itself which, to maintain some communicative integrity, gives the illusion of direction, definition and orientation. But what language creates, language can deconstruct and recreate; hence, postmodernism urges us to reconceptualize hierarchies and binaries.

Deconstructive practice challenges us to recognize the Other, but, of course, refutes any resort to foundational principles which tell us whether the Other should be dominated, colonized, co-opted or subjugated. For Feldman, the paradox of postmodernism is that because it cannot provide us with such foundations, its practice is fundamentally political. For postmodernists, this political essence requires us to speak in the language of the Other to try to see from the Other's perspective and to evaluate how our actions may affect the Other. The postmodern prescription is to use language as well as our prejudices to cause us to conceptualize and create new social ordering.

***

And what of mediation? What is the language of mediation? Can the self find transformation from within, and does mediation offer us some unique form of discourse?

To be sure, mediation celebrates its uniqueness from law. In a postmodern sense, mediation is law's "Other". Law and mediation are tied to each other, but their relationship mirrors their sameness and difference simultaneously. In a certain sense, law and mediation form a binary, but there is, nonetheless, a gap

---

[35] *Ibid.* at 199.

[36] J. Zerzan, "The Catastrophe of Postmodernism" (1998) <http://elaine.teleport.com/-jaheriot/pomo.htm> (as of publication, web site not found), <http://www.subsitu.com/kr/pomo.htm> and <http://www.primitivism.com/postmodernism.htm>.

or space between them, a zone of indeterminacy where both share a certain vocabulary and seek similar ends, though they remain fundamentally different.[37]

Mediation theory purports to liberate us from law's seeming preoccupation with "rights" talk. The theory says that rights talk is misleading and is an exercise in obfuscation.[38] The appropriate subject of debate, according to mediation theory, should be "interests" or "values"; hence, we are urged to substitute a discourse centered on rights with one that seeks ways of discovering, articulating and bartering interests. It is argued that such a shift in this discourse would also serve to obviate or, at least, lessen the role of representatives or agents to speak for those whose story must be told.

Mediation also offers us an escape from law's categories and hierarchies, for it is prepared to grant a voice to those who might not have the right of articulation in law and may be prepared to recognize entitlements whose law would not otherwise legitimate. Hence, mediation gives the potential for robust debate and for the direct exchange and compromise of what we perceive to be the essentials of our existence.

Moreover, mediation theory seeks to seduce us with the notion that compensation, redistribution and other outcomes can be fashioned in a way which parallels the "interests" of the parties; therefore, substantive outcomes move closer to the reality of human experience. Eschewing the need for a vocabulary which must speak in generalizations, mediation engages in a discourse which reflects the uniqueness of the self and the Other.

Finally, mediation theory purports to dispense with the need for the search for truth, objectivity and fact finding. There is no need to appeal to normative standards such as the "reasonable man", and no need to rely on binary opposites. Mediation language is that of the narrative, or that of the story, that the self must tell. Myth and narrative, without pretense to universalism and determinacy, are what mediation language seems to be about.[39]

At first blush, therefore, mediation ideology tantalizes us with the promise that it can do better than law. Certainly, mediation ideology appears to carry us forward some way toward a postmodern new world. Focusing on "interests" rather than rights, and on remedies that would appear to go beyond law's aversion to the deconstruction and rearrangement of institutional configurations, mediation seems to offer us a direct dialogue between self and Other, and between interests and deliberative action. Mediation's agenda is centred on the language of the narrative which offers the self and the Other the potential to recreate and rectify.

---

[37] For a look at the discursive borderline between law and history, see W. MacNeil, "Living On: Borderlines — Law/History" (1995) 6 Law and Critique 167.

[38] S. Silbey and A. Sarat, "Dispute Processing in Law and Legal Scholarship: From Institutional Critique to the Reconstitution of the Judicial Subject" (Madison, Wis.: Institute for Legal Studies, University of Wisconsin-Madison, Law School, 1988).

[39] For a discussion of myths and peace building, see B. Blaustone, "Myth: The Conflicts of Diversity, Justice and Peace in the Theories of Dispute Resolution; A Myth: Bridge Makers Who Face The Great Mystery" (1994) 25 U. of Tol. L. Rev. 253.

Contemporary mediation practice is legitimized and justified on two pillars: consent and neutrality.[40] The former ensures that, absent perceived unequal bargaining power and other debilitating factors, consent provides us with the gateway to justice. Negotiated or bargained outcomes are seen, in the eyes of mediation theory, to be legitimate, just and fair because they are consensual. Justice is achieved because the parties have contracted for and have consented to a bargain which reflects their interests.

The latter is promoted as reflective of an allegedly value-free process which is a precondition for a communication context in which interests can be discovered, explained, understood, exchanged and compromised. This value-free and neutral process, so the theory goes, will serve to empower the narrators and generate creative ideas and outcomes which reflect the uniqueness of individuals. This neutrality contains a number of elements: the mediator promotes the notion that he or she is impartial, non-biased and detached; the narrators are told that the process belongs to them, and they will be responsible for their own agreement; and conflict and emotion, such as anger, are all managed and mediated through the use of certain processes (caucus, venting, *etc.*) and linguistic manoeuvres (active listening, reframing, *etc.*) which are aimed at insuring the appearance of procedural fairness and decorum.

Nevertheless, mediation's belief that consent must have priority over justice is surely misplaced. Consent alone cannot be the criterion of validity, truth or justice. Consent may be of interest because it may signal to us that the procedure for attaining agreement may be fair, but it does not necessarily follow that the outcome derived from such consent is the correct one.[41] Mediation ideology ignores this distinction and appears to suggest that substantive justice flows from the consensual act.

Similarly, mediation's presence in the face of neutrality hides the reality that mediation, like law, provides a forum which mediates and compromises conflict. Just as the "reasonable man" provides us with a normative construction to approach, but which we never quite reach, so too the "neutral mediator" provides us with a standard to which to aspire. The very involvement of the mediator serves to infect the process and shape the contours of the exchange of narratives.[42]

Moreover, because the stories advanced by narrators conflict, with each trying to dominate, colonize and subjugate the other, narrators resort to rhetorical tools that appeal to morality, law, ethics, rationality and emotion to dominate the other. By employing an ideology which professes neutrality, and by using techniques which also serve to legitimize a neutral process, mediation silently aids and abets the hegemony of some narratives over others. In the end, mediation is simply another form of mystified politics, where dominant ideologies colonize

---

[40] For the deconstruction of the rhetoric of neutrality in mediation, see S. Cobb and J. Rifkin, "Practice and Paradox: Deconstructing Neutrality in Mediation" (1991) 16 L. & Soc. Inquiry 35.

[41] S. Benhabib, "In the Shadow of Aristotle and Hegel: Communicative Ethics and Current Controversies in Practical Philosophy" in M. Kelly, ed., *Hermeneutics and Critical Theory in Ethics and Politics* (Cambridge: MIT Press, 1991) at 12.

[42] See the discussion of the effect of mediator involvement in S. Cobb and J. Rifkin, "Practice and Paradox: Deconstructing Neutrality in Mediation (1991) 16 L. & Soc. Inquiry 35 at 39-40 and D. Luban, "The Quality of Justice" (1989) 66 Denv. U.L. Rev. 381.

the marginalized. Hence, the danger that is inherent in mediation is that its language functions not so much to represent reality, but to form and constitute it. Mediation language only serves to facilitate dominance and existing hierarchies. Narrators are seduced into the belief that they are engaging in a rational, value-neutral discourse in which their "interests" can be identified and exchanged, when they are, in fact, unknowingly and unwittingly compromised and co-opted. In a postmodern sense, the narrators are urged to do the impossible, that is, step outside of themselves and place their fate in the hands of what is in essence a political process.

From a postmodern perspective, therefore, mediation, like law, fails to deliver the goods. Trapped in its rhetoric of neutrality and consent, mediation ideology fails to face up to the notion that mediation discourse aims at the production of "conversational endings", agreed-upon propositions and conclusions whose justice, truth, value and moral rightness are to be accepted by all.[43] Mediation ideology has failed to grapple with how competing narratives can be ordered, or with the content of substantive justice. Until mediation ideology confronts its true self and strips away its pretense to neutrality and consent, and admits that it is, in the end, a process of politics and of ordering, its transformative potential will remain as blunted as that of law.

To take us beyond this stalled enterprise, mediation must develop its own communicative ethic and notions of justice that not only recognize the uniqueness of the Other and develop strategies whereby the voice of the Other can be understood and internalized, but also which develop the appropriate moral and political blueprint to permit the self and the Other to transform each other in a new context of shared meaning and experience.

To accomplish this, postmodernist thinking directs us to create a justice which recognizes the singularity of the Other and which uses a vocabulary to understand the Other's point of view. With respect to the former, we are urged to recognize that the Other is both similar to and different from us. We are challenged to understand both their similarity and difference, and to bridge the two.

> ...Every attempt at understanding is a simultaneous assertion of commonality with and difference from the Other. If we unthinkingly assume that the Other is too much like us, we will never understand her actions when they diverge from our own; if we insist on our absolute difference from her, she will never be able to understand us.[44]

The second prescription of postmodernist thought is that we must remain open to the possibility that the world view of the Other may be superior to our own. In short, we must be prepared to change, and we must assume the responsibility of attempting to speak in the language of the Other; conversely, the Other must reciprocate by learning to speak in ours. A precondition to this symmetry requires that we treat each other with respect and without force, violence or

---

[43] M. Walzer, "A Critique of Philosophical Conversation" in M. Kelly, ed., *Hermeneutics and Critical Theory in Ethics and Politics* (Cambridge: MIT Press, 1991) at 182.

[44] J.M. Balkin, "Transcendental Deconstruction, Transcendent Justice" (1994) 92 Mich. L. Rev. 1132 at 1161.

dominance. In this way, we can come to understand how the Other experiences his or her world, although perhaps, the best way of putting it might be that we come to understand what it would be like for *us* to experience the Other's world. It may be impossible for us to know how the Other experiences his or her world, but it may be possible for us to come to know how we would experience the context in which the Other dwells. Consequently, by experiencing the language of the Other, we can create a subjective nature of experience and move closer to the experience of the Other as well as transform ourselves in the midst of pluralist practices and local communities.[45]

CONCLUSION

In a popular film, *The Truman Show,* the lead character Truman is born, grows up, and lives in what appears to be a perfect island community. He holds a respectable job, is married to a seemingly loving wife and is surrounded by what appear to be warm and supportive neighbours and friends. What he does not realize, however, is that the island is an immense television studio, each person on the island a mere actor, and the entire community the creation of a media studio broadcasting Truman's life to a worldwide audience. Truman lives what he believes is a rational life, in a well-ordered community where conflict is minimal: in short, a paradise or garden of Eden.

But, when Truman tries to leave the island and explore the world outside, he finds resistance from those around him, and he slowly comes to appreciate that his world is not what it appears to be. He comes to understand that he has been exploited and that his life has been staged. He eventually escapes from the island studio to the "real world", leaving behind a safe and ordered existence, and armed with new knowledge and awareness of himself and those around him.

When we examine our own world, can we say that our own experiences and perceptions accord with "reality"? We live in a world of language, symbols and representation that appear to ground our experience and meaning. Classical philosophy theory holds that meaning or truth precedes the representations and symbols that communicate truth. The self, armed with free will and consciousness, encounters and embraces these signs and representations in order to uncover truth and meaning.[46]

But in the postmodern world, meaning and truth do not precede representation. Instead, meaning and truth are created and constrained by language and tradition. The self lives in a world of contingency, a world without foundational principles, where meanings and symbols do not form the gateway to truth and understanding. As Truman discovered, his world was a mere creation, a construction whose language, relations, and context were false. One might wonder

---

[45] *Ibid.* And see also the discussion in F. Ankersmit, "Experience, Transcendentalism and the Limits of Interpretation" (1997), online: Rice University <http:www.ruf.rice.edu/-culture/papers/Ankersmit.html>.

[46] J. Zerzan, "The Catastrophe of Postmodernism" (1998) <http://elaine.teleport.com/~jaheriot/pomo.htm> (as of publication, web site not found), <http://www.subsitu.com/kr/pomo.htm> and <http://www.primitivism.com/postmodernism.htm>.

parenthetically whether Truman, upon leaving his studio world and entering into the "real world", might have come to appreciate that the "real world" might itself be a false one, and that another better, more "truthful" world might lie beyond it. And perhaps, that is how we change and transform. We come to discard "truths" and their symbols and language, and we substitute fresh ones as we strive to approach a new truth and order.

Law and mediation constitute worlds composed of symbols, representations and language, and they both promise to transport us to another world. We might conceive of them as forms and forums of discourse. Each offers us the hope and promise of transformation, but each is trapped in a paradox: each engages in the language or vocabulary which aspires to neutrality and "justice", but the practice of each serves only to extend and reinforce the conflict that arises from difference. Each purports to mediate conflict by engaging in ordering and in employing a language which may appear to serve justice but which, in the end, may only serve to perpetutate conflict.

We might conceive of law and mediation as each other's binary. In both, we conceive that their respective languages serve not so much as a representation of reality, but as a reality itself. To this extent, the language of each is neither neutral nor innocent, but rather enables and constrains understanding, knowledge and experience.

Although transformation may be the reflection of our cultural tradition of critique and dialogue, mediation must develop a communications ethic which can serve as a guide in our quest for a more perfect justice. We must abandon the rhetoric of consensus, neutrality and foundational principles, and embark upon a new project which readily admits that narratives, stories, interests and legal positions seek dominance and hegemony. We need to develop new strategies of deconstructive and hermeneutic practice which sensitize us to the predicament of the Other so that in the end, we can transform ourselves in a free and unencumbered way.

Appendix III

Dispute Resolution Success Stories

The following is a series of case studies based on actual negotiations that the author mediated. These nine cases resolved on the basis of interest-based negotiation, and they serve as examples of what creativity and a departure from positional bargaining can achieve.[1]

Which of the parties' interests did each settlement address? Why did these settlements work for the parties? The following cases settled in the manner in which they did because rather than fight solely over the money at issue in the dispute, the parties looked hard at what really mattered to them and came to settlements which recognized their primary needs. All the rest — the merits of the arguments in the dispute, the machinations of the litigious process — were secondary.

CASE #1

A lawyer that had dealt with his accountants for many years brought an action against them for allegedly overcharging him and for incompetent work, which allegedly caused damages in the nature of lost tax savings and penalties from Revenue Canada. He had not paid a number of substantial invoices, so there was a claim for the amount of the outstanding fees

The two sides disliked each other intensely and were steadfast in their positions. The case would have been expensive to litigate because it would have required the court to examine several years of detailed and messy accounting records. Neither side could tolerate any kind of payment to the other.

However, the parties could agree that their local nursing home was a worthwhile charity, and they agreed to make matching contributions, for a discounted amount of each of their respective claims against the other.

CASE #2

A high school student was walking up a ramp at school, on which some other kids had earlier splashed an oily substance as a joke. The student slipped and fell, injuring herself. She eventually brought forth a claim; however, there was a serious issue that she had not brought it within the statutory limitation period.

---

[1]   The names and references have been modified to protect confidentiality.

The school's insurer felt that it did not owe anything due to the expiry of the limitation period, the fact that the oil was placed on the ramp by others, and because there was a reasonable cleaning procedure in place.

The injured student revealed that she had a two-year-old daughter and that she was a single mother. Because of the severity of the injury and the impact it had on her future earning capacity, she was very concerned as to how her daughter would ultimately receive a good education. She specifically wanted her child to be able to go to university.

A settlement was achieved whereby the school's insurer paid $6,000 into a structured settlement. The money would be invested for 16 years, in which time it would increase to $23,000; this would be sufficient to put the daughter through a Bachelor's degree program in an Ontario university or college. If the child did not pursue a post secondary education, the mother would get the money.

CASE #3

A large well-known company had received some very bad press about the manner in which it treated people involved with the corporation, and in respect of how it ran its internal affairs. A media entity reported a story concerning these affairs, and the large company sued for libel. The media entity relied on the defence of the truth of story and on public comment.

The media entity was completely convinced of the truth and impartiality of its story, much of which was comprised of interviews with the people involved.

The company, though, wanted to improve its public image, which had recently suffered. The media entity, however, did not want to back off its story.

The settlement included the media entity agreeing to do a story on a major, real example of the company's "good works". The company was to develop a charitable or public-spirited project, thereby creating a new and positive corporate reality to be the subject of the story.

CASE #4

A contractor sued a municipal corporation for moneys owing on a job to construct a park. The municipality had a counterclaim for problems in the work that was done.

The monetary values to the claims were less than the likely non-recoverable legal costs if the case continued. The parties had had a very good business relationship prior to the lawsuit, and there was the potential for a lot of future work.

The case was settled by having each party drop its claim and enter into an agreement with respect to future work.

CASE #5

A passenger of a major airline received a terrible fright when on landing, the aircraft took an abrupt turn upwards, aborting the landing and circling back to land again. She was startled, and, consequently, her fear of flying was reinforced. She then claimed damages for mental anguish.

The manoeuvre had been instigated by the aircraft's computer as a safety precaution in relation to the angle of descent, winds and speed. The airline denied any negligence and, in fact, took the position that not to have initiated the manoeuvre could have been negligent.

The case settled with an agreement whereby the airline would give her time with a trained pilot in the simulator to have all her questions about flight and the safety regimens of the aircraft answered.

CASE #6

A plaintiff bank brought an action on a farmer's guarantee in respect of the debts of the farmer's cooperative. Until 1987, a guarantee had been obtained for each crop year, but then, in 1987, a continuing guarantee was put in place. The form was the same, and the change to a continuing guarantee was not explained to the farmers. There was, however, evidence that the co-op board knew of the contingent liability (*i.e.*, that the guarantees could be called upon).

This particular claim was only one of nearly 50 claims against individual farmers on the guarantees. Several of the defendant farmers were board members who had varying degrees of knowledge regarding the guarantee. Among the non-board farmers, there was a mix of guarantee dates, attendances at meetings and receipt of information, which would have made many of the cases different from one another, likely requiring different trials.

There was little likelihood of the plaintiff bank being able to enforce the guarantees against all the different farmers, many of whom would have had different defences available.

One of the defendant farmers attended a mediation with co-op board members. There was a strong sense of collective identity and a desire to act in concert. However, the board members feared recrimination from the members of the co-op if things got out of control. The plaintiff bank was reluctant to settle any one case piecemeal, isolated from the rest.

At this point, there was an impasse, with neither side wanting to make any proposals or committing itself in any way.

Finally, all the cases were mediated together, a global settlement was reached, and all the cases were settled (including one that had consolidated a large number of actions).

CASE #7

A claim was made against a ski hill owner for flooding the land below, the flood having been caused by artificial snow. The remedial measures that had been taken by the hill owner were alleged to be insufficient. There had been previous recommendations which had not been adhered to, and a number of different options existed regarding berns and drainage systems.

The main issues were whether the ski hill owner was responsible for the water as well as the cost of an appropriate drainage plan.

The parties were full of acrimony, and counsel exacerbated the bickering. The mediator let the parties vent for a while and then jointly and separately facilitated brainstorming with the parties to devise creative drainage solutions. The parties eventually presented their plans to one another and jointly modified them to adhere to some mutually acceptable standards that had been pointed out by a consultant.

Each party was going to pay 50 per cent of the cost to have the consultant come back and determine the compliance with a previous set of recommendations. Instead of an expensive fence, trees would be planted to create a barrier and to absorb moisture.

CASE #8

Two partners had a falling out and were making claims against each other for a shotgun purchase of the other's interest in the partnership, and for various other things, including the depletion of partnership property.

It became apparent that they still liked each other and would take back certain things that they had said and done to one another if they could somehow go back six months in time.

Accordingly, that is precisely what they decided to do — to go back in time as if the six months had never happened and they were still in business together. They also agreed to write up a partnership agreement, which they had not done before.

CASE #9

A financial institution which held a $5 million mortgage that had gone into default, and pursuant to which it had taken possession of the property, sued the mortgagor which happened to be a property investment company. The company's building was a downtown office building whose value had plummeted millions of dollars since 1988, when it had been purchased.

The dispute centered on whether the financial institution could sue the property investment company for the deficiency (the amount owing on the mortgage after the property was sold and the proceeds given to the mortgagee), given that the financial institution had assumed an existing mortgage which provided that its only recourse was seizure of the property. However, the assumption agreement seemed to suggest that a new covenant had been created, allowing the financial institution to sue for the deficiency.

Instead of letting a judge decide the narrow interpretive problem for them, the parties agreed to explore ways in which to do business with one another, either going into partnership on an acquisition, or one party acquiring property from the other or lending money to the other for an acquisition.

These case studies illustrate how enforcing rights does not always offer the best result to either party; however, negotiation with a thorough canvassing of interests can open the door to creative, flexible solutions that are custom-made for the parties.

Appendix IV

AGREEMENT TO MEDIATE

The parties hereto have agreed to convene before a mediator for the purpose of attempting to settle the dispute between them. The parties agree to the following:

1. ROLE OF THE MEDIATOR

The mediator is a third-party neutral who is not a judge and is not able to give legal advice to the parties.

2. CONFIDENTIALITY

The parties agree that all communications and documents shared, which are not otherwise discoverable, shall be without prejudice and shall be kept confidential as against the outside world, and shall not be used in discovery, cross examination, in an affidavit, at trial, in this or any other proceeding, or in any other way.

The mediator's notes and recollections cannot be subpoenaed in this or any other proceeding.

3. LIABILITY

The mediator shall not be liable for anything done or omitted with respect to the mediation and has the immunity granted to a judge under the *Courts of Justice Act.*

4. RULE REGARDING FULL AUTHORITY TO SETTLE

The parties shall bring to the mediation the individuals/representatives who have full knowledge of the events in issue and who have full authority to settle. Full authority to settle means the complete discretion to consider and decide upon (at the mediation) a wide range of monetary and non-monetary settlement options.

Only with the consent of all the other parties and the mediator, and the pledge that the relevant individual/representative will be available by phone during the mediation, can an exception be made to this rule.

5. SETTLEMENT

The parties or their counsel will draft any settlement documentation/Minutes of Settlement and any releases.

6. TERMINATION

The mediator can exercise the discretion to terminate the mediation at any time.

7. FEES

The parties and/or their counsel are liable for the fees arranged with the mediator.

_____   _____

Plaintiff   Defendant

_____   _____

Counsel   Counsel

Appendix V

CANADIAN BAR ASSOCIATION — ONTARIO ADR SECTION MODEL CODE OF CONDUCT FOR MEDIATORS*

I. OBJECTIVE FOR MODEL CODE OF CONDUCT FOR MEDIATORS

The main objectives of this Model Code of Conduct for mediators arc as follows:

    (a) to provide guiding principles for mediators' conduct;

    (b) to provide a means of protection for the public; and

    (c) to promote confidence in mediation as a process for resolving disputes.

II. DEFINITIONS

In this Model Code of Conduct:

"mediation" means a process in which an impartial person, a mediator, helps disputing parties to try to reach a voluntary, mutually acceptable resolution of some or all of the issues of their dispute.

"mediator" means an impartial person whose role in mediation is to assist and encourage parties to a dispute:

- to communicate and negotiate in good faith with each other;
- to identify and convey their interests to one another;
- to assess risks;
- to consider possible settlement options; and
- to resolve voluntarily their dispute.

---

* The CBAO Model Code of Conduct was adopted by the Mandatory Mediation Program, except for section IX. Fees.

"impartial" means being and being seen as unbiased toward parties to a dispute, toward their interests and toward the options they present for settlement.

"conflict of interest" means direct or indirect financial or personal interest in the outcome of the dispute or any existing or past financial, business, professional, family or social relationship which is likely to affect impartiality or reasonably create an appearance of partiality or bias.

III. PRINCIPLE OF SELF-DETERMINATION

1. Self-determination is the right of parties in a mediation to make their own voluntary and non-coerced decisions regarding the possible resolution of any issue in dispute. It is a fundamental principle of mediation which mediators shall respect and encourage.

2. Mediators shall provide information about their role in the mediation before mediation commences, including the fact that authority for decision-making rests with the parties, not mediators.

3. Mediators shall not provide legal advice to the parties.

4. Mediators have the responsibility to advise unrepresented parties to obtain independent legal advice, where appropriate. Mediators also have the responsibility to advise parties of the need to consult other professionals to help parties make informed decisions.

IV. IMPARTIALITY

1. Mediators shall serve only in those matters in which they can remain impartial.

2. Mediators have a duty to remain impartial throughout the course of the mediation process.

3. If mediators become aware of their lack of impartiality, they shall immediately disclose to the parties that they can no longer remain impartial and shall withdraw from the mediation.

V. CONFLICT OF INTEREST

1. Mediators have a responsibility to disclose to the parties in dispute any conflict of interest reasonably known to the mediator, as soon as possible.

2. Mediators who have disclosed a conflict of interest to the parties shall withdraw as mediator, unless the parties consent to retain the mediator.

3. Mediators or their associates or partners shall not establish a professional relationship with any of the parties in a matter related to the mediation which could give rise to a conflict of interest, without the consent of all parties.

4. Mediators' commitment is to the parties and the process and they shall not allow pressure or influence from third parties (persons, service providers, mediation facilities, organizations, or agencies) to compromise the independence of the mediator.

VI. CONFIDENTIALITY

1. Mediators shall inform the parties of the confidential nature of mediation.

2. Mediators shall not disclose to anyone who is not a party to the mediation any information or documents that are exchanged for or during the mediation process except:

    (a) with the mediating parties' written consent;
    (b) when ordered to do so by a court or otherwise required to do so by law;
    (c) when the information/documentation discloses an actual or potential threat to human life;
    (d) any report or summary that is required to be prepared by mediators; or
    (e) when the information/documentation is non-identifiable, (unless all of the parties otherwise authorize identification), and is used for research, statistical, accreditation, or educational purposes and is limited only to what is required to achieve these purposes.

3. If mediators hold private sessions (breakout meetings, caucuses) with a party, they shall discuss the nature of such sessions with all parties prior to commencing such sessions. In particular, mediators shall inform parties of any limits to confidentiality applicable to information disclosed during private sessions.

4. Mediators shall maintain confidentiality in the storage and disposal of mediation notes, records and files.

VII. QUALITY OF THE PROCESS

1. Mediators shall make reasonable efforts to ensure the parties understand the mediation process before mediation commences.

2. Mediators have a duty to ensure that they conduct a process which provides parties with the opportunity to participate in the mediation and which encourages respect among the parties.

3. Mediators shall inform parties to a dispute that mediation is most effective when the parties with full authority to settle are in attendance and when they are willing to consider options for settlement.

4. Mediators who are lawyers shall not represent any party(ies) to the mediation.

5. Mediators have an obligation to acquire and maintain professional skills and abilities required to uphold the quality of the mediation process.

VIII. ADVERTISING

In advertising or offering services to clients or potential clients:

1. Mediators shall refrain from guaranteeing settlement or promising specific results.

2. Mediators shall provide accurate information about their education, background, mediation training and experience in any representation, biographical or promotional material and in any oral explanation of same.

IX. FEES

This section has been deleted for the purposes of the Mandatory Mediation Program and replaced by the fee regulation under the *Administration of Justice Act* and Part 3 of the MMP Code of Conduct.

X. AGREEMENT TO MEDIATE

Mediators shall ensure before the mediation commences that the parties understand the terms of mediation whether or not they are contained in a written agreement/contract to mediate, which terms shall include but not be limited to the following:

(a) confidentiality of communications and documents;
(b) the right of the mediator and parties to terminate or suspend mediation;
(c) fees, expenses, retainer, method of payment and what, if any, fee there is for cancellation, lateness or delay; and
(d) the fact that the mediator is not compellable as a witness in court proceedings by any parties to the mediation.

XI. TERMINATION OR SUSPENSION OF MEDIATION

1. Mediators shall withdraw from mediation for the reasons referred to in paragraphs IV.3 and V.2.

2. Mediators may suspend or terminate mediation if requested by one or more of the parties;

3. Mediators may suspend mediation if in their opinion:

   (a) the process is likely to prejudice one or more of the parties;
   (b) one or more of the parties is using the process inappropriately;
   (c) one or more of the parties is delaying the process to the detriment of another party or parties;
   (d) the mediation process is detrimental to one or more of the parties or the mediator;
   (e) it appears that a party is not acting in good faith; or
   (f) there are other reasons that are or appear to be counterproductive to the process.

4. Mediators shall terminate mediation if the conditions referred to in XI.3(a)-(f) are not rectified.

XII. OTHER CONDUCT OBLIGATIONS

Nothing in this Model Code of Conduct replaces, supersedes or alienates ethical standards and codes which may be imposed or additionally imposed upon any mediator by virtue of the mediator's professional calling.

INDEX